# ENGLISH COUNTRY LIFE IN THE EIGHTEENTH CENTURY

THE HUNTSMAN

# ENGLISH COUNTRY LIFE IN THE EIGHTEENTH CENTURY

BY

ROSAMOND BAYNE-POWELL

LONDON

JOHN MURRAY, ALBEMARLE STREET, W.

*First Edition . . . 1935*

# CONTENTS

vi CONTENTS

# LIST OF ILLUSTRATIONS

vii

# INTRODUCTION

COUNTLESS books have been written about the eighteenth century; but they treat chiefly of urban life and manners, of politics and the court, of the wits and the coffee houses. The urbane man was the town dweller. He despised the rustic, the boor, the bumpkin. He satirized him as Tony Lumpkin or Squire Booby, and was convinced that wit and taste and learning could only flourish in a town. There was some truth in his contention. Countrymen, whether they were squires or peasants, farmers or parsons, were often brutal, boorish and ignorant. They lived isolated lives, how isolated it is difficult for us to realize. The squire and the parson sometimes penetrated to the county town, the farmer went no farther than the nearest market, and the labourer seldom stirred beyond his own village. The inhabitants of other parishes were foreigners, with whom it was not well to intermarry, and who were regarded with deep dislike and suspicion. The countryman had, however, one great advantage over the townsman, whether he were squire, farmer or peasant—he had been brought up on the land. The soil gave him his daily bread, and in so doing taught him much. He had learnt about crops and pasture, beasts and birds, the weather and the winds. He had preserved old tales and legends, old customs and traditions. When men and women cannot read, or read but seldom, the story-teller and the fiddler, the mummers and the ballad singers are welcome guests, and their plays and tunes and songs are remembered and preserved. Old traditions, curious folk-lore, handed down from ancient pagan Britain, are taught to every child, and in turn related to children and grandchildren. These old traditions and superstitions are part of the daily life. Wars and politics and the changes of dynasty passed unheeded. Whether Dutch William or English Anne or the " German lairdie " occupied the throne was a matter of complete indifference to Farmer Flamborough when he sat over the fire and drank his lambswool. The novels of the time tell us little of wars and politics. Fielding scarcely mentions the Jacobite rebellion, which put all London in a panic and nearly sent George II scuttling back to his beloved Hanover.

It was not until the end of the century that the war which England then waged upon the Continent began to affect prices, and had some influence upon the daily life of the country. The enclosures were the only political measure which really changed the life of the people, and these, as we shall see, had a very deplorable influence upon the lot of the labouring man. In other respects, the daily life of the people continued in much the same grooves. There were changes and improvements ; but nothing of that gradual march of progress and civilization which was characteristic of the nineteenth century, nor of the cataclysmic changes, which are the feature of our own unhappy times.

Village life [Trevelyan tells us] embraced the chief daily concerns of the majority of Englishmen. It was the principal nursery of the national character. The village was not then a moribund society, as in the nineteenth century, nor was it, as in our day, a society hoping to revive by the backwash of life returning to it from the towns.

The village and the country town, for the latter was only the village writ larger, were the nucleus and core of national life. London stood apart as the centre of government, the place where statesmen, authors and journalists congregated; the Universities of Oxford and Cambridge carried on some traditions of scholarship and learning, but the bulk of the nation lived rural lives, and even those men whose avocations took them to the metropolis, or the Universities, had often been born and nurtured in the country, and returned to it at intervals during their lives.

Our times are times of great changes, to which we have accustomed ourselves for good or for evil, but it is difficult for us, inured as we are to the mutations of contemporary history, to realize the prodigious changes which have taken place in the last 150 or 200 years.

England in the eighteenth century was a small island with a sparse population of some 5 million to 9 million persons.[1] It was governed by the King, whose prerogative, though much curtailed, was still far greater than at present, for many years by a Whig oligarchy, and all through the century by the aristocracy and the country gentlemen. The county franchise was only given to freeholders of 40s. a year. The rotten boroughs, of which there became an increasing number, returned a member as they were bidden, and though here and there a cry like " Wilkes and Liberty " was raised by a free electorate, for the

[1] Statistics of population in the eighteenth century are not very reliable ; but 5,475,000 in 1700 and 9,160,000 in 1801 are probably more or less correct figures.

most part, Parliament entirely represented the upper classes.

No Roman Catholic or Nonconformist was eligible for any national or municipal office, nor could he enter the Universities unless he were prepared to take the Test Oath.

The rigour of the criminal law strikes us with horror. One hundred and sixty offences could be punished with death, and though juries might acquit for some of these petty misdemeanours, in the teeth of the most convincing evidence, an enormous number of men and women were hanged for such things as sheep stealing or robbery to the value of 40*s*. Prisons were noisome abodes of iniquity where innocent and guilty alike were herded together at the mercy of rapacious gaolers. The press gang ravaged the country-side, and many an inland town and village was scoured for men to man the fleets of Rodney and Nelson. There were a few weak protests; but the majority of people looked upon these things as necessary evils like the smallpox and the typhus which ravaged the country. The conscience of the nation slept. Even the Society for the Propagation of the Gospel kept slaves in Barbados, and it was not until the following century, when the teaching of Wesley, the evangelical revival, and the humanitarian doctrines of Rousseau and the Encylopædists had permeated the nation, that reform became possible.

In spite of many evils and abuses, the eighteenth century was a great age. It was free from the civil wars and religious persecutions which characterized the previous century. Comparatively speaking, it was an era of peace and prosperity, when international trade, the mother of our colonial empire, grew from small beginnings to world-wide enterprises.

Art and Literature, freed from the shackles of Puritanism and the turmoils of civil war, began to flourish and the country emerged from the shell of the little agricultural England of 5 million people to a great empire stretching beyond the seas. It is of this little country and its few inhabitants, living for the most part quiet uneventful lives in little villages and country towns, of whom we purpose now to write.

# CHAPTER I

## AGRICULTURE

### CONDITIONS OF AGRICULTURE AT THE BEGIN-NING OF THE EIGHTEENTH CENTURY

THE year 1700 in rural England opened upon a prosperous scene. The years since the Restoration had been mainly peaceful; trade was good, and, despite change of rulers and an uncertain political future, there was a sense of security and wealth. In 1645 the Feudal Dues, which till then had been paid (though intermittently), were abolished by the legislature and the Restoration parliament confirmed the Act. Landowners were freed from burdens, the price of corn was forced up by a protectionist policy, which put a duty of 16s. a quarter on foreign wheat when the price did not exceed £2 3s. 4d. per quarter. An Act of 1688 gave a bounty of 5s. per quarter on the export of home-grown corn whenever the price fell below 48s. Land became a good investment when investments, good and bad, were scarce and fortunes made in the city or in trading enterprises abroad were put into the soil.

It is interesting to picture this country of ours when Queen Anne ascended the throne.

The population of England and Wales was reckoned at 5,475,000 people, of whom only 1,400,000 were urban. Therefore some 4 millions in England alone were living upon the soil, getting a good living from it and exporting large quantities of grain to the Continent. We may note that now the number of the agricultural population is reckoned at 1 million.

How did this large rural population exist and how did it manage to thrive? To answer this we must look back over two centuries upon a country so unlike our own that we should scarcely recognize it if we should see it. An enormous part of England (Gregory King had estimated it at over a quarter) was given to bare heaths, moorlands, wastes and swamps.

Within the last thirty years, it is true the wolf and the wild boar had been exterminated, but herds of red deer roamed through the country. All kinds of game were plentiful, so plentiful that preserving as it was practised later was unknown. The old English wild cattle were still to be found roaming in some of the southern forests.

Writing in 1773 Arthur Young pointed out that there were at least 600,000 acres of waste land in the county of Northumberland alone.

In those of Cumberland and Westmorland there are many more. In the north and part of the west riding of Yorkshire and the contiguous ones of Lancashire and in the west parts of Durham are yet greater tracts. You may draw a line from the north point of Derbyshire to the extremity of Northumberland of 150 miles as the crow flies which shall be entirely across waste lands, the exception of small cultivated spots very trifling.

It is extremely melancholy (he writes as he travels through Yorkshire) to view such tracts of land as are indisputably capable of yielding many beneficial crops, lie totally waste.

Even Enfield Chase, though it lay so near London, was nothing but waste land covered with mole hills and ant hills, where the deer roamed and the badger had his earth. Epping and Hainault Forests were

impenetrable tracts of woodland infested by robbers
and broken men. Sherwood Forest occupied a large
part of Nottinghamshire and was nearly as wild as it
had been in the days of Robin Hood. The great
bustard and the bittern flew over the sandy wastes of
Norfolk. At Barton-upon-Humber they rang the
church bells after sundown to guide the hapless
traveller across those tractless wilds. The fen country, despite the efforts of Vermuyden and Dela
Pryme to drain it in the previous century, was, for
the most part, a black uncultivated swamp producing
nothing but stunted willow trees, the fen eagle and
the ague.

In the weald of Surrey there were stuck up here and
there tall posts to guide letter carriers and the few other
travellers there might be across the heaths. Sedge-
moor was a swamp in which " King Monmouth's "
hapless army had foundered, and as for Devonshire,
no wheeled vehicle was known in the rural parts for
the very good reason that there were no roads.

The total acreage of England and Wales, according
to King, was rather more than 37 million acres, of
which 11 million were arable.

The same authority made a census of the live stock
of the country. Much of this must have been mere
guess-work, but it is interesting to know what an
agricultural authority at the close of the seventeenth
century believed to be probable.

Horses and asses, we are surprised to learn, did not
number more than 60,000 ; but the day of general
and rapid horse traffic had not yet dawned. On the
other hand there were 4½ million cattle, about one cow
to each member of the rural population, which we may
remember was the aim of Joseph Chamberlain, though

he wished to add three acres to it. Sheep, King estimated at 11 millions, and pigs at 2 millions.

It was, therefore, a pleasant smiling rural England, full for the most part of prosperity and content, that the traveller would have found in the year 1700. England is still a beautiful country; in those days it was far more beautiful. The towns with their cordons of ash-heaps and dunghills were a blot on the landscape; but the blots were few. There were millions of acres of unspoilt woodland, great rolling heaths purple with heather and yellow with the dying bracken, lovely little streams where the yellow iris grew and the trout leapt—a paradise for sportsmen with its wealth of game and a paradise for naturalists, of whom there must have been many like Gilbert White, who, later in the century, loved the countryside. They would have found the badger there and the marten and the beaver and the polecat and birds that we see resplendent in the pages of Gould—the golden oriole and the rose-coloured pastor and the eagle and the great bustard.

A number of roads, all almost entirely bad, intersected the country, and by the side of these, here and there were villages, hamlets and small country towns. The surroundings would have had a curious aspect to modern eyes, for at least half the land in 1700 was unenclosed. As the traveller came towards the village he would have seen first the woodland where the commoner had the right to cut what wood he wanted, then there was the waste as it was called, rough common pasture or sometimes heath where peat might be cut and where small starved sheep made what living they could all the year round. Down by the stream, if there was one (and the old villages had established themselves by rivers when they could), were to be found the meadow lands, " ings " as they were often called, where the hay was grown and gathered, a poor, sparse crop, and where the cows grazed. Up above were big, open ploughlands for growing the village crops, divided into strips and scraps of land by boundaries of coarse grass. On the ploughlands were grown barley, oats and rye and, except at high altitudes and in the extreme north, a great deal of wheat. Such crops as clover, turnips, sainfoin and potatoes were certainly grown, but only here and there by the large farmer or great landowner. The small man with his strip of ploughland had not the room nor the money for experiments, and even if he had, he could not have grown what he wished. The whole system of agriculture in the unenclosed villages was settled by the twelve jurymen who were chosen annually at the meeting of the court leet, or by the vestry. These men were given absolute power as far as agricultural matters were concerned, and being themselves farmers of some age and experience inclined to a rigid conservatism.

There were the three staple crops : wheat for export and for bread for the bettermost people ; barley for the brewers, and for the poor man's loaf ; and oats for the horses, and, in the north, Cumberland, Northumberland and Durham, for cakes and bannocks. These crops the jurymen said should be grown with unfailing regularity. A few beans for the horses, rye in districts where it was customary to grow it, these were perhaps allowed ; but no newfangled crops, no turnips or mangolds for winter keep.

The jury made the laws, and appointed the village herdsman, swineherd and shepherd to look after the beasts and the village pinder who searched out stray animals and drove them into the pound. In addition to these there were the Foremen of the fields, certain farmers who looked after the whole village, and saw that no one sent more beasts to pasture than he should, and that men mended the hedges over against their land or they would call in the hayward to do it for them, and that they kept their pigs ringed and did not let their geese stray. With a bounty upon exported corn it is not surprising that much land was under the plough and a great deal which would have made good pasture was turned into indifferent arable. Drainage was generally impossible, for if one man drained his neighbour might block his outfall. The fields were banked into high ridges so that the furrows between might carry off some of the moisture. There were generally one or two village ploughs which at the time appointed by the jurymen were used by the village ploughman to plough the whole of the arable. It did not matter what the land was, a heavy, water-logged clay or a light sand, it all had to be ploughed at the same time. The ploughs were heavy wooden implements. It was not until the middle of the century that the plough with the metal share was at all generally used. These cumbrous things had to be drawn by four horses and on heavy clay land a yoke of as many as twelve oxen might be used.

The strips of land were so narrow that it was difficult to turn the plough. A man might have the right to turn on his neighbour's strip; but this was not general, so that cross ploughing and cross harrowing were impossible, which on heavy land was a serious drawback. The lands being ploughed, the seed was then sown broadcast—the drill, though invented, was not used till much later. When seed is sown broadcast the difficulty of cleaning the land is insurmountable.

Jethro Tull in 1733 published his book upon horse hoeing husbandry, advocating the use of the drill and the necessity of hoeing, but no one paid the slightest attention to him. Weeds grew apace; if one man attempted to clean his land his neighbour's thistles and dandelions seeded themselves on him, and his labour was in vain.

The custom, which was necessary in those days when there was little manure, of allowing each strip of land to lie fallow every three years, encouraged the growth of weeds, and the coarse grass which formed the boundaries spread and seeded itself upon the cultivated land. When haytime came all who owned arable plots went down to the meadows to claim their share. These grass fields were divided by posts or pegs driven at intervals into the ground. (The clause in the Commination Service about the removing of a neighbour's landmark is thus explained.)

In some villages each commoner had his own plot which he claimed every year; in others lots were drawn for the parcels of land; but it was always arranged that the man who had the most arable had also the largest area of meadow hay. The hay was, of course, cut with the scythe, the whole village population turning out into the vast hay field. The cottager, or smallholder as we should call him, cut his own small plot, his wife and children helping in the raking and carrying. The large farmer brought his labourers, and if he had a very large plot would hire in help : 9d. a day and food is mentioned as a wage for outside labour during hay harvest, or in some districts 1s. 4d. and beer—generally small beer is specified.

This is about 2*d*. a day less than the sum offered for harvest labour, which required greater knowledge and dexterity. It may be asked where all this extra labour was to be found ; but in Queen Anne's reign, and indeed all through the century, the discharged soldier —when he did not take to the highway and evil courses—was glad enough of a job, and the poorer villager when he had garnered his own scanty crop would assist the larger farmer to get in his. It was not possible for the small commoner to live on his holding. He must do something else as well. He might be the village carpenter, blacksmith or wheel-wright, or a day labourer ready with his help at hay- or harvest-time, or when the corn was threshed. The quality of the hay was very poor. It was not till 1760 that Benjamin Stillingfleet wrote his treatise on herbage, showing by illustration the difference between grasses, and the importance of sowing the best. Before this, if a farmer wished to renew his pasture, or lay arable land down to grass, he drew a quantity of hay out of his rick, shook it over the barn floor, and had the seeds collected in a bag to be spread broadcast. He might be sowing grass or thistles, he could not tell, but, no doubt, he hoped for the best.

The lack of manure was an even more serious draw-back. Few milch cows seem to have been kept, and what there were, fed upon the common land with the sheep by day, and folded on the fallows at night. The consequent loss of manure is constantly deplored by Arthur Young, who insists upon the necessity of stall feeding cattle for the sake of the manure they pro-duce. The hay harvest was, however, a secondary affair ; the getting in of the corn was the crowning work of the year. On this the countryman lived :

the large farmer who sent his grain for export to the Low Countries or the Baltic equally with the cottager who took his sacks of corn to the mill to be ground as his staple food for the winter.

In the south and south-west the rye was cut in July, and the fields were bare stubble by September; but in the north of England the harvest often lingered through cold and rain and floods until late in the autumn, in some districts of Northumberland the last sheaf not being carried till All Hallows Eve (Oct. 31st). This may possibly have been owing to a superstition that the man who cut the last sheaf would have ill-luck throughout the year; but in any case the harvest was a long lingering affair.

Barley and oats were cut with the scythe, and a sufficiently tedious process this seems to a generation brought up on machines; but the rye and the wheat were cut with the sickle, which must have been a far slower affair. The reaper could only grasp a few stalks of corn in his hand, which he proceeded to cut about half-way down, leaving a foot or so of stubble standing in the field. Everyone in the village turned out in the harvest field: the blacksmith left his forge and the miller his mill; the farmer if he had well-grown children at school sent for them home. It has even been said that the long vacations at the Universities and at the Bar were instituted so that undergraduates and barristers might hasten home to the paternal roof, and assist in getting in the corn. When the last sheaf had been gathered in, and the widow and her children had often gleaned corn enough to last her for the winter, the harvest home was held with the greatest feasting and merry-making. The hardest labour of the year was over. The stock was turned into the stubble field, to eat the stalks of the standing corn and manure the fields. This precluded any autumn sowing of wheat, except, of course, upon fallow, and made farmers averse from sowing such crops as mangolds, swedes and turnips. Having very little hay, and no other keep, for such foods as cotton cake and oil cake had not been invented, the farmer was forced to kill the greater part of his stock. A milch cow or two he kept, a bull perhaps if he were a large farmer or breeder (though as a rule bulls and rams were the property of the parish), and enough sheep to replenish his fields in the spring; but the rest of the animals were killed and salted down for winter food. It had often been difficult on the crowded commons to get food enough for the beasts in summer; many were half starved, undersized and weak, falling a ready prey to scab and foot rot or to the mysterious cattle plague which devastated England. " In a single year," says Lord Ernle, " the government, paying one-third of the value, expended £135,000 in compensation " for slaughtered animals.

Throughout the eighteenth century the political economist condemned the common field system as wasteful, extravagant and hopelessly uneconomic, and yet under that system the peasant was well fed, contented and prosperous; agricultural wages were higher than they had ever been since the reign of Henry VI, commodities were cheap, and a large export trade in grain was carried on with the Continent. At the close of the century, the agricultural labourer was earning a wretched pittance and was half supported by the rates, while food was nearly twice as dear. The population, it is true, had enormously increased. In 1700 it was 5,475,000. At the close of the century it was about 9 millions but England had lost her export trade in corn, and had been driven to import grain from the Continent.

In 1700 the price of wheat was 36s. 7d. per imperial quarter; in 1800, a war year, it had risen to the monstrous price of £5 13s. 10d. ! The great agriculturists of the century might sing pæans in favour of enclosure, men like Coke and Bakewell and Arthur Young might spend themselves on improving the industry, there is no doubt that the quality and quantity of live stock, and consequently of milk, butter and cheese, enormously increased; and yet at the end of it all, the man who lived on the land—the agricultural labourer—had sunk to a condition of abject poverty and starvation, and farming, once the staple industry of England, was soon going down the hill towards that slough of despond in which it is at present foundering. It is very interesting to speculate what might have been the consequences if all the enclosure bills of the eighteenth and nineteenth centuries had never been passed and if England had remained the small agricultural country of Queen Anne's reign.

We have already pointed out that agriculture was the principal industry in eighteenth-century England, and that much capital was invested in it. Naturally it occurred to the large landowner and farmer that the unenclosed system of farming was extremely uneconomic. It would be far better, they thought, that the old common field system, with its small plots of land, should go, that the fields should be fenced and owned by men who could work them properly, grow the new crops that were being introduced from abroad, have winter feed for beasts and so possess milch cows and fat stock all the year round. The machinery was there to effect the change. During the sixteenth and seventeenth centuries lands had been enclosed in spite of bitter remonstrances, and often armed resistance ; but it had been done infrequently, spasmodically, and not in consequence of any settled plan. Now it became the policy of agriculturists and landowners in general. During the course of the century enclosure bill after enclosure bill [1] was passed by the Commons, and the old village with its common fields passed away.

An enclosure bill began by a petition to Parliament from some local person, generally a big landowner who was lord of the manor. His signature alone was sufficient to set a bill in motion, and before the year 1774 he was not even obliged to acquaint his neighbours that he proposed to divide up their property afresh. After this date a copy of the petition was affixed to the church door, so that such as could read in the parish might be apprised of their fate. Parliament, having heard the petition, granted leave for a bill to be introduced ; which was twice read and then referred to a committee. In the eighteenth century, the member in charge of a private bill, presided and packed the committee with his friends and supporters. It is true that any member of parliament, who cared to do so, might attend these committees, and being there, he was allowed to vote. This was a check on legislation by private member, and, in the case of the enclosure bills, which we are now considering, often curbed the enthusiasm of the lord of the manor. There were other interests represented in Parliament. The rector might be concerned about his tithes, which in enclosure bills were often commuted, and if he were

[1] Between 1700 and 1801 1,631 enclosure bills were passed by Parliament dealing with 3,473,214 acres.

a man of family he would have the ear of his own member, or of some other. Neighbouring gentry might consider that their claims had not been considered, and in this way a sort of justice was meted out between the richer folk. The man who was not represented was the smaller farmer and the cottager. It is true that consent had to be obtained from parties concerned and that a majority, sometimes of three-fourths, sometimes of four-fifths of these, was necessary for the passing of an enclosure bill ; but the proportion was not counted in persons but in the number of acres or on the annual value of the land. Thus the man who owned four-fifths of the unenclosed land of the parish had four-fifths of the votes, and so in proportion. Anyone in the parish was entitled to send petitions to Parliament against the enclosure ; but in many cases the common people were too ignorant to do anything of the kind, and often the distance from London was an insuperable deterrent.

Occasionally if we look through old newspapers we find such an entry as this which is taken from the Annual Register for 1767.

On Tuesday a great number of farmers were observed going along Pall Mall with cockades in their hats. On inquiring the reason, it appeared they all lived in or near the parish of Stanwell in the county of Middlesex, and they were returning to their wives and families to carry them the agreeable news of a Bill being rejected for enclosing the said common which, if carried into execution, might have been the ruin of a great number of families.

Stanwell is, however, very near London. When it took the best part of a week to get from York to London, and the journey was known to be dangerous, few countrymen would have had the hardihood to

attempt it.   Much abuse has been hurled at the heads
of the country gentlemen of the time.   They have been
called rapacious, predatory and unscrupulous and have
been depicted by some modern writers as so many
Ahabs, coveting Naboth's vineyards.   The charge is
generally absurd.   We cannot seriously suppose that
men who owned or farmed thousands of acres were
setting the law in motion so that they might filch a
few parcels of land from their humble neighbours.
Undoubtedly these men were actuated by worthy
motives.   They saw, as Arthur Young saw when he
made his famous tours through England, that thousands of acres were lying waste, that much land was
badly farmed, and that obviously no improvement
could be looked for under the common field system.
The remedy lay beneath their hand in an enclosure
bill.   In some of the acts the enclosures were said to
be " for the better maintenance of the poor of the
parish."

That they were destroying the poor man's independence, and in so doing destroying his character,
would have occurred to very few of them.

Arthur Young indeed, keen advocate of enclosures
as he was, expressed his sympathy with the under dog.

The small proprietor [he says], whose property in the township
is perhaps his all, has little or no weight in regulating the clauses
of the Act of Parliament, has seldom if ever an opportunity of
putting a single one in the bill favourable to his rights, and has
as little influence in the choice of commissioners, and, of consequence, they have seldom any great inducement to be attentive
to his interest.

> " A sin it is in man or woman
>     To steal the goose from off the Common,
>     But what then is his excuse
>     Who steals the Common from the goose ? "

Such sympathy and understanding were, however, un-usual. Independence was not looked upon favour-ably. " An independent person, a saucy fellow." We often find the phrase in records of the day. Although the country gentleman of England who had been brought up among the sons of farmers and villagers might have a practical sympathy with the poor which the French aristocracy never possessed, he was also quite convinced that he was the best judge of what was good for them.

The enclosure bill having been passed, commis-sioners appointed by Parliament would arrive at the village and proceed to redivide all the lands. A pro-portion of the land was given to the lord of the manor, a proportion to the holder of tithes, and other and smaller lots to others who may have had claims. The power of these commissioners was very great; in many cases they could even prescribe the course of husbandry that was to be pursued.

Thus [says Arthur Young] is the property of the proprietors, and especially of the poor ones, entirely at their mercy; every passion of resentment and prejudice may be gratified without control, for they are invested with a despotic power known to no other branch of business in this free country.

There is no remedy against the impositions and blunders of the commissioners but that which is perhaps as bad as the disease: viz., filing a bill in Chancery.

The plight of the villagers was a sad one, and the bitter consequences are to be felt even at the present day; but there is no doubt that as more and more land was enclosed so agriculture improved and prospered. Arthur Young computes the acreage of agricultural land at 32 million acres. He commenced his tours in 1767 and has much to say in praise of farming. He describes the new crops that were being grown, turnips, cabbages, mangold-wurzels, such manures as they had, how they were practising ensilage, or growing fat stock. He mentions the great improvements made by drainage, in so much that land which had once been let from 6d. to 5s. an acre, let, after it was drained, from 12s. to 35s.

A modern improvement in this county (Rutland) [he says] is the laying their lands down with clover and trefoil for two years, and keeping it well fed down with sheep, by which means many pernicious weeds which used to trouble them are greatly got under.

He waxes enthusiastic about the growing of cabbages.

This gentleman [he says, speaking of a farmer near Grantham] has likewise planted large quantities of cabbages. . . . The sorts he has planted most the turnip, the Battersea and the Winter Green Globe, the first rose to 5 lbs. weight, the second to 10 or 12 lbs. . . . A man sets 1000 or 1500 in a day.

He does not always mention that the land was enclosed; but when we find in his pages descriptions (and there are plenty of them) of unproductive farms, bad husbandry and waste lands, we generally find that the open field system is in force.

In very many instances the effect of the enclosures was to turn indifferent arable into pasture. Marshall, writing of Leicestershire in 1786, says, "It was not long ago an open arable country, now it is a continuous sheet of greensward."

We shall presently mention Coke's experiments in growing merinos, shorthorns and Devon cattle, and Jethro Tull's achievements in the teeth of misfortune were a lesson to the more prosperous farmers of his day. Lord Townsend, who had had a brilliant career as Minister and Ambassador, settled down in 1730 upon his estates at Raynham in Norfolk and devoted himself to agriculture. It was said that his land would produce nothing but thistles and warrens, but he soon proved it was possible to grow clover and turnips. He was the originator of the Norfolk system, as it was called. This was the four-course rotation of crops, in which corn, grasses and roots were raised alternately. Townsend was repeatedly advocating the growing of turnips, as he saw that the roots, fed on the ground by sheep, improved and enriched the light, sandy soil. He gained the nickname of "Turnip Townsend" and was celebrated by Pope in his Horation Illustrations.

> Why of two brothers rich and restless one
> Ploughs, turns, manures and toils from sun to sun.

Everywhere the English country gentleman was taking the lead in agriculture. His sons went as pupils to farmers.

George III declared that he was more indebted to Arthur Young than to any other man in his dominions, and justified his nickname by contributing to the *Agricultural Magazine* under the pseudonym of Ralph Robinson. He was much criticized for selling his stock at auction, which was considered most undignified conduct in a sovereign; but justified himself with the sturdy common sense which he showed in his domestic concerns.

"Anyone might accept a sheep and neglect it," he said, "but no one would buy one, who did not mean to take care of it."

Lord Erskine, when he had left the Bench, was found by his friend who came to visit him in his rural retreat at Hampstead, spade in hand among his potatoes. "Here you find me," he exclaimed, "in my *otium cum dignitate*."

Agriculture, in short, had become a fashionable pursuit; landowners and farmers became rich and prosperous and the only man who suffered by the changes was the unfortunate cottager, who had sunk from his state of comfortable independence to a condition of beggary and starvation. It has been supposed that Goldsmith's "Deserted Village" was a description of a village before and after enclosure. It begins, as we all know, with a description of peace, happiness and prosperity.

> Sweet Auburn, loveliest village of the plain.
> Where health and plenty cheer'd the labouring swain.
> Where smiling spring its earliest visit paid,
> And parting summer's lingering blooms delayed.
> Dear lovely bowers of innocence and ease
> Seats of my youth where every sport could please.
> How often have I lingered o'er thy green,
> Where humble happiness endeared each scene.
> How often have I paused on every charm
> The sheltered cot, the cultivated farm.

The end is a description of desolation, and the poem closes with an invocation to Poetry to—

> Aid slighted truth with thy persuasive strain
> Teach erring man to spurn the rage of gain
> Teach him that states of native strength possest
> Though very poor may still be very blest.

# CHAPTER II

## THE VILLAGE AND ITS GOVERNMENT

IN a previous chapter we have touched upon the agricultural management of an enclosed village. We now propose to inquire into its government. From feudal times onward, until well into the seventeenth century, the manor was the centre of authority. The lord of the manor lived in his hall, court or manor, owning the land about it, and also having his share or demesne both in the common fields and in the meadows. The tenants, who had been villeins in feudal days, held their lands from the lord of the manor, and paid for them either in kind or by labour. They also rendered him certain dues, such as merchet, which was paid upon the marriage of a daughter, and fines upon entering upon a tenancy. There were manor courts, presided over by the steward of the lord of the manor, and known sometimes as the court leets or court manors. The bailiff of the court acted as a kind of public prosecutor, and the business attended to was various. Manorial offences such as bad husbandry, taking of wood from the lord's woodlands, moving of landmarks and other such matters were tried in this court. So, too, were petty civil disputes and small criminal offences.

As the seventeenth century progressed, and the English country gentlemen had perished in the civil war or were exiled abroad, the power which had rested in the manor court fell more and more into the hands of the magistrates, and matters which had been settled in the manorial courts were settled in the vestry of the parish.   Still, even in the eighteenth century, manor courts still lingered, especially in the north of England, and occasionally we read of the court leet settling affairs and appointing officers instead of the vestry of the parish.

In 1785 Marshall, writing of the Midlands, says that manor courts are pretty generally held.   The division of England into parishes has been attributed to Archbishop Theodore in the seventh century and is extremely ancient.[1]   The parish was the area for which an appointed priest was responsible : the inhabitants had the right to his ministrations, and to worship in their parish church.   When the boundaries had been settled, we do not know ;  but they were fixed by ancient custom, and in most parishes there was an annual perambulation of the bounds, generally with some ceremony.   The steward of the lord of the manor, or some official chosen by the parish-meeting or vestry, would take several men and luckless boys and proceed to walk round the skirts of the parish.

A writer in *Hones Year Book* thus describes it :

A perambulation or, as it might more accurately be called a circumambulation, is the custom of going round the boundaries of a manor or parish with witnesses to determine and preserve recollection of its extent, and to see that no encroachments have been made upon it, and that the landmarks have not been taken away.   It is a proceeding, commonly regulated by the steward ;

---

[1] Some authorities hold that the area ruled over by a thane constituted a parish.

who takes with him a few men and several boys, who are required
to particularly observe the boundary lines traced out, and thereby
qualify themselves for witnesses in the event of any dispute about
the landmarks or extent of the manor, at a future day. In order
that they may not forget the lines and marks of separation, they
" take pains " at almost every turning.

For instance, if the boundary be a stream one, one of the boys
is tossed into it ; if a broad ditch, the boys are offered money to
jump over it, in which they of course fail, and pitch into the mud
where they stick as firmly as if they had been rooted there for the
season ; if a hedge, a sapling is cut out of it, and used in afflicting
that part of their bodies upon which they rest in the posture
between standing and lying ; if a wall they are to have a race on
the top of it, when in trying to pass each other they fall over on
each side—descending, perhaps into the still, Stygian waters of
a ditch, and others thrusting " the human face divine " into a bed
of nettles ; if the boundary be a sunny bank, they sit down upon
it and get a treat of beer and bread and cheese, and perhaps a
glass of spirits. When these boys grow up to be men, if it
happens that one of them should be asked if a particular stream
were the boundary of the manor he had perambulated, he
would be sure to say in the manner of Sancho Panza, " Ees,
that 'tis, I'm sure o't by the same token that I was tossed
into 't and paddled about there like a water rat till I wore
half dead."

If he should be asked if the aforesaid bank were a boundary,
" oh, it be," he would say, " that where we squat down and
tucked in a skinful of vittles and drink."

With regard to any boundary perambulations after that, he
would most likely declare, " I won't be sartin ; I got so muddled
up top o' the banks, that don' know where we ambulated after
that."

It is estimated that at the beginning of the eighteenth
century there were about 9,000 parishes in England.
Some of these were very large, 100 square miles being
often the area in Northumberland and Yorkshire, and
some were merely a handful of houses and a few acres
of land around some tiny church. Each parish, however, had its own government, and it is with this

that we now propose to deal. The centre of the government was the town vestry or meeting. By law, as well as by ancient custom, the inhabitants of the parish had the right to be summoned, at least once a year, at Easter, and oftener if it were deemed necessary, to the vestry meeting.

A bell was tolled for half an hour, called in some parishes the " mote " or " meeting bell," and the vestry assembled generally in the parish church. The word " inhabitant " was variously interpreted. Towards the close of the century and then for the most part in large towns, anyone living in the parish considered that he had a right to attend the vestry meeting, but the right was generally confined to rate-payers. In some cases a very efficient and thoroughly democratic government was evolved ; but too often the open vestry meeting degenerated into a shouting, turbulent assembly, and often ended in a free fight. At the other end of the scale was the close vestry. These were variously constituted. Some had always been close vestries by immemorial custom ; others had been so constituted by bishop's faculty or by a local act ; but however they had been formed, their constitution and procedure were the same. The members of this body were variously styled " the gentlemen " or " the company of the four and twenty," " the ancients " or " the elders," or more appropriately " the masters of the parish," and this is indeed what they were. They occupied their position on the vestry for life, and co-opted others to fill any vacancies. These close vestries were found in quite a number of rural parishes ; but in the country the so-called open vestry was the more general.

The parishes were usually small, having perhaps

200 or 300 inhabitants, and the number of rate-
payers who came to the vestry, when the bell sounded
on Easter Monday, might number, perhaps, a dozen.
There would be the Squire, of course, and the parson,
who, *ex officio*, was a member, though he did not
pay rates, three or four farmers, and perhaps the innkeeper, the miller and the smith. No cottage was
rated, so the labourer had no voice in the government
of his parish.

As a rule the vestry only met once a year, at Easter.
It would proceed to elect the churchwardens, two
or three or four or even more, or, in a few cases, only
one. The office of churchwarden was one of honour
and responsibility, and no difficulty was experienced
in inducing men to accept it.

The principal farmers, or some freeholder of substance, would generally be elected ; though there were
other methods of choosing the wardens. The next
official to be chosen was the constable, though in
some parts, particularly in the north of England,
the constable was still chosen by the court leet, and
had duties extending over a larger area than the
parish.

In most cases he was, however, a parochial servant,
and as this, like all the three other offices of which
we are speaking, was unpaid, the vestry would find
difficulty in getting a man voluntarily to undertake
arduous and unpleasing duties. Consequently, men
were chosen in turn by " house row " as it was called,
and were obliged to serve for a year. There were
still two other officials to be chosen, the Surveyor of
the Highway and the Overseer of the Poor. These
were appointed by the Justices of the Peace, though
in the case of the surveyors, the vestry had the right

to submit a list of names. Besides these officials, whose functions we shall presently consider, most parish vestries appointed some paid officials such as the parish clerk, the vestry clerk, the organist and bellows blower, a beadle, and a host of minor officials inherited from the ancient court leets.

We find an aleconner appointed, a scavenger, or town's husband, surely a most necessary man, a hayward or driver, a neatherd and hogwarden to tend the cattle and pigs on the common fields, a pinder to impound straying animals, a waywarden to look to the roads, and a dog whipper, who kept quiet the dogs of worshippers during divine service. These various officials, or some of them, were appointed each year at the Easter Vestry, which would then proceed to other business. The churchwardens would present their accounts, which, if they were in order, the vestry must pass and find the money to meet. This money and other parish funds were almost entirely raised by the church rate, which all rate-payers, whether they were church people or non-conformists, had to pay under penalty of distraint. The vestry, therefore, levied the rates, agreed as to the assessments on which they should be levied, made such by-laws as they thought desirable ; and in the unenclosed village when the authority of manor and leet courts was dead or dying, they administered the common lands as we have described in a previous chapter. It will thus be seen that much power lay in the hands of these village assemblies and that the well managed open vestry was the only really democratic institution in England.

Besides levying rates, appointing officials, and passing by-laws the vestry seems to have attended to

a multiplicity of business.   Some of the account books
of ancient vestries have been preserved and they make
curious and interesting reading.   At Havering-at-
Bower, in Essex, the vestry generously allowed " a
pint of sack to the Minister that officiates the Lord's
Day the winter season," while at Bitton in Gloucestershire they parsimoniously object to the poor man
having a new hood.   Rewards were given for the
destruction of such vermin as sparrows, chuffs, pole-
cats and foxes.[1]

At Weston-super-Mare, then a tiny village, the
Squire objects to payment being made for hedgehogs,
of which sixty-four had been destroyed, not because
the hedgehog is a harmless and curious animal, but
" because by this allowance they seem rather to
increase."   A whip for the dog whipper costs 4d.,
and at Almondbury in Yorkshire he varies his
customary occupation :  " For walking in the church
on Sunday and keep people from sleeping, and whipping of the dogs 2s. 6d," is the entry.   We find
numerous items of poor relief which were often on a
generous scale.   As a matter of fact, however, the
vestry was often very niggardly as regards outdoor
relief, instructing the overseer to refuse it whenever
possible and to force applicants into the workhouse.
It was also extremely chary of allowing any to settle
in the parish who might become chargeable to
it.   The poor man, however, had his remedy.   He
could go to the nearest justice and complain and the
English country gentleman, being, for the most part,
free-handed with his own money, had no compunction
about spending other people's.   He ordered relief

[1] This was in 1701.   Later in the century it became as great a
crime to destroy a fox as it is now.

upon a lavish scale.   We therefore find such entries as the following :

Ordered Mary Nalls, two shifts, a gowne, a Petty Coate, a woolen apron and a pair of shoes.   To Thos. Gardiner's wife for mending Sam Wood's cloathing 6d.
William Bragge a shirt and shee a shift.

Parish coffins would be ordered at 7s. 6d. each " great and small " and such things as " cotin coverings and sheetes."

That Sarah Tower be relieved at Discretion for cloathing her boy and Mr. Kempe have notice that if he doe not repaire ye house ye parish will remove it.

They made short work with slum property owners. In this same parish of Finchinfield in Essex, twenty-two persons, chiefly widows, had their rents paid by the overseer in the year, and the Vestry also ordered " that Gowlatt's Boy doe have a pair of breeches and a fear-nothing coat."   " Ye Widdy Beals boy a baze wasecote " and later for " bringing ye Widdy Beal to ye grave 2s."

" Given to Widdow Parry to go to the doctor with her sore eyes and a horse to carry her " and "Sixpence for candles " are other items.   The candles were for a pauper funeral which, like the funerals of the wealthy, was held at night.   " Given to four men who had lost their tongues " we read though we are not told how such a grievous accident befell them.   We find many cases in which shifts, coats and breeches are bestowed on the poor, coals or loads of wood or a strike of barley.

On the other side we find reflected the barbarities of the penal laws.   The constable of the parish of Great Staughton in Huntingdonshire reported that he had spent on Nurse Loudon, for searching the woman, to see if she was with child, before she was whipped, 2s.

"Paid Thos. Hawkins for whipping three people yt had the small pox 8d." "Paid for watching the victuals and drink for Mrs. Mitchel 2s. 6d. For whipping her 4d." "For whipping Goody Brady 4d." Great Staughton seems to have been a vindictive parish.

Thomas Turner, whose diary we shall presently consider, has the following note concerning a vestry meeting, which shows how far a parish would go in removing what might have been a charge to it.

It was the unanimous consent of all present to give to Thos. Dawe upon condition that he should buy the house in the Parish of Waldron for which he hath been treating, by reason that he would then be an inhabitant of Waldron and clear of our parish, half a ton of iron ; a caldron of coal, etc. £2 ; in cash £8 and find him the sum of £20 for which he is to pay interest, for to buy the said house.

A fine present for a man who has already about £80 ; but yet I believe a very prudent step in the parish, for he is a man with but one leg and very contrary withall, and his wife being entirely deprived of that great blessing, eyesight, there is great room to suspect there would be one time or other happen a great charge to the parish, there being a very increasing family ; and I doubt the man is none of the most prudent, he having followed smuggling very much in the past, which has brought him into a very trifling way of life.

Something must now be said of the principal officials. The office of churchwarden had been, since Reformation days, one of honour and authority. In many country parishes the occupiers of certain farms were always chosen as churchwardens, and women could thus be elected ; but they usually appointed a deputy. In the same way a nonconformist was sometimes warden, for there was no religious test for any of the parish officers. In other cases where service, in respect of tenure of lands, was not the custom, the churchwardens might be elected by the open vestry, or co-opted in the case of a close vestry. Occasionally the incumbent chose the wardens, and there was an ancient custom in many parishes that one should always be a rector's or vicar's warden.

In 1604 Convocation sought to make this the universal practice; but Convocation was powerless against ancient custom, supported as it usually was by the law of the land. The new churchwarden would have to present himself before the archdeacon at his annual visitation in order to take the necessary oaths; but the archdeacon could not refuse to swear him, however unsuitable he might appear to be.

The duties of a churchwarden were various. He was responsible to the bishop or his archdeacon, and to the Ecclesiastical Court, for the upkeep and repair of the church, excepting the chancel, which was usually in the care of rectors, lay or clerical. He had to see that everything was provided that was necessary for the conduct of divine service, that seats were allocated according to custom, and that the church was decently kept. He had, moreover, to keep an eye on the incumbent and upon the parish, and to report to the archdeacon upon his visitation whether the services were properly conducted, and whether the parishioners went to church and lived decent, moral lives. It is improbable that any churchwarden carried out the latter duties very seriously. To complain of the clergyman, in whose parish he was living, would have been an invidious task, and one seldom undertaken, and as he was one of the parishioners he probably turned a blind eye to many failings and, for the honour of the parish, held his tongue. Another of the duties of the churchwarden was to co-operate with the overseer for the relief of destitution, the apprentising of children, and the control of beggars.

For this and for the repair and maintenance of the church, funds were necessary. Endowments seldom covered more than the stipend of the clergy, and offertories in country churches were infrequent. All other money was raised by the church rate. This rate was levied by the vestry, and although, curiously enough, it was never authorized by statute, except for a few years during the Commonwealth, the man who did not pay it would be served with a distress warrant and possibly lodged in gaol.

The next official to be considered was the constable appointed sometimes by the vestries, sometimes by the court leet, where this still existed, sometimes by the justices of the peace, and generally, as we have said, by "house row" rotation. This functionary had great authority, and the staff which he carried, and sometimes hung before the door of his dwelling, was no empty symbol. Like a policeman of the present day, he would have the duty of executing magistrate's warrants, of apprehending prisoners and of attending at sessions; but, unlike the police, he was not paid.

A man, thus chosen, at haphazard, and compelled to serve, would be very unlikely to make a good officer. He would either be inert and incompetent, unwilling to embroil himself with his neighbours by reporting their delinquencies, or in some cases harsh and vindictive.

The other two principal officers of the parish, the

overseers, were chosen by the justices, who had also
the power to reverse their decisions and order relief
on any scale they saw fit. In all parishes there were
at least two of these overseers. They had an immense
deal of unpleasant work, such as removing paupers
to their original settlements, obtaining affiliation
orders, apprentising destitute children ; they would
have to listen to the abuse of their fellow-parishioners
if their scale of relief raised the rates, and to the rebuke
of the justices if it were niggardly. Often the nature
and extent of the relief is left to the overseers and they
are bidden " to assist William Smith for his daughter
being a little out of ye waye in her senses at Discretion
of ye Overseers," or the vestry gives a vague order
that " Old Glascock bee looked after."

In some villages where the squire or the parson
kept a watchful eye, old Glascock would have had
everything he wanted, but Sir John Fielding called
the overseer " the stepfather of the parish," and undoubtedly he would have a natural tendency to keep
down the rates, and so to stand well with the rate-
payers in his parish, and, if neighbouring justices did
not intervene, this might result in great hardship.
It is significant that a law was passed, by which the
overseer might be indicted for manslaughter if a
parishioner, to whom he had refused relief, actually
starved to death.

The last member of the great unpaid, the surveyor
of the highways, was often called the Waywarden.
He, as we have said, was chosen by the justices from
a list of names submitted by the vestry. He was
responsible, under the justices, for the roads, and
could even be indicted at the Assizes for disobedience
to a magistrate's order. In spite of this, the roads

were in such a disgraceful state that the custom grew, during the eighteenth century, of letting out the main roads to Turnpike Trusts, who were responsible for their upkeep.

Before Telford and Macadam the practice of road-making and mending was elementary. The well-to-do inhabitants of the parish would be forced to send their carts and horses and the cottager must work for six days in every year upon the roads. In the parish of Finchinfield in Essex, it was agreed in the vestry that every " parishioner shall pick and carry in one load and half of stones for every five which he is rated to the Poore Rate for. And in lieu of his statute work in ye King's highway for ye present year." This was early in the century. In 1772 the parish spent £97 18s. 6d. on the roads, and in 1768 over £100. The stage coaches were becoming more numerous and rapid.

In the Horefield rate book is the following entry :

Paid to Aldwin, being one of the surveyors of the highway for ye year last, 1701, for picking of stone and drinck for the labourers, but for the time to come no drinck allowed. £1 1 6. For picking of stones 41 loads and one shillin for drincking. 14s. 8d.

In addition a highway rate might be levied, by order of the magistrates ; but the condition of the roads of England, until the close of the century, remained as bad as it could be, and to take a journey in winter was reckoned to be flying in the face of Providence.

As we have seen, the offices, other than that of churchwarden, were most unpopular, and few men would willingly have filled them. Those who did so often had an axe to grind.

" If there is a greater rogue or villain than ordinary," says the Rev. Wm. Jones, " he usually elbows and shoulders himself into the chief parish offices." Men of any position were exempt. No peers, clergymen, members of parliament, barristers, attorneys, justices of the peace, apothecaries, dissenting ministers, or officers in the army or navy need fill any parochial office. There were, moreover, other ways of avoiding office. The man who was elected could refuse to serve, and pay a fine to the vestry for the default, or he could choose a substitute, who for payment, would act for him.

By an act of parliament of 1699, the person prosecuting a felon, who was afterwards convicted, was exempted from holding parish office. This privilege could be and often was, sold for a large sum, and was generally known as the " Tyburn Ticket." It certainly offered an incentive to the prosecution of felons, and enabled the well-to-do to shirk an onerous duty.

We have thus described something of the cumbrous machinery by which an eighteenth-century parish was worked ; we shall now proceed to consider who and what the people were who lived in it.

## CHAPTER III

## THE COUNTRY GENTLEMAN

### I

"To Gentlemen of fortune and estates who being born to large possessions and have no other avocations, it's indeed lawful to spend their spare hours on horseback with their hounds or hawks, pursuing their game or on foot with their gun or their net, and their dogs to kill hares, birds, etc."

DEFOE.

THERE is a story told of George III being stopped out riding by a country squire and accused of trespassing.

"Sir," said the startled monarch, "do you know whom you address?"

"Yes," answered the squire, by no means abashed, "I know that I have the King of England talking to me; but I, too, am king upon my own property."

This story, though probably untrue, illustrates the position of the English country gentlemen. They had great power upon their own property; but, like a constitutional monarch, they were amenable to the law of the land, and an immense deal of public business was thrust upon them. We shall presently notice their duties as magistrates, which were often exceedingly onerous, and shall now consider how they lived, and what manner of men they often were.

A large number of very beautiful country houses

33

were built during the reign of Anne. They were
followed by others—less beautiful certainly, but often
stately and dignified, enclosed in large, well timbered
parks with beautiful gardens. That those houses
were well built, warm and very comfortable, the
fortunate owners know to this day. Fielding in *Tom
Jones* describes such a house as he was born in, and
where he lived, in the intervals between the Hay-
market and Bow Street.

> The Gothic style of building could produce nothing nobler
> than Mr. Alworthy's house.   There was an air of grandeur in it,
> that struck you with awe, and rivalled the beauties of the best
> Grecian architecture ;   and it was as commodious within as
> venerable without.

From Grecian to Gothic seems to us a far cry ; but
the term in the eighteenth century is vague. It
may be applied to Salisbury Cathedral, or to Pope's
Villa at Strawberry Hill, or as a term of contempt.

Every century decries the one just behind it, as we
need scarcely be reminded ; and neither the buildings
nor the literature of the sixteen hundreds were thought
much of, after the new century had dawned. The
low rambling dwellings of Elizabethan and Jacobean
times, beautiful though they were, were found to lack
the most ordinary comforts and amenities. The
leaded casement windows did not fit, the large open
chimneys smoked, low ceilings and oak panelling
made the rooms very dark, and each room opened into
another, making privacy impossible. The newer
houses were well and solidly built, over ample cellars.
The rooms were large and loftier, and were fitted with
sash windows, which let in light and occasionally air ;
though that element, much lauded by poets, was
regarded with dread by the ordinary householder.   In

passing, and in connection with windows, we must note one change which was certainly no improvement.

The window tax was first levied in 1695, and was then so light as to be scarcely noticed ; but during the eighteenth century it was made considerably heavier, and it applied to all houses which had more than seven windows. We find Barbara Kerrich, the wife of a country parson, describing her husband as " busy as a bee looking after ye stopping up of ye windows. In this great rambling house we shall pay for about forty, do what we will." To this day, we may find old houses with their windows blocked up, and with sham windows painted on the walls.

For the most part, however, the eighteenth-century dwellings were superior to those of the previous century. It cannot be claimed that they were more beautiful. The custom of panelling in dark oak was largely going out. If rooms were lined with oak it was painted a light colour and the fashion of covering the walls with fabrics and wall papers was coming in. The new furniture was lighter than the old. Spindle legged sofas and chairs, satin wood cabinets with their incomparable golden lustre, the works of Hepple-waite and Sheraton fill our museums, and their imitators fill our shops. The large open hearth, with its settle on either side of the fire, gave place to grates of iron and steel, often beautifully wrought and finely polished. The old virginals and spinet had become the harpsichord, upon which Handel and Hayden played, until at the end of the century that instrument, too, went its way and was replaced by the pianoforte. The rooms did not now so often open out of each other. In the previous century the custom had been for the daughters of the household to sleep all together in one large chamber, and the sons in another. The maid-servants also slept together in a dormitory, and the men-servants dispersed themselves where they could, in hall or kitchen, upon straw or mattress.

Sir John Verney, writing to his steward about their home-coming, says that the foot boy " may lie in the hole within the passage over the scullery."

This custom still lingered on into the eighteenth century, in the houses which lacked bedrooms, and among the conservative who clung to old customs. Among the wealthier, however, separate bedrooms for the family, at least, became the rule, though servants were still herded together, two and three in a bed. The much travelled English milord brought back the French innovation of the *cabinet de toilette*. The English dressing-room, however, was large, and often contained the bed as well as the wash-hand stand.

These beds were of wood, and generally large four-posters, with elaborate curtains and hangings, often embroidered by the ladies of the family ; though by the middle of the century the half-tester bed was coming in.

Children and servants slept upon low, curtainless, wooden beds. Each year in careful households all these beds would be taken to pieces, the feather mattresses and pillows put out in the sun to bake, and the wood thoroughly washed with vinegar and water. The necessity for these precautions is obvious when we read such an entry as this in Lady Cowper's journal, " Was bit in the night, I am afraid by a bug."

The feather mattresses were frequently made and stuffed at home. Mrs. Stone of Brightwell bought 54 pounds of superfine, seasoned, swan's feathers for this purpose, which at 2*s*. 3*d*. the pound cost £6 1*s*. 3*d*., but most people contented themselves with the feathers of the common fowl.

The country was infinitely cleaner and healthier than the towns in that age when sanitation, as we know it, did not exist and when water was often scarce and difficult to obtain.

The country squire could live a happy, spacious life in his fine house with its park, its trees and its gardens. He could ride to hounds, keep his town house in the nearest country town, to resort to in winter, collect pictures and books, and give his wife a present of the new musical instrument, the harpsichord. He could do all these things if he had the taste and the money. At the beginning of the century, there were many country squires living comfortably though quietly upon £200 or £300 a year. That sum in Queen Anne's reign would be worth £1,000 or £1,200 in our present currency ; but as the century advanced money depreciated. The small squire found that his income admitted very little in the way of culture or the amenities of life. Travel and books were out of the question. He could go no farther than the nearest market town, where he would sit in a tavern drinking, with other small squires, and perhaps look in at the market or at a bull baiting or a cockfight. Such men were generally too poor or too ignorant to care to take out their dedimus as a justice of the peace, so that the training and education of public work was denied them. They spoke the dialect of their county with a strong accent. Fielding's Squire Western speaks broad Somerset, and with his boorish manners, his violent temper, his ignorance and coarseness, his love of field sports and a certain generous kind of courage,

may be considered typical of the more uneducated of
the country gentlemen.

Squire Western, however, had money. The small
man, with his two or three hundred a year, had nothing
to spare, to spend upon the improvement of the land or
upon agricultural experiments. Fielding, who knew
this type of man well, having lived among them,
speaks with disgust of their boorishness, their drunken
obscenity and their coarse practical jokes ; and though
many hard things have been said of Fielding he has
never been called squeamish. He admits, however,
that by the middle of the century matters had been
improved.

The small squire had been squeezed out by the rise
in the cost of living. Sometimes he had become a
mere hanger-on like Will Wimble,

who lives with his older brother as superintendent of his game.
He hunts a pack of dogs better than any man in the country,
and is very famous for finding out a hare. He is extremely well-
versed in all the little handicrafts of an idle man. He makes
mayflies to a miracle, and furnishes the whole country with angle
rods. . . . He carries a tulip root in his pocket from one to
another, or exchanges a puppy between a couple of friends that
live, perhaps, in the opposite sides of the county.

More often, however, the small squire had declined
into the ranks of the yeoman farmer where his brains
and his morals were improved by hard work. As the
century grew older, the roads became less bad.
Visits to London were generally confined to the
aristocracy, and to members of parliament and place
hunters ; the country gentleman and his family
journeyed to the country town for balls and theatrical
entertainments ; which were held in most large towns
whenever the assizes or a race meeting afforded an

excuse. In the winter it was quite usual for the family to adjourn to their town house or to some inland watering-place. The circulating libraries and book clubs, which by the middle of the century had been set up in most country neighbourhoods, were sources of enlightenment; papers like the *Spectator*, the *Tatler* and the *Gentleman's Magazine* penetrated into the country and the result was the increase of knowledge, and a softening of manners.

The sports of our ancestors must be considered presently. It may be noted, however, in passing, that the hunting coat, as now worn, comes down to us from the reign of Queen Anne, when it was the ordinary dress of the country gentleman, worn then with a black Steinkirk cravat, a black hat with a wide brim and a short black wig. The country fashions, during the first half of the century, were much behind the town. We read in the *Spectator* of a " justice of the peace's lady near Salisbury, who was at least ten years behind hand in her dress, and looked like one of those animals which in the country are called a Friesland hen."

We also hear of

the greatest beau at our next country sessions who was dressed in a most monstrous flaxen periwig that was made in King William's reign. The wearer of it goes, it seems, in his own hair when at home, and lets the wig lie in buckle for a whole half year, that he may put it on, upon occasion to meet the judges in it.

Wigs were a necessity for any sort of ceremonious occasion even in the country, and were always worn in town by people of condition. When John Byrom went up to Cambridge, his sister sacrificed her own hair to make him a wig. Wigs were often very expensive, a large periwig costing as much as £60, and even ordinary wigs, grizzle majors, great ties and bag wigs cost from 15s. to 25s. Frequently, they would be handed down from father to son, and be carefully brushed and powdered. The Purefoys send to London more than once for grounds with which to powder wigs.

The wig finally gave way to powdered hair, and in some old houses powdering closets may still be found.

This powdered hair must have been an intolerable nuisance, particularly in country houses far away from hairdressers. Towards the close of the century heads became very elaborate. There were monstrous erections of horsehair with powder laid on as a paste, and crowned with birds of paradise, men of war, post chaises and flower gardens.

" Three weeks is as long as a head can go in summer without being opened," says a hairdresser. Special cases were made for enclosing the heads at night, but the discomfort must have been extreme. To what horrors will not women submit in the name of fashion. They will even endure the reproof and ridicule of their menkind.

The riding habit when it was first introduced from France evoked nearly as much disgusted comment as the short skirt of our own century.

" The rider's sex," says Richardson, " could not easily be distinguished. She looked neither like a modest girl nor an agreeable boy." Yet after all these diatribes we find quiet country women like Lydia Thackeray, the daughter of the headmaster of Harrow, being married in a scarlet riding habit with a white hat and feathers ; and very well she must have looked, we may be sure. On the whole the cost of dress and of dress materials seems to have been very high. Timothy Burrell allowed his daughter £80 a year for her clothes, a large sum in those days, and paid £40 9s. for mantua petticoats, stockings, linen hood, gloves and gowns.

The country lady at the beginning of the century would wear a canvas petticoat over a whalebone hoop, and a little linen cap. In the town hoops might be larger or smaller as the fashion dictated and the head-dresses of very great height.

" Women were of such enormous stature," says the *Spectator*, " that we appeared as grass-hoppers before them. I remember ladies that were seven feet high."

This great height was a transient fashion, but the wide hoop persisted, and coaches had to be made larger to accommodate these monstrosities. Some country gentlemen, like Lord Verney, even went so far as to build bigger and better coach-houses to hold their enormous vehicles.

London fashions penetrated into the country by slow degrees, and though beaver hats, made in the reign of Charles II, were seen in church in the reign of the second George, persons of condition affected a sumptuousness of apparel on occasions of ceremony. Dr. Johnson, whom we know as a snuffy old man in a dirty tie wig on ordinary days, went to the first appearance of his *Irene* in a scarlet waistcoat, laced with gold, and a gold-laced hat.

Dr. Farmer, Master of Emmanuel, wore a scarlet cloak on Sundays, with a three-cornered hat and a gold-headed cane, though he spoiled the full effect of this splendour by putting on pattens when the Cambridge streets were muddy. No wonder undergraduates waited outside Great St. Mary's to see him come forth.

Patches were worn in Queen Anne's reign, and indicated the politics of the wearer, the Tory ladies putting them on the right cheek and the Whigs on the left ; just as, later in the century, the gentlemen who supported Pitt wore scarlet waistcoats, and those who followed Fox wore buff. Patches were also worn much later in the century and looked extremely well with the powdered hair.

" From beef without mustard, from a servant who overvalueth herself, from a woman who painteth herself, good Lord deliver us." This was a much-quoted saying, and all moralists condemned the practice, yet cosmetics were as much used in periods of the eighteenth century as they are to-day.

The great change in the century, which enormously affected the poorer classes, scarcely touched the rich. This was the invention of cheap cotton goods. Well-to-do people still clung to linen for underclothing and household use. In the country this linen would be made at home. Flax was grown in large quantities in various parts of England ; which was a far damper country then than now. The preparing of the flax was a village industry, and in every country house the maids spun it into yarn upon a spinning-wheel. Careful housewives were very particular as to the hemp and flax they used. We find Mrs. Purefoy returning some and complaining of it " being no better than 8*d*. hemp. She desires you will send her a pound of your best 12*d*. hemp."

In some cases the yarn was sent away to be woven into linen ; but more often the mistress of the house would wait until the itinerant weaver, who spent his time between neighbouring parishes, should call at the back door. This man was never called by his name, but was always known as " the Weaver." He stayed in the house for as many weeks as were necessary to spin the flax yarn into linen, and often, in the north, he would weave woollen goods. No wonder that the material lasted and that tablecloths of the eighteenth century have come down to the present day.

The spinning-wheel may remind us of the large amount of work which was done in country houses, and, of necessity, superintended by the mistress of it. The bread was baked at home, and every other kind of food made and prepared. At the beginning of the century fresh meat was often unobtainable in the winter, even in the homes of the well-to-do, and an immense amount of beef, pork and mutton was put into pickle every autumn to last the family till the spring.

Jams were made and fruit was bottled as is done at the present time, but in addition to this many medicines, cordials and cosmetics were made at home. Every country house had its still-room, devoted in later times to making cakes, but in early days used as its name implies, for the distillation of essences, cordials and medicaments. There the still-room maid, under the superintendence of her mistress, would make juleps, electuaries and purges for the good of the poor ; strong waters and surfeit waters, and cowslip, elderberry and many other kinds of wine. Beer was brewed at home and a large supply made to last the whole year.

In the apple counties, cider would be made instead of beer, and at the beginning of the century mead was still drunk.

Sir Roger de Coverley, when he was walking in Spring Gardens, and thinking of the widow, was aroused by a " mask " who came behind him, gave him a gentle tap on the shoulder and asked him if he would drink a bottle of mead with her.

Ink was another thing which was made at home. Three ounces of powdered galls, picked off the oak tree, were to be mixed with $\frac{1}{2}$ an ounce of camphor, in two lumps, and a pint and a half of water. The liquid was to be put in a bottle, which had an iron rod through the cork, and with this the ink was to be stirred night and morning for a fortnight or a month, it did not seem to matter which. There were many complaints about the quality and colour of these home-made inks ; but the letters of the eighteenth century have survived and are legible down to the present day.

The kitchen premises in a country house were very extensive. The kitchen had its great open fire with its roasting jack, turned sometimes by the kitchen boy, sometimes by a turnspit dog ; its wide chimney where hams and bacon could be smoked, though in some places the smoking was done in a separate house, reserved for the purpose. Wood fuel was used for smoking, and as coal was increasingly used in kitchen grates, a separate fire and chimney became necessary for the hams and bacon. Separate larders for the keeping of home killed meat, game and cooked viands were a necessity at a time when country houses were largely self-supporting. The dairy was no less important, and there would also be a brew house for the beer, and sometimes an ice house, where ice was stored, wrapped in flannel and salt, from winter frosts to the hot days of summer. In the store-room were preserved the jams and cordials, the home-made soap and candles and the fruit, which began to be preserved at the end of the century, when war and privation made housewives more careful.   Here, too, were found the mortars where the great loaves of hard sugar were pounded to powder, and the strong chipper which cut it into pieces.

Clothes were washed in country houses thrice a year, as is still the custom in some parts of Europe, and this vast laundering was called a " bucking."

Timothy Burrell writing at the beginning of the century says, " I washed in soap.   Bought blew 1/–. I payed for 18 stone hard soap at 2/3 the dozen £1 6."

Timothy Burrell was a widower and there was no lady to superintend his household.   A notable housewife would have made the soap at home, or used wood ashes or soapwort.

Candles were also home-made.   The bees' wax was poured into moulds ; but the tallow candles were made by dipping the wicks into mutton fat.   These tallow dips were considered quite good enough for children and servants, who were sometimes put off with rush lights.   The latter were made of the piths of rushes dipped into scalding fat or bear's grease.   Gilbert White declared that " a poor family will enjoy $5\frac{1}{2}$ hours of comfortable light for a farthing."   A very small modicum of comfort was thought sufficient for the poor, and even the light from wax candles would be considered a miserable thing in these days.   What lamps there were, in the eighteenth century, were wretched things, giving a feeble, smoky light, and much fine sewing, embroidery, and exquisite penmanship was executed by the light of two wax candles.

A visit to town was taken full advantage of. Catherine Verney writing to her husband sends a long list of things required in the house :

cloth for the liveries, and a hat for Robin and one for Natt. Stove to burn coals in, in the little parlour and a coal basket. A pound of coffee, be sure do not forget that, and also 2 pnds of salt petre and one pnd of salt.   Prunella, and one pnd of citron and half a pnd of oring and half a pnd of Lemon peeles, and a brush to rubb the great parlour.

" Bye some writing paper and a few smelts," she adds as a postscript.   Fish was often sent immense distances.   John Byrom despatched oysters from London to Manchester for his daughter's birthday. One wonders in what state they arrived . . . rather like Parson Woodforde's skate " indifferent and dark," one imagines.

There was often a constant interchange of presents between the country squire and his friends and relations in town.   The squire sent a dozen hog's puddings, a chine, a brace of leverets, or a cock turkey ; the town responded with a barrel of oysters, a pot of sturgeon, or a gallon of Jamaica rum.   Sometimes there were disappointments.   The coach was late, the oysters were put out on the road, the rum mysteriously leaked out of the keg, but, on the whole, the presents from town were a welcome addition to the country larder.

The superintendence of a large country house was no light matter, and the mistress of it must often have been glad of the services of a waiting gentlewoman to relieve her of some of the responsibility.   These women were the unmarried daughters of good family, and the post of waiting gentlewoman was the only one to which they might condescend.   They are often mentioned in the Verney letters, and not always with approval. In the houses of relatives their lot may have been happy ; but among strangers it must often have been a sad one. They were poorly paid, if paid at all, and were at the beck and call of their employers, whose equal they socially were ; but who often treated them as upper servants and made them take their meals in the housekeeper's room. Fortunately, most women married and went to serve husbands and children of their own.

The novels of the eighteenth century are full of elopements and parental opposition to marriages. It is a fine romantic subject which the novelist of modern manners must miss.

In the earlier years of the century the marriage law made such elopements easy. There were many churches and chapels where couples could be married without banns or licence or formalities of any kind. Clarissa Harlowe runs away with her scoundrel of a lover. In real life Mary Granville is coerced into marrying at seventeen a man of sixty, whom she confessed to finding " rather disgusting than engaging." When her elderly husband had drunk himself to death, she for a long time refused to marry Dr. Delaney, whom she really loved, because her brother, now head of the family, objected to the match.

A bridegroom was often chosen because his family or estates commended themselves to the bride's family, and the woman was expected to fall in with these arrangements.

When a friend writes to Lord Fermanagh proposing Lord Hatton's daughter as a bride for his son, the father declines the alliance as a poor bargain financially. " You see," he writes, " the cheapness of the sex . . .

my son is very young, and I hope may deserve more if he carries himself discreetly."

There was a strong protest in the *Tatler* against love being left out of these arrangements, and

young men and women not being permitted the least relish of that exquisite gladness at meeting, that sweet inquietude at parting, together with the charms of voice, look, gesture and that general benevolence between well-chosen lovers, which makes all things please, and leaves not the least trifle indifferent.

There has, however, always been a romantic strain in the English nation and love matches and elopements were common. In the letters and memoirs of the time we catch many a glimpse of married happiness and content.

" Women in the plural," said Sir Thomas in the Verney letters, " had little attraction for him, because woman in the singular was so dear to him."

In the case of unhappy marriages, the parties concerned made the best of it. The husband might seek for consolation elsewhere, but, with very few exceptions, English country ladies were virtuous. Divorce, which involved an Act of Parliament, and was enormously costly and troublesome, was almost unheard of. It was certainly never resorted to by the class of which we are writing.

Marriage ceremonies were in some ways simpler than our own and in some ways more elaborate. The custom of inviting hordes of people to weddings, and the wholesale giving of presents is more or less modern.

" The Bride received from her mother," we read in a memoir dealing with the end of the century, " a new piano, from her eldest brother, a silver teapot, and from her eldest sister a tea service of Worcesterchina," and this was apparently all that the much loved daughter of a large family was given by her relatives or friends.

On the other hand there was much feasting, dancing and drinking at a wedding. The bride was brought home to her husband's house with ceremony, and after supper was undressed and put to bed by her brides-maids. There was then the ceremony of throwing the stocking, which is thus described in a book entitled *Hymen*, dated 1760.

> The men take the bride's stockings and the women those of the bridegroom; they then seat themselves at the bed's feet and throw the stockings over their heads, and whenever anyone hits the owner of them, it is looked upon as an omen that the person will be marrying in a short time. Meantime the sack posset is got ready and given to the married couple.

On the following day the bride and bridegroom might be awakened by a serenade of marrow bones and cleavers, tin kettles, pans and shovels being played and rattled beneath their windows. Thus the butcher boys and other urchins were wont to felicitate the newly wed, and to solicit largesse for themselves.

Such ceremonies among the gentry fell gradually into disuse, "and to spare the ladies's blushes," as Fielding said, the wedding trip or honeymoon was instituted. The happy couple journeyed perhaps to Bath or Brighthelmstone; the bride, who could not be left to the solitary and savage society of her own husband, always taking a bridesmaid with her.

If marriage customs altered, those of funerals were preserved with conventional rigour. Heavy mourn-ing clothes were worn for months after a bereavement. People even blackened the soles of their boots, and the edges of their underlinen. They bought mourning furniture, hung the parlour with black hangings and, in some cases, had a special black bed in which the dead or dying member of the family was laid. The Verneys had such a bed, which they obligingly lent round to sickly relatives.

Mrs. Pendarves, writing to her sister about three months after the death of their father, says,

you should, if you keep strictly to the rules of mourning, wear your shammy gloves two months longer; but in the country if it is more convenient to you, you may wear black silk : you might have worn black ear rings and necklaces these two months.

The law of Charles II, which, to encourage the wool trade, ordered everybody to be buried in woollens, was still observed. Funerals among the gentry generally took place at night, the friends or mourners walking behind the coffin, with a torch in one hand and a sprig of rosemary in the other. When the coffin had been lowered into the grave, the branches of rosemary were thrown upon it and the torches were put out.

" When Hopkins dies a thousand lights attend the wretch who, living, saved a candle's end."

These funerals were often enormously expensive. This is the bill for a funeral in 1789, one of very moderate expenditure, costing £68 in all.

To 32 persons for carrying ye lights at 2/6.
To 32 branches for ditto 5/4.
68 lbs. of wax candles for ditto at 3/- per lb. £10 4.
To 2 beadles attending ye coaches with silk dressing gowns £1 10.

This bill says nothing of gloves and scarves which were distributed to the mourners, nor does it mention mourning rings, which were often beautiful and costly, and which were given to all near relations and friends.

A Mr. Dinsdale, a Yorkshire squire, writing to a friend, says : " I was one of 12 pall bearers ; the entrance into the hall was very solemn indeed. It was all hung with black cloth, even the pillars from top to bottom. The coffin was highly ornamented with large plumes of feathers from London."

An enormous meal was provided for those who attended, many of whom had come from great distances.

The duel, so much resorted to by men of fashion, was less common among country people. Men might insult each other in their cups ; but the cause of offence would be forgotten next morning. A man could not shoot his neighbour or run through the man with whom he rode to hounds. Only a great offence, committed in cold blood, would call for a settlement by arms.

The open-handed hospitality of the country gentry was universal. The squire kept open house for his friends, though, owing to distance, these might be few.

Cowper speaks of the " ceremonious civility of the country gentlepeople," but Cowper was a poet and a man of letters, to be set by the squires in the same category with Frenchmen, dancing dogs and other little known phenomena. What was to be made of a fellow who kept tame hares and had written a poem about a sofa ? No wonder that they were stiff with him, and if they ever came to pay a morning call, wondered how soon they could decently go.

The large landowner entertained his neighbours on a very handsome scale. Lord Fermanagh, we are told, in the Verney letters, entertained four hundred people in one day at Christmastide, " with drums, trumpetts, hautboys, pipes and fiddles " ; on the top of all this hospitality his tenants came to demand reductions in rent.

" I am very glad Xmas is ended," he adds bitterly. Besides the visitors from the neighbourhood, the larger country houses could be filled with friends or relatives from a distance.    Sons who were in London sent their wives and children to spend the summer under the paternal roof.

When Ralph Verney brings home his bride he writes to tell his father that " there will be 10 coach horses, 4 saddle horses, and Mr. Herring, coachman and butler . . . my wife's maid will come down with us."  This was the sort of cavalcade for which a country hostess had to be prepared.

Old friends came immense distances and stayed an immense time.    When it took a week or ten days to reach a place, guests did not content themselves with a three days' visit.    They probably stayed three months.

To judge from the novels of the time, country manners were hearty, rough and boisterous.    There was much dancing and practical joking, and plenty of what was called good fellowship, which meant inordinate drinking.

Fanny Burney, who held the mirror up to her times, according to the verdict of her contemporaries, describes how a cruel practical joke was played by a host upon an elderly lady actually staying in his house. Sir Robert Walpole said that, whenever he was at a loss for conversation, he " always talked bawdy," which he found acceptable in all kinds of society. On the other hand there are charming pictures of country life depicted in many memoirs and letters of the time.

Amusements in the country chiefly consisted of field sports and of dancing, and in those days as in these, everybody danced. Dances were often informal affairs—a few couples from the immediate neighbourhood would dance to the music of the village fiddler, or the squire's lady would play upon the spinet. Large parties and the constant paying of calls became the fashion at the close of the century when the roads had been improved; but near neighbours kept up a close intimacy and constantly invited each other to dinner or to drink tea.

Tea would be served about four or five after the dinner was over and the gentlemen seldom partook of it. Sometimes they joined the ladies in the parlour for cards, though the taste for these was not so great in the country as in London. Among the games played whist (whisk as it was then called) and piquet have lasted into the present day; but there were others, of which we never hear, such as : ombre, loo, quadrille, pope joan, bassett, passage, costly colours, Queen Nazareau, Post and pair. Ombre seems to have been a most elaborate game and had its own curious terms, such as matadores, beasts, spadil, nimil, codil and basto.

Sometimes the tea visitor would be entertained for supper, which was a meal more eaten in the country than in town. Nor did people always wait for an invitation. The open-handed hospitality of the country welcomed uninvited guests.

"If it is agreeable to you and Miss Birt," writes Mrs. Purefoy to a neighbour, "I will take a commons with you between 1 and 2 o'clock."

In London the dinner hour was getting later and later. "The landmarks of our fathers," said Richard

Steele, " are removed and planted further up in the day
. . . in my memory the dinner hour has crept from
12 o'clock till 3."

" I do not like dining at near 6," says Horace
Walpole later in the century.

In the country the dinner hour probably remained
where Pope put it at twelve o'clock.

> She went to plain work and purling brooks
> Old fashioned halls, dull aunts and croaking rooks,
> To pass her time t'wixt reading and Bohea
> To muse and spill her solitary tea.
> And o'er cold coffee trifle with the spoon
> Count the slow clock and dine exact at noon.

This mention of solitary tea reminds us that when
Pope wrote, it had not been long established in England and would scarcely have penetrated into the
country.   John Byrom having heard of such things
as silver tea kettles, took a drawing of one to a silver-
smith that he might make a kettle for Mrs. Byrom.

The whole tribe of philosophers, economists and
sermonizers fastened upon tea as the most pernicious
beverage of the age.   In this straining at gnats, they
overlooked the terrible part which intemperance
played in English life.

A country clergyman writes to remonstrate with a
nephew at Cambridge for running up a long bill, not
at a wine merchant's, which might have been pardoned,
but at a chandler's shop ; which bill he declares is too
high " by reason of ye foolish custom you have got
of drinking and treating with tea, wch. is not only very
chargable ; but is ye occasion of misspending a great
deal of time."

In spite, however, of the diatribes of the clergy and
of the medical profession, who considered tea most

prejudicial to health, the drinking of it increased. Tea, or its cousins, chocolate and coffee, ousted beer from the breakfast table. We should consider the price paid for it enormous. Byrom speaks of Bohea at 16*s*. a pound, and he always drank green tea, thinking that the black was often dyed. Sixteen shillings was quite a modest price ; the best Bohea often fetched 30*s*. a pound or 35*s*.

Tea among the poor was concocted of many kinds of leaves, and even the well-to-do drank sage tea and, as medicines, dandelion and nettle tea.

Mrs. Kerrich, writing to her husband, who had gone to Cambridge to take his doctor's degree, says, " We have plenty of fine radishes in the garden now. Miss and I sup of 'em sometimes and we have drank sage tea every morning since she came. I don't know but yt may be as good as ye ale."

If tea was expensive, food seems to us to have been amazingly cheap ; but we must always remember the difference in the value of money. Even as the century advanced the purchasing power of money decreased.

In 1743 a writer asserts that King William and Queen Anne possessed an income of £700,000, and adds that " they both lived in times when that income would have supported a greater expense than a million would do now ; for the truth of which I appeal to the experience of every private family and to the known advance in all commodities."

Food does not seem to have increased much in price until the last thirty years of the century. The squire could produce the bulk of what he ate upon his own estates, and the plenty of the English table became proverbial.

When Mrs. Purefoy wants a cook she stipulates that the woman shall be able to cook from five to ten dishes of meat upon occasion.

Timothy Burrell had four friends to dinner and he gave them the following menu :

A peas pottage, which being taken off,
A haunch of venison
salad
Lemon pudding on one side.　Scotch collops on the other.
Leg of mutton rost.
Cutlets at lower end
A venison pasty
Two large chickens rosted.
Scotch pancakes.　　　Kidney pies.
Gooseberry tart
Raspis in cream jelly
Imperial cream
Flummery.　　　Plain cream
Codlings.

This was a dinner for five people.　No wonder, if such was the scale of housekeeping, that a cheese weighing 18 pounds, which Burrell had bought for 2¾d. a pound, was all eaten in his kitchen in ten days.

Such a dinner does not seem to have been anything out of the way.　James Woodforde, who, though a parson, was of the country gentry, and lived like a squire, gave the following dinner to a party of four who came in to play cards.

Our dinner was boiled skate and fryed eels, peas soup, rump of beef, roasted ham and three boiled chickens, with turnips, french beans, cabbage and potatoes.　Second course fricasseed Rabbits and a couple of ducks roasted, a batter pudding with currant jelly, cherry and bullace tart.

By way of dessert, we gave them some grapes, pears, walnuts and filberts, with some Morelle cherries that had been preserved in brandy.　The skate [the parson adds], that I sent to Norwich for, turned out very indifferent and looked very dark.

No wonder that Defoe, who pointed out his countrymen's faults with unfailing regularity, declared that the English " consumed more flesh than half Europe besides," and that " there was more waste of provisions in England than in any other nation in the world," the kind of remark which has been repeated by subsequent critics with a wearying monotony.

Wine was another commodity which was consumed in vast quantities, and as a result of the Methuen treaty in 1703, port wine was let into the country almost duty free. It could be bought in its new heady state at 1s. 4d. a quart in any tavern and the country gentleman laid down pipes and tuns of it.

> Valiant and firm the Caledonian stood
> Old was his mutton and his claret good.
> "Let him drink port," the English statesman cried.
> He drank the poison and his spirit died.

Neither the Englishman's spirit, nor for the matter of that, the Scotsman's, showed any sign of dying ; but this import of heavy cheap wine ousted the old English beer and mead from the tables of the gentry, and greatly checked the consumption of light French wines. Incidentally, it must have tended to the serious increase of drunkenness.

Much of our knowledge of the life of the country gentry has come down to us in their letters. Beautifully written with faded ink upon many pages, crossed and recrossed, they tell the story of the times.

> The distemper among the horned cattle which prevails to a dreadful degree.
> I had a very bad coming down ; we were overturned, but, thank God, none of us had no hurt ; the next day ye coach stook

fast and we were all forced to get out in ye mire and dirt, and so late before we got to ye inn. *Verney Letters.*

My neckclothes being all worn out I intend to wear stocks, but not unless they are more fashionable than the former. In that case I shall be obliged to you if you will buy me a handsome stock buckle for very little money; for twenty or twenty-five shillings, perhaps, a second hand affair may be purchased that will make a good figure at Olney. *Cowper's Letters.*

Nobody has such a thing as silk buttons to a silk waistcoat, and if you have it done with silver it will be very handsome, and my lord thinks so too. You have sent up one half of your britches, and I must have the other half of them sent up, for the britches is too long, and we want that which is too much for the britches, to make the wescote compleat, and can't do without it, so pray don't fail to send it by John Innes the carryer next week. *Verney Letters.*

We received your kind present of a codling and oysters. The codling was very good; but the oysters, half of them were as black as ink and the other half was poisoned with the stench, for they were all of a ffroth and your ffishmonger should give you your money again. We return you hearty thanks for them. *Purefoy Letters.*

Such entries as these carry us back into the intimate life of the century. Long some of these letters are, and we may wonder if people often cared to pay 10*d.* or 1*s.* for the privilege of reading the ordinary gossip of the daily life. Very few, however, in the higher classes, paid much for their letters. In a single year Timothy Burrell, a man of many friends and of good education, paid 5*s.*

All members of parliament had the privilege of sending letters free, and they were also permitted to sign as many covers or sheets of writing paper as they pleased. These they gave to their friends, or occasionally sold, or allowed their servants to sell.

In 1715 the value of franks amounted to £24,000 and by 1763 it had increased to the enormous sum of £170,000. A country gentleman, wanting a horse or a couple of hounds, would have them franked half across England.

In writing to friends it was thought more polite to have the letter franked by a member of their party.

Political feeling ran very high, and in the earlier years of the century the strife can be well understood. The Jacobite, though he was always romantic, and often brave and gallant, stood in the eyes of the Whig for the support of tyranny and alliance with a foreign power.

" Huzza for old England," says Fielding's Jacobite squire, " twenty thousand Frenchmen be landed in Kent."

Jacobitism, however, never really took hold in England, and as the country progressed it gradually faded out into a pretty empty thing, a drinking of the King's health " over the water," and wearing white roses on the 10th of June.

" The principal difference," says Mr. Drinkwater, " between the Whigs and the Tories, was that the Whigs were in office, while the Tories coveted it, and that the Tories, once their Jacobite passions had subsided, would have employed power in all essential respects as it was employed by the Whigs."

The passions engendered by politics were, however, fierce and abiding. Politics broke friendships, divided families, and were responsible for duels, feuds and financial ruin.

" Pray, Mamma," said a little girl, the daughter of a famous Whig house, " are Tories born bad or do they become so ? " To which her mother gravely replied,

" They are born bad, my dear, and they become worse."

We hear of a Welsh baronet, Sir George Williams and his son, both posting up to Cambridge with four horses to vote at a parliamentary election. Sir George was a Tory and his son was a Whig, but they did not trust each other sufficiently to pair.

The money spent upon elections was enormous. The bribing of voters, which is said to have commenced in the reign of Charles II, was naturally greatest in the towns. In the country, tenants as a rule voted for their landlords, though they were not always returned.

> I was in great hope [says Elizabeth Adams, writing one of her delicious letters to Sir John Verney] my countrymen would have made themselves hapy in their choys of you, but I see men as well as wimen often chuses to the worst, and so has my felow bumcins done now.

What the squire so often ruined himself over was the buying of a seat in Parliament.

" Perhaps it will be the best way," says Lady Mary Montague, writing to her husband in 1714, " to deposit a certain sum in some friend's hands and to buy some little Cornish borough." When Lady Mary wrote the practice was in its infancy. Later in the century the country was invaded by the " nabob," the business man or trader, who had made a vast fortune in India. The nabob considered the best way to establish himself in the country was to buy a seat in Parliament. The price of boroughs consequently rose, and enormous sums were paid for them.

Something has been said in another chapter of the changes and improvements in agriculture. These improvements were entirely due to the energy and generosity of the country gentlemen. If they had not found the money for the necessary agricultural experiments, it is quite certain that no one else would. By so doing, they greatly improved the value of their properties ; but in the majority of cases this was not their chief motive.

" Thirty years ago," says Arthur Young, speaking of a district in Norfolk, " it was an extensive heath, without either tree or shrub. Now there is an excellent turnpike road . . . and the whole laid out in enclosures and cultivated in the Norfolk system in superior style. The whole is let at 15/8 an acre, ten times the original value."

In the following chapter, some account is given of Thomas Coke of Holkham. The agriculture of his time owed more to him than to any other man ; but Coke was only doing on a large scale and with great ability what many a squire, up and down the country, was trying to do in a lesser way and with smaller means.

Sir Thomas Parkyns, of Bunny in Nottinghamshire, was an excellent and active country gentleman, most versatile in his talents. Besides building his own enormous house, he erected a school, a hospital for four widows, and a vicarage. He put a new roof on the parish church, compiled a Latin grammar, wrote a treatise on wrestling, and a pamphlet upon the duties of servants, in which he declared that " by a notorious reverse of nature, masters were vilely and contemptibly become the slaves of their servants, and the equal of their slaves." To assist these slavish masters, he drew up a list of wages to be paid in most industries in the country, which the Court of Quarter Sessions embodied in its own assessment of wages in 1723.

On the other hand he was eager to relieve distress and right injustice.

He wrote as follows :

To the Constable and Churchwardens and others, the Overseers of the poor of the parish of Burton Joyce, Greeting :

Whereas complaint hath been made unto me, Sir Thos. Parkyns, Bart. one of His Majesty's Justices of the Peace . . . that George Merston of your town, who appears to me to be an inhabitant, legally settled in your sd. parish, is in great need and poverty, and likely to perish for want of employment to maintain himself and family. These are therefore, in His Majesty's name, to command you the CH. Wardens, etc. to set ye said George Merston on work, or pay unto him two shillings weekly forth and out of your publick levy for ye use of ye poor made . . . otherwise to come before me, and show cause to the contrary. Here of fail not at your peril.

A fierce letter ! We are not surprised to learn that the writer of it took a great interest in wrestling. He used to have a number of young men in to wrestle on the hearthrug in his drawing-room, " beefeaters, all of them, for he could scarce tolerate a sheep biter or anyone else with the sign of a pap bottle about him." He was a fine old Diehard and he did his duty as he saw it.

One of the chief avocations of a country gentleman was that of a justice of the peace, a position in the eighteenth century of some honour and distinction.

It has been computed that at the beginning of the eighteenth century there were 3,000 magistrates in England and Wales.

For the most part they were men of wealth and good family, although there were exceptions. Bishop Burnet had complained in 1691 that " none were left, either on the bench or the militia, that did not with zeal go into the humour of the court."

This meant that in a district where the country gentlemen were Catholics or Jacobites, shopkeepers and other small freeholders might sit upon the bench. Such men were often admirably suited to the office ; but they were regarded with much disapprobation and contempt by their confreres.

I remember [says Oldmixton in his *History of England*] a west country baronet, distinguished alike by his fiery face and fiery zeal, being opposed on the bench by a Justice who had the reason on his side, said in answer to his reason, "Fine times indeed when gentlemen must be taken up by Blue Apron men," alluding to his brother justice having been a shopkeeper. The latter retorted, "Whatever the Blue Apron man has is his own," alluding to a very heavy incumbrance which the baronet could never clear his estate of.

The retort was not likely to soothe the fiery magistrate and it must be admitted that in some cases the strictures of the country gentlemen were justified.

An honest thriving farmer or tradesman had seldom time to attend to magisterial duties, and the man who pushed himself forward had often his own axe to grind. The custom of the time allowed the justice to reimburse himself for his trouble and expenditure of time by taking for himself certain small fees. They were so small that a respectable stipend could only be assured by numerous convictions and very often by the most unblushing acceptance of bribes. Fielding's predecessor at Bow Street had made a thousand a year by his office, "the dirtiest money on earth," good Henry Fielding called it.

These "trading justices" were, chiefly, if not entirely, to be found in the towns, and more particularly in London. When honest Matt. Bramble, fresh from the country bench, encounters such a creature on his visit to town he is quite nonplussed.

He cannot conceive why the magistrate keeps on remanding the case against Humphrey Clinker. A friend at last drops a hint that the justice is waiting for a bribe, and Bramble is as righteously indignant and astonished as any man need be.

The country magistrates for the most part disdained bribes; the best of them indeed refused to take the small fees which the law allowed them.

" The magistrate," one of them observed, " should not only refrain from taking any money. He should be above the possibility of such a suspicion."

The faults of the rural justice, at any rate in the earlier years of the century, were prejudice and ignorance. Sometimes he acted with extreme harshness and cruelty, especially when any infringement of the game laws was in question.

"I know," says the rascally Scout in *Joseph Andrews*, " some justices who make as much of committing a man to Bridewell as his Lordship at ' size ' would of hanging him. But it would do a man good to see his Worship, our justice, commit a fellow to Bridewell. He takes so much pleasure in it ; and when once we ha' 'un there we seldom hear any more of 'un. He's either starved or eat up by vermin in a month's time."

We may hope such things were rare. The milder manners, which years of settled prosperity brought, the spread of education and the custom, which grew up during the century, for clergymen to be magistrates, raised the tone of the county bench and mitigated its severity. Nowadays the work of the rural justice is not onerous, but in the eighteenth century an immense deal of business was thrown upon him.

He attended at Quarter Sessions, at Highway Sessions, when the state of the roads was inquired

into, and perhaps occasionally improved ; at Brewster
Sessions, and, in addition, he had the right, and was
indeed enjoined, to try cases, and settle disputes in
his own house. The diaries and notes of some
justices have come down to us, and the impression
they give is that an immense deal of petty crime and
litigation existed through the century.

We find magistrates with four or five cases to settle
in a day, and in addition, the issuing of warrants and
summonses ; the signing of the parish accounts ;
inquiring into cases of settlement, or giving passes
to labourers and wayfarers to proceed to other
parishes ; granting relief to necessitous persons
which the overseer may have refused ; issuing affiliation orders ; swearing affidavits ; advising the surveyor as to the state of the roads and enforcing
statute labour for the purpose of mending them.
These and many other duties fell upon the rural
justice.

Early in the century when religious influences were
strong, we find the magistrates very actively engaged
in putting down Sunday amusement, trading and
travelling ; also brothels, gaming houses and the
practice of swearing (a magistrate hearing a man swear
could then and there fine him for it), and vice and
immorality generally. This enthusiasm was short-
lived ; but the magistrate had plenty to do in the
ordinary execution of his duty. People poured into
his house at all hours, with complaints, accusations
and requests. The constable dragged thither his
prisoners, often with an excited mob of villagers at
his heels.

The unfortunate magistrate, who had no clerk, was
expected to take coherent notes of all these proceed-

ings. It is not surprising that this was not always done, and we find an unfortunate young magistrate who had had his case removed by certiorari to the King's Bench, where it was subsequently quashed, lamenting his neglect of his notes. "I regret," he says, "that I kept only loose minutes of what passed before me at the hearing instead of taking down the evidence in full and correctly, as ought always to be done. For this omission, I must plead that I was but little conversant with business; and secondly, the interruption and distraction occasioned by the clamour and contention of the parties, completely bothered me."

In some cases it was enacted that magistrates must sit in pairs, so we have what were called "double justices." For such matters as the appointment of Surveyors of the Highway and Overseers of the Poor, for fixing the poor rate, and, early in the century, for licensing, it was necessary that two justices should sit. This they did quite informally in their own houses.

The burthen of so much business became at last intolerable, and the petty sessions was established, with a fixed meeting-place and a clerk. This reform had been established for some time in towns before it was set up in the country, and must have been a boon to magistrates, and an aid to a better administration of the law.

When the squire of the parish was a magistrate his power over the people was very great; and even when he had not been put upon the bench he exercised a very wide paternal influence. That there were some boorish and cruel men and a few rapacious scoundrels cannot be denied; but in many if not in most parishes the squire tried to do his duty as he saw it. He protected his people against overseers and other oppressors, gave generally in time of need with an open hand, and recognized that he had a duty towards the men whom he employed, and the people who lived upon his land.

## II

## COKE OF NORFOLK

IN the year 1759 a little boy of five years was
painted by Sir Joshua Reynolds as the young
Hannibal. When that boy, Thomas Coke of Holkham, came to manhood he was destined to fight as
important battles as Hannibal on the stony infertile
soil of Norfolk.

For a few years after he grew up he lived the usual
life, socially and politically, of the young man of his
age and position ; though naturally fond of the country and all field sports. Then the Tories swept the
country at a general election and Coke, who was a
Whig and a firm supporter of Fox, found himself
without a seat in the House. He was already, from
his possession of Holkham and many barren acres, a
man of importance in the county, and looking round
for further outlet for his great activities, chance
guided him to agriculture.

Two tenants on his estate asked for a renewal of
their leases, and Coke demanded a yearly rental of
5s. an acre for the land. Even allowing for the immense depreciation of the value of money, the
rent was low ; but the farmers refused to pay it,
one of them, indeed, declaring that the land was
not worth more than 1s. 6d. an acre, which his
father had paid. Coke, with characteristic energy,

HOLKHAM HALL

took over the land himself and proceeded to farm it. A large part of the Holkham estate was salt marshes, reclaimed from the sea in the seventeenth century, and the rest was little better than a rabbit warren.

When Mrs. Coke told Lady Townsend, Walpole's beautiful Statira, that she was going into Norfolk, the old lady's comment was a perfect description of the county.

" Going into Norfolk, are you, my dear ? Then all you will see will be one blade of grass and two rabbits fighting for that."

In few parts of England was agriculture so poor. In what is now, even in these depressing years, a rich corn-growing country, not an ear of wheat was raised. A little rye was miserably grown, about 800 sheep were fed with difficulty on Coke's 3,000 acres, and it was thought quite impossible to keep milch cows, or indeed any kind of cattle. When Coke asked neighbouring farmers the reason for this state of things, they blamed the seasons and the weather, and the import of foreign corn to Blakeney and Cley, and, above all, they blamed the sandy, worthless, Norfolk soil. Coke retorted with the old Norfolk proverb that " Muck is the mother of money." They must keep more beasts, he said, and better beasts.

At Dishley there lived a breeder named Robert Bakewell, of whom the envious said that his animals were " too dear for anyone to buy, and too fat for anyone to eat." Him Coke invited to Holkham, and when the breeder informed him that the Norfolk sheep had backs like rabbits, and were the very worst in England, he asked for his help and advice. Bakewell took him home to Leicestershire with him and showed him his own sleek beasts.

" Mr. Coke," he said, " give me your hand and I will guide it," and taking his hand in his own, he passed it over the cattle, and taught him how to judge an animal. Coke promptly increased the number of sheep upon his farm, trying various breeds, including merinos, with which, and with Southdowns, he had his greatest success.

When he had improved his breed of sheep, Coke set about importing cattle, at first Shorthorns, and then Devons, which he found most suited to the country. The problem of manure had still to be solved. The " muck which was the mother of money " was insufficient to manure that arid soil, chemical manures were not yet invented, and it was not until 1794 that a Lancashire farmer ground bones in his mill and sold his surplus to his neighbours.

Coke turned his attention to the sub-soil—a rich marl. He caused deep pits to be dug, and covered the sandy surface with the fertile earth. In 1760 Stillingfleet had pointed out the difference between good and bad herbage ; but no farmer had hitherto paid any attention to him. When the grasses were in flower, Coke called the village children around him, showed them what he wanted, and despatched them to scour the country for the necessary seed. By such means, clover and good grasses were made to flourish, and Lady Townsend's rabbits would have found their one blade of grass multiplied a thousand-fold. He next experimented with the drill on 3,000 acres of corn lands, and, discovering the advantage of this in labour saving, economy of seed and facility of cleaning the land, he adopted it. In the same way, after experiment, he introduced the use of oil cake, the growing of swedes and potatoes—of which latter crop his neighbours had said " that perhaps they would not poison the pigs."

Coke certainly did not belong to that particular class of fools who think they can farm without hard work and by the light of nature.

Early and late he was in the fields, labouring in his smock frock like any peasant, and he set himself to learn his job with the most self-sacrificing industry. Robert Bakewell was only one of his teachers. He picked the brains, such as they were, of all the farmers in the neighbourhood. He then mounted his horse, and rode through the length and breadth of England, braving bad roads, bad inns, and highwaymen. He came back at once cheered and despondent—cheered because Norfolk was, at least, no worse than many other counties in England, and despondent at the crass ignorance, stupidity, and conservatism of the countryside. In Yorkshire he had seen fertile meadows, thick with such grasses as he had only dreamed of, and in a score of these only one donkey had been grazing. In Shropshire he had ridden many miles and had seen two sheep, one being driven along the road, and the other in a field it is true, but chained up on account of its dangerous propensities.

It was estimated that during his life Coke spent more than half a million upon his farms, cottages and agricultural buildings. It is true that his revenue also increased. When he began his farming career, the annual gross rental from his estates was £2,200; in 1816 it had risen to £20,000. His rents were not excessive, though much higher than in most parts of the country, and his leases contained management clauses, till then almost unknown. His tenants prospered with him, it being urged against him that his farmers lived like gentlemen, driving their curricles and drinking port wine.

The population of Holkham, which in 1776 was under 200, had swelled to 1,100 by the nineteenth century. The two ale houses in the village had gone, and a deputation had waited on Mr. Coke to suggest that, as the neighbouring workhouse was always empty, it had better be pulled down. Even Cobbett, who hated landlords, admitted that Coke was an exception.

" Everyone," he declared, after a visit to Holkham, " made use of the expressions towards him which affectionate children use towards their parents."

The annual sheep shearings were great events. They took the place of the modern agricultural show. Tenants brought their best animals and received substantial prizes and visitors came from all parts of the country, and even from America. Jonathan Binns, a Quaker farmer of Lancashire, thus describes a visit to Holkham :

Having borrowed a saddle and bridle I rode to Holkham and had the pleasure of finding Mr. Coke at home & met with every civility & attention. Mr. C. was engaged for the day ; but directed his bailiff to show me round the farm in his occupation, consisting of 2,000 acres, . . . Mr. C. invited me to dine, but as I had ridden on horseback along limestone, splashy roads & had no change of dress, intending to return in the evening, I could not accept the invitation. He would not hear of this, as he had arranged to ride round the farms with me next day, & he kindly said he would provide me with a clean shirt and what was necessary, & as his steward was away from home I might have his room, & I must stop 2 or 3 days, I could not see all in less time. Of course I had neither the power nor the wish to decline such unexpected hospitality. I dined at Holkham that day. The company consisted of the Lady and two Miss Hunlokes, Lady & two Miss Fords, Mrs. & three Miss Blackwells, Miss Coke, Miss Arbuthnot, Miss Anson, Sir Thomas Arbuthnot, Coll Ponsonby, Coll Cheney, Mrs. Newcombe, Mrs. Odell or Odie. I spent the evening most agreeably & never found less ceremony in any house that I ever was in. The next morning I accompanied Mr. C. on horseback thro' the parks and grounds . . . called on some of the tenants, the two Mr. Moores. He remarked to me afterwards that they looked too well, & that this was caused by their good living, & said he should like all his tenants to be able to drink their pint of wine to dinner and keep their hunter. . . .

Dined again at Mr. C.'s and met nearly the same persons as yesterday. Mr. C.'s friends come without invitation, his house being open to all ; they went away also without taking formal leave ; at the dinner table Mr. C. noticed the newcomers & used to say O. such a one has left. Those who wished to leave before dinner had something provided for them in a room for the purpose, & anyone who wished to go out shooting had an early breakfast ready, they had only to help themselves. Mr. C.'s friends sat as long as each liked at the dinner table, & dropped off one by one to join the ladies. Tea & coffee were in the adjoining room & anyone that wished for it, went and took it ; in the evening candles were brought into the next room & without the ceremony of taking leave you took one & retired to your bedroom. Thus throughout in this noble mansion, there was the greatest liberty, united with the greatest simplicity and liberality. Mr. Coke was a very handsome man of about 70. Some of the ladies at the dinner table were remarking on his fine handsome countenance in which not a wrinkle could be seen. He was desirous that a nephew should marry a daughter of the Earl of Albemarle & was recommending him to her, & she said she would rather marry him than his nephew. He took her at her word & they were soon married. This of course was since I was there. This lady brought him six children, sons and daughters.

It may be urged with truth that Coke was an unusual man, and not typical of the ordinary landowner.

Few, if any, equalled him, but in their own way, and according to their means and abilities, the country gentlemen of England were doing the work which Coke did, though on a smaller scale, and without his extraordinary genius.

# CHAPTER IV

## THE COUNTRY PARSON

### I

HE liveth like an honest plain farmer, as his wife is dressed but little better than a goody. He is sometimes graciously invited by the squire, where he sits at an humble distance. If he gets the love of his people, they often make him little useful presents. He is happy by being born to no higher expectation, for he is usually the son of some ordinary tradesman or middling farmer. His learning is much of a size with his birth and education, no more of either than a poor hungry servitor can be expected to bring with him from college.

This is Swift's description of the country parson of his time. That gloomy dean lived in the reign of Anne, the good queen whose bounty every clergyman and tithe payer, nowadays, has cause to remember. A wave of strong religious feeling passed over England in the reign of Anne. It was evanescent and was succeeded by an age of complacent torpor. In the reign of Anne were founded the religious societies. The S.P.C.K. and the S.P.G. had been started in 1698 and in 1701; but various other societies for the reformation of manners, and for the leading of a godly life, were founded by ardent youth. Daily services and frequent celebrations of the Holy Communion were advocated, and in the towns, at least, were often adopted. It became apparent, moreover, to thoughtful churchmen that stipends of £20 and £30 per annum, which had possibly been more nearly sufficient, when money had a greater purchasing power, were now wholly inadequate. The queen, with a generosity which is often forgotten, bestowed upon the clergy the first fruits and tenths, which, originally the property of the Pope, were appropriated at the Reformation by Henry VIII.

The Bounty, when first instituted, was computed to amount to £17,000 a year, a modest sum, even in those days, with which to relieve so many indigent.

In 1716 the *Stamford Mercury* included the following among its advertisements :

If any clergyman of good character has the misfortune to be destitute of preferment and will accept of a curacy of £27 in money yearly and a house kept, let him with speed, send to Mr. Wilson, Bookseller in Louth or the Rev. Mr. Charles Burnett of Burgh in the Marsh, near Spilsbury, in the county of Lincoln, and he may be further satisfied.

It does not seem that his satisfaction could have been great, but there were clergymen even worse off.

The cheapest curates [wrote Archbishop Tenison to Queen Anne] are too often chosen . . . by lay improprietors some of whom have allowed but £5 to £6 a year for the services of the church. Such having no fixed place of abode, are powerfully tempted to a kind of vagrant and dishonourable life, wandering for better subsistence from parish to parish.

Some were hired by the nobility and others to read prayers at 10*s*. a month. They were known as trencher chaplains, and it is some of these men whom Macaulay lashes in his attack on the clergy of the seventeenth and eighteenth centuries. He describes them as the toadies and hangers-on of great men, condoning and even encouraging their vices, feeding on their broken meats, and marrying their cast-off mistresses. The picture is, no doubt, over-drawn : there were chaplains who were honourable men, the friends and mentors of their employers. As the century advanced and religion became less and less regarded, the keeping of private chaplains was looked upon as a waste of money, which might be more profitably spent on rearing pheasants, or on putting down a pipe or two of port. It was not surprising that the poor country parson looked for other ways of earning his living. Some who had sufficient learning took in pupils. That pathetic and wholly delightful man, William Jones, who was at first curate and then Vicar of Broxbourne, in Hert-fordshire, eked out his dismal stipend by attempting to put some learning into the heads of dunces. His pupils were a great trial to him ; but he could not live without them.

" It struck a damp upon my spirits," he writes, " when casting up my accounts, I found that the expenses of the last quarter exceed £36, which sum is almost double my income for the same quarter." He wrote, besides his journal, *A Book of Domestic Lamentations*, which, as he had a shrewish wife and every kind of domestic affliction, is the sort of book we should expect him to write. What we should not expect are such entries as this : " The more children the more blessings, I will not despair." Poor man ! he had nine of these blessings and they were not particularly satisfactory. " I have every-thing I can wish for, at least, everything I ought to wish for," he adds, thinking perhaps of his shrew of a wife and of the arrogance of pupils, and the

stinginess of some of his parishioners. He was a
man of deep spiritual fervour, and full of charity
and loving kindness, well educated and with social
gifts. He is often asked out to dine or sup or play
cards. The latter, with dancing, he had eschewed at
Oxford, and about the propriety of dinner and
supper parties he is very doubtful.

"A clergyman's life," he says, "should be chiefly
spent among his books . . . whatever time he can
spare should be laid out in exhortory advising, com-
forting and assisting his poor parishioners, especially
those who are sick."

It is curious to our thinking that such an excellent
clergyman as Jones should consider that his life
should be spent "chiefly among his books." How
few parish priests in our own day find time for even
the most necessary study. In the eighteenth century,
however, a parson was not expected to do more
than read the service and preach once or twice on
Sunday. If he made friends with, and visited his
people, so much the better, but he had not the multi-
farious duties of the modern clergyman. He never
served tables. There were none to serve. Men of
the calibre of William Jones occupied themselves
with their books, others were less harmlessly employed.

Jones had one enemy: "this great mushroom
man" as he calls him, who had sprung from being
a groom in Lord Monson's stables to a position of
some authority and affluence in the parish. He tries
to prevent Jones from becoming the Vicar, but in
this is fortunately unsuccessful.

"Fiend Rogers," is the clergyman's opening to a
letter to this man; but he pities and visits him when

he is ill. He lives on good terms with all other men, even with the dissenters, who were too often regarded with suspicion and dislike by the country clergy. He even opposes the hell-fire doctrine of his time.

The Lord [he writes] is good to all and his tender mercies are over all his works. I confess I know not how to reconcile this most benevolent declaration of Holy Scripture with the eternal damnation of any soul which a wise, just and all perfect God has formed. . . . Many poor outcasts, whom these Jonahs, these religionists, or shall I write damnationists seem to consider in a state of reprobacy will, I firmly believe, be cheered with as welcome a greeting to the right hand of their Redeemer and Judge as they themselves can possibly expect.

Jones tells us nothing of his house, but there is a charming description of Dr. Primrose's vicarage in the *Vicar of Wakefield* which Goldsmith probably copied from life.

My house consisted of but one storey, and was covered with thatch, which gave it a great air of snugness. The walls on the inside were nicely whitewashed and my daughters undertook to adorn them with pictures of their own designing. Though the same room served for parlour and kitchen that only made it the warmer. Besides, as it was kept with the utmost neatness, the dishes, plates and coppers being well scoured, and disposed in bright rows on the shelves, the eye was agreeably relieved, and did not want richer furniture. There were three other apartments, one for my wife and me, another for our two daughters, within our own; and the third with two beds for the rest of the children.

Jones' stipend was better than that of Dr. Primrose, who had only £15 a year, but he augmented his living by farming about 20 acres of excellent land.

Such men as Jones, and many others with far less learning and piety, might eke out their miserable stipends by taking pupils; there were others who lived like Dr. Primrose or Swift's "honest plain farmer," or as the village tradesman. Such a man was Robert Walker (1709–1802), the curate-in-charge of Buttermere and afterwards Vicar of Seathwaite in Cumberland. He was the youngest son of a farm labourer, used to poverty and hardship in his own home ; but he found his stipend of £30 a year somewhat inadequate. He was an expert weaver and set up his looms in the very church itself, where he also taught as a schoolmaster for eight hours a day, using the altar as a table. When he died he was worth £2,000 and had gained the name of Wonderful Walker, and the respect of William Wordsworth, who wrote of him that " his good works formed an endless retinue."

" A journeyman in almost any trade or business, even a bricklayer's labourer, or the turner of a razor grinder's wheel, all circumstances considered, is generally better paid than a stipendiary curate." This was written in the eighteenth century, and if for curate, we should substitute vicar, the words would be true of the present day. In those days as in these the chief remedy proposed for the poverty of the clergy was pluralism. When two or more livings were held together they were not supposed to be more than forty miles apart, an impossible distance even in these days, and in the eighteenth century it often meant that the incumbent never entered a parish from one year's end to another. He put in a poor curate, paid him a miserable pittance and appropriated the rest of the stipend. It was calculated that of all the parishes in England only 4,412 had resident parish clergymen.

Dr. Willes, who was Bishop of St. David's, was

also Canon of Westminster, Canon and Dean of
Lincoln, and the Rector of one London and two
country livings. Watson, Bishop of Llandaff, finding
no episcopal residence there, went to Westmorland,
where, as he said, he made a great success of agriculture, improved his own health, and amassed a
very comfortable provision for his family.

These were extreme cases of pluralism and non-
residence. Some attention was usually paid to the
Canons. When a clergyman applied to Archbishop
Potter for a dispensation to hold two livings in the
same county, the horrified Archbishop pointed out
that they were " out of distance."

" If Your Grace," said the bold cleric, " will look
into the map of Kent, you will find they are nearer
than Lydd and Wrotham." As the Archbishop had
just presented these two livings to his own son, he
presently considered that the least that was said about
the Canons the better, and gave the clergyman his
dispensation.

The Bishops may have been pluralists ; they may
have passed their days in translating Greek plays and
writing philosophy, or like Lord Bristol, that peri-
patetic prelate, in travelling half over Europe ; but
they were men of respectable lives and of decent
though torpid morals. Of all the clergy this could
not be said. Many of them lived a life of pleasure,
hunting and shooting, drinking, cock fighting and
dicing.

Fine gentlemen [a contemporary describes them] who are far
more anxious to attain the fame of being excellent shots, giving
the view halloo, well mounted in the field, and being in at the
death, than raising their voices at the desk or pulpit, or feeding
the flock, whom they are eager to fleece.

They were sometimes men of the lowest moral character, too drunken to read the service, too fuddled to preach, reeling against the altar as they administered the sacrament.    They robbed and filched from their parishioners, they seduced their neighbours' daughters, their lives were a by-word and a scandal, and yet it was very seldom that such men were indicted in the ecclesiastical courts.    The social position of the clergy differed enormously.    Some, like Fielding's Parson Adams, were entertained in the squire's kitchen with a cup of ale, others might be asked to dine with the gentry, but they were expected to retire before the pudding was put upon the table.    Clergymen, like Parson Woodforde and his friend Mr. Du Quesne, were neighbours and friends to all around them, entertaining and being entertained on terms of equality by the squire and his wife, and all the gentry in the neighbourhood. Their position depended entirely upon their birth and education.    Swift's parson, who was the son of an ordinary tradesman or middling farmer, would have felt out of his element at the squire's table.

William Jones was continually refusing invitations to the houses of the neighbouring gentry.

The decline of religion and morality after the death of Queen Anne is very remarkable.    It was even more sudden and astonishing than the decline of religion and morals in our own day.    In the reign of Anne churches were re-built and restored ; there were daily services, in many places of worship the Holy Communion was frequently administered, the poor were cared for, prisoners were visited, schools and libraries were founded, missionaries were sent out to the heathen, and various religious societies were formed by young men desirous of leading godly lives. A generation or so later there was a great change. The churches were shut up all the week, and opened for one service on a Sunday. The Holy Communion was celebrated thrice a year and dirt, decay and general neglect characterized the House of God.[1]

The little associations for religious study and the practice of a good life had ceased to exist, or, like Wesley's band, were jeered at as they went to weekly communion. Various reasons have been assigned for this disastrous change. The non-jurors had been cast out, and in these men the church lost a zeal for godliness and sound learning which was not easily replaced.

Because of an attack by Convocation upon a book by the Bishop of Bangor, that meeting was suppressed in 1717 and the clergy, having now no religious centre, where they could discuss matters pertaining to their calling, sank into sloth and indifference. The social influence of the Court, which has always been great in England, was not directed towards religion and morality. Good Queen Anne was dead, and the influence of the first two Georges was certainly neither religious nor moral. It is, however, very easy to overpaint any picture, and we must remember that the finest portraits of clergymen since the time of Chaucer were painted by eighteenth-century novelists. If the kindly Goldsmith may be accused of sentimentality, the author of *Joseph Andrews* certainly never minced his words, and his Parson Adams is even more attractive than the Vicar of

---

[1] We are speaking generally. There were many exceptions; but it is the memory and tradition of scandals which comes down through History.

Wakefield.   There were certainly many parishes where
the parson lived an absolutely careless or even a dis-
solute life, where the church was dirty, and the service
gabbled over once a Sunday was the extent of his
ministrations.   There were individuals and communi-
ties who, then as now, were virtually heathen.   At
the close of the eighteenth century, a lady staying
in West Yorkshire noticed a woman on Good Friday
sitting at her cottage door spinning.   She stopped
and spoke of the events which the day commemorated
and of our Lord's life and works.

" Pray, ma'am," said the woman, " did you know
him ? "

Lest we should think that we have gone far upon
the road of religious knowledge, the reply of an
East London woman to a clergyman who spoke to
her on the same subject is worth quoting.

" Oh well, sir, it all happened a long time ago,
p'raps it is not true ! "

There were, however, many men who did their
duty as they saw it.   They may not have acted with
any great enthusiasm, for enthusiasm was not the
order of the day ; but they saw that things were
done decently, and that the church was kept clean
even if it were not beautifully adorned.   They read
the service twice on a Sunday, and celebrated
the Sacrament at least thrice a year.   They visited
the poor, and relieved them as far as their means
would allow.   They admonished those whom they
considered unworthy.   Many of them were University men, who had brought away from college
rather more learning than Swift's poor hungry
servitor.   Countless sermons were published in the
eighteenth century, besides other theological works,

and a large number of these were written by the country clergy. Parson Woodforde, whom we shall consider presently, may be considered a typical country clergyman of the better sort. He was no saint. He seems to care more for his dinner than for his church; but he was a decent honourable man, very generous and hospitable, and his parishioners were fortunate in their parson. Cowper writes of a Mr. Nicholson, a north country cleric, very poor, but very good and very happy. " He reads prayers here twice a day all the year round, and travels on foot to serve two churches every Sunday through the year, his journey out and home again being sixteen miles." Such men too often leave no journal or record behind them. We read their names in the list of incumbents hanging in our parish Church; but their good deeds have not been written in any book on earth. It must also be remembered that amid the brutal immorality of the populace, and the supine indifference of a large section of the Church, was lighted the great lamp of faith and missionary endeavour, which was called Methodism. That the English Church should reject the ministry of such men as Whitefield and the two Wesleys need not surprise us. Had not the Catholic Church rejected Savonarola ? Did not the Jewish Church crucify its Master ? We must remember in explanation of this attitude that the wild enthusiasm and ranting eloquence of some of the followers of Wesley, though he himself never indulged in such extravagances, had very pernicious effects on many hearers. Religious mania is a very terrible thing, and the terror of the message, as it was sometimes delivered, had driven men out of their senses. It was said that after a sermon by

Whitefield fifteen people went mad. The mob, which was at that time unbelievably brutal and cruel, was generally actuated by a ferocious love of violence ; but behind this may have lain memories of a Puritan reign in England, when the theatres as well as the churches were shut, and sports and pastimes forbidden. They feared, that if they listened to these new preachers, it might mean that the alehouses would be closed, and the revelry at fair and feast forbidden. It would certainly mean that they were called upon to live godly, righteous and sober lives. Everywhere in England howling mobs set upon the Methodists. Their houses were burnt, they were stoned, beaten, ducked in horse ponds ; their women were subjected to the foulest outrage. In spite of such treatment, which was often connived at and sometimes even instigated by the clergy and country gentlemen, Methodism spread like a flame of fire through the land. Literally thousands flocked to hear John Wesley and Whitefield. They preached upon the hillsides, in disused quarries, on village greens, and after a while, as the faith and power of these men did its work, opposition melted, and the gospel which they preached spread over the English speaking world and beyond. Their influence was even greater, and the Evangelical revival in the English Church, the agitation for the abolition of slavery, the spread of education and religious knowledge, which all conduced to a humaner outlook in the next century, were largely due to the heroic labours and the burning faith of John Wesley and his followers.

A contributor to the *Gentlemen's Magazine* in 1799 complains that all the churches in England had had their interiors covered with whitewash.

I make little scruple in declaring that this job work, which is carried on in every part of the kingdom, is a mean makeshift, to give a delusive appearance of repair and cleanliness to the walls, when in general this wash is resorted to to hide neglect or perpetrated fractures.

The whitewash certainly hid many beauties which eighteenth-century eyes would have regarded as " Gothic and uncouth " ; but it has preserved much, which later ages have brought to light again. Many a fresco would have been destroyed as Popish ; many a piece of oak or fine carved stone put to other uses or defaced, if it had not been hidden by whitewash.

The fabric of the churches was in a most precarious state. Defoe speaks of Ely Cathedral as " tottering so much with every gale of wind . . . that whenever it does fall, all that 'tis likely will be thought strange in it, will be, that it did not fall a hundred years sooner."

Bishop Secker, speaking of the country churches in one of his charges, says, " Some I fear have scarce been kept in necessary present repair, and others by no means duly cleared of annoyances, which must gradually bring them to decay : water undermining and rotting the foundations, earth heaped up against the outside, weeds and shrubs growing upon them . . . too frequently the floors are meanly paved, or the walls dirty or patched, and the windows ill glazed and it may be in part stopped up."

These animadversions call to our minds a gloomy picture, which too often would have been a true one. The churches were frequently bare and dirty, their walls whitewashed with perhaps a painting of "Moses and Aaron upon a church wall holding up the Commandments for fear they should fall," or rows of mouldering escutcheons as their chief ornaments.

The altar was often a small table with a moth-eaten velvet cloth, closely hemmed in by railings, and without candlesticks or other ornament.   As we have seen in the case of " Wonderful Walker " it was some-times used for secular purposes, and it was quite common for the parishioners to put their hats upon it.

There were, however, many country churches which were kept in excellent order.   Henry Purefoy writes with much care and detail about the repairs of the church he attended.

Our church at Shelstone is so much out of repair, and one of the main beams broke, which is now forced to be propt to pre-vent its falling on the people and unless there is a new beam ye Revd., Mr. Harris can't repair his chancel.   The pews of the church are likewise out of repair, and must be repaired soon, and the church floor must be paved with stone, and likewise the church windows must be re-glazed there must also be a new church Bible.   I consider the tenants to have great losses in their cattle, etc. and 'tis hard times with them, so entreat you will let Mr. Taylor know that if he will condescend to give an oak tree to repair the church pews, and three guineas towards glazing the church windows, I will give an oak tree for a beam for the church and a church Bible.   Then there will be the paving of the church left for the parish to do, which will come to about £4, besides ye workmanship.

Perhaps Mr. Purefoy was not so generous as he sounded.   The oak tree came off his estate, and in another letter to a friend in London, he asks him to look out for a second-hand Bible.

It was not every parish that was blessed by a squire like Sir Roger de Coverley.

My friend Sir Roger, being a good churchman, has beautified the inside of his church with several texts of his own choosing. He has, likewise, given a handsome pulpit cloth and railed in

A Typical Country Church,
Chislehurst

the Communion table at his own expense. He has often told me that at his coming to his estate he found his parishioners very irregular, and in order to make them kneel and join in the responses he gave everyone of them a hassock and a Common Prayer Book, and at the same time employed an itinerant singing master who goes about the country for this purpose.

The one really handsome piece of furniture in the church was the great three-decker pulpit, with its immense sounding board. At the bottom sat the clerk, the next tier had the reading desk and in the highest of all the parson preached for an hour or so, by the hour glass beside him. These pulpits were often of beautiful workmanship, and it is a great pity that they should have been swept away, in that wave of iconoclastic zeal in the last century. Their height was then a necessity as nearly all churches had wooden pews, often five or six feet high, from which a view of the church was impossible. These pews were much reprobated, and have been almost entirely swept away together with the three-decker pulpit, and the west gallery. In town churches where pew rents were charged, and the poor were not admitted, or put upon hard benches under galleries, the system became a scandal. In country churches, however, each man had his own pew allotted to him. They were never paid for, but went with the houses. The squire, whoever he might be, sat in the squire's pew, and the farmer and the wheelwright in his. The squire's pew was certainly the largest and was comfortably furnished with carpets and cushions. Sometimes it had a fireplace and the footman brought in refreshments on a tray before the sermon began. These old stone churches were terribly cold in winter, for there was no form of heating, and the services

were very long. Morning prayer, litany, Ante-
Communion and sermon were the order of the day.
It was no wonder that the squire appreciated a glass
of sherry or a cup of mead, or that the congregation
was apt to slumber in the pews. In some parishes
an official was appointed to stir people up with a long
wand, or to hit them on the head if their social position
permitted. He generally combined this office with
that of dog whipper. Dogs apparently wandered in
with their masters, and hid in the pews. They were
generally whipped out again, or snatched up with the
dog tongs that were kept in some churches, and
deposited outside. Still they came, it seems undis-
couraged, for the office of dog whipper continued,
and dog tongs are now to be found in some churches
and museums.

When Thomas Hardy's father came to Stinsford
Church, he found one old man in the gallery, playing
upon the oboe. This old man was the last of a fine
band of musicians. In most country churches there
was a band in the West Gallery. They played Tate
and Brady's Psalms in verse; no doubt they were
frequently out of tune; but the interest in the services
such a practice gave, and the stimulus to music in
the parish, should not be overlooked. It is a great
pity that the eighteenth-century church band has been
swept away, in the zeal for church improvement in
the nineteenth century.

The dress of the country clergy was the cassock.
Fielding describes his Parson Adams as striding about
the countryside, with his cassock belted up above his
knees. By the end of the century the parson's cassock
was disappearing, and the parson's wig was only seen
upon the episcopal bench.

The authority of the clergy was also dwindling. Excommunications and public penances had become very rare. In the early years of the century, it was a not unusual sight for a man or woman to do penance in the church porch in a white sheet with bare feet and carrying a white rod.

" One Sarah Gore," says Parson Woodforde, " came to me this morning and brought me an instrument from the Court of Wells to perform public penance next Sunday in Castle Carey Church for having a child, which I am to administer to her publicly next Sunday after Divine Service."

Penance was usually inflicted for incontinence ; but other offences were occasionally taken notice of. Bishop Fleetwood reminded the clergy and church-wardens that rebuke and even penance should be inflicted for such offences as non-attendance at public worship, for neglecting to send children apprentices and servants to be catechised, for the non-payment of church rates, and for teaching without a licence. Slander could likewise be dealt with, as the following confession shows. It was repeated before the congregation in church : " Good people, whereas I, contrary to good manners and Christian charity, have unjustly reproached and defamed Elizabeth Bridges . . . by saying to her ' You are a strumpet, and I knew you when you lay on the Botley Road,' of which I am convicted by the same court (the Archdeacon's) by my own confession and by the decree of that court, am come hither to acknowledge my fault, which I hereby do, and am very sorry I have so defamed and injured the said Elizabeth Bridges, and do hereby ask forgiveness of the same."

This seems an admirable substitute for an action for slander.

We have already alluded to the great decline in religion and morals, which took place during the eighteenth century.   Amid much sloth and indifference, one thing stands out in sharp contrast to the customs of to-day—the observance of Sunday.   In London it is true, there was a certain amount of Sunday trading, over and above that in milk and mackerel, which was permitted by a statute of Charles II.   In London a bishop might play at cards on Sunday and receive a letter of rebuke from the King; but in the country the day was observed with great strictness.   No unnecessary work was done of any kind; Parson Woodforde was no precisian; but when his razor breaks in his hand on a Sunday, he notes it in his diary as follows:

" May it be a warning to me not to shave on the Lord's Day, or to do any other work to profane it, *pro futuro*."

Sunday travelling was unknown at the beginning of the century, and at the end was only resorted to in emergency, or to escape the attentions of highwaymen, who never took the road on a Sunday.

In a chapter given to the Church and clergy, a few words must be said for the clerk.   There had been parish clerks in England since Saxon times, and they were, in their own eyes at least, most important persons.   The saying of all the responses in church devolved upon them, the congregation for the most part remaining dumb.   On the clerk also fell the duty of keeping the books and setting down a record of baptisms, marriages and funerals, and the fees charged for these ceremonies.

John Spence, the parish clerk of Iver, kept a most interesting book. He notes that when Mr. Henry Allen dyed Jan. 7th that "the charge for the vaut was 6/8, the bell 5/4, the cerimony 4/, the minister 8/, the Barers and Bier 8/." He also notes down unusual details connected with any deaths in the parish, and some of them seem to have been most remarkable.

"Henry Beasley dyed, drowned in a hogtub. Richard Butter dyed by misfortune of a piece of timber falling on him at Hillington. Samuel Grantham dyed, unfortunately by being shott with a gun in attempting to kill a snake." Another man "dyed suddenly gooing home from church." "Sarah Hatson was drowned in a well at Sutton. William Carter dyed by being stung by bees. James Pain dyed by excessive drinking and blows by W.F. Robert Batting wilfully hanged himself in the cage, being overcome by drink and pashion."

John Hemce of Finchinfield, who enjoyed a salary of £2 1s. a year, charges 1s. 6d. for "whishing the surpets." He receives 5s. "for burying my mistress Trepe" and "10/- for burying my Master Trepe." When Pope wrote his satire which he called P.P. clerk of the parish, he was writing a satire more on Bishop Burnet's History, than upon such a humble servant as the Parish Clerk. His description of the clerk is probably very accurate. No parish clerk could have written as Pope wrote; but many a one may have said within himself to much the same effect,

Remember Paul, thou standest before men of high worship, the wise Mr. Justice Freeman, the grave Mr. Justice Tonson, the good Lady Jones, and the two virtuous gentlewomen her daughters, nay the great Sir Thomas Truby, Knight and Baronet, and my young master the Squire, who shall one day be Lord of this Manor.

Where there was no dog-whipper appointed no doubt the clerk was equally severe in " whipping forth dogs from the Temple all excepting the lap dog of the good widow Howard, a sober Dog, which yelped not nor was there offence in his mouth."

P.P. even proceeds " to moroseness, tho' sore against my heart unto poor babes in tearing from them the half-eaten apples, which they privily munched in church, but verily it pitied me, for I remembered the days of my youth."

He causes pews and benches, which had formerly been swept out once in three years, every Saturday to be swept with a besom and trimmed.

" With the sweat of my own hands I did make plain and smooth the dog's ears throughout our great Bible."

No money could be sent out of the parish without a notice to this effect from the Bishop being read in the church. These notices were called briefs, and P.P. " collected at 9 several times for 9 churches 2/- and 7¾$d$." In the Devonshire parish of Broad Clyst they collected " four shillings and two pence " towards the " Briefe for Chatteris in the Isle of Ely " which had " a losse by fire 178 lbs. up wards." The difference in money values must be remembered before we accuse the congregation of stinginess.

Pope is describing an officious, bustling creature with a good opinion of himself; but his clerk at least does his duty, even to the extent of laying the surplices in lavender, and sometimes sprinkling them with rose water.

William Jones was less happy with his clerk. "If there is a man in the parish," he says, "who reads and sings worse than anybody else it is used to make him church clerk."

## PARSON WOODFORDE

JAMES WOODFORDE, the author of the volu-
minous diary, was born at Ansford in Somersetshire in 1740. He was the son of the Vicar of that
parish, and came of learned and diary-writing stock.
His grandfather, Samuel Woodforde, was a man of
learning and the friend of painters and poets, and
he and his wife both wrote diaries, as did other
members of his family.

James Woodforde was no great scholar, though
he was fellow of his college, nor did he mix in the
great world like Pepys and Evelyn. Mr. Beresford,
who edited his diary, describes him as " that very
rare and beautiful bird, a typical Englishman." He
was certainly a typical eighteenth-century parson of
the better type.

From the time that he was ordained, till the day
of his death, he lived in small country villages, and
his diary deals entirely with the daily life of a country
clergyman. He was no saint like William Jones, no
mystic like Fletcher of Madely. After the first few
pages, personal religion is scarcely mentioned in his
diary. On the other hand he is no bigot. There
are no diatribes against the nonconformists, and he
gives with great generosity to the fund which was
raised for the exiled French priests. He reads prayers

and preaches every Sunday in the parish church, and
he celebrates the Holy Communion rather more frequently than is usual. He will ride many miles at
night in order to baptize a sick child, and he regards
Saturday night as " a very improper time to spend
the evening out anywhere." Though a peace-loving
man, he can speak his mind should the occasion need
it, whether it were to a servant " who came home
in liquor and behaved very rudely and impudently "
or to his brother-in-law to whom he lends *A Sure
Guide to Hell,* " a very good moral book if taken
properly." He was friendly and courteous to women,
but there was never a breath of scandal concerning
his moral character. In the whole of his long diary
there is nothing suggestive of evil, no salacious story,
no jest or innuendo inappropriate to his profession.
He has certainly the moral ideas of his age. He goes
out fishing with his squire's brother and the latter's
mistress, and sees nothing unbecoming in this ;
though he made a poor woman do penance in church
in " a white sheet for the sin of incontinence." He
employs a smuggler to bring him bags of hyson tea,
and though a very kindly humane man, will yet
attend bear-baitings, and go to see a hanging. To
the poor his generosity was unbounded, and his
kindness extended beyond the confines of his own
parish.

The diary begins in the year 1758 when Woodforde was an undergraduate at Oxford, and opens
characteristically with an account of various expenses.
He had paid £4 10*s*. for a superfine blue suit of
cloathes, very good cloth, and £3 for a " bad chocolate suit." A pair of curling tongs and a " wigg "
had cost 2*s*. 8*d*. and a guinea respectively, and he

had bought "two Logick books for 6/– and a sack of coal for 4/9."

He becomes a scholar of New College, and his description of the daily life of an undergraduate is most interesting.

He tells us how he " played crickett in Port Meadow, the Winchester against the Eton, and we Winton beat them " ; and he makes a pleasant friendship with two Oxford girls, Nancy and Betty Bignell, one of whom hems his handkerchiefs, and to whom he gives silver thimbles. In the free kindly fashion of the day, before strict propriety had laid a deadening hand upon social intercourse, he goes for walks with the two girls. He even pays 4d. to a man who had made verses upon them. These verses were better received than some which were made upon him by a saddler's apprentice " whom I threshed."

In 1761 Woodforde becomes a Fellow of New College, and two years later he is ordained deacon. His first curacy is at Thurloxton in Somersetshire. After vainly attempting to find lodgings, he arranges to live with his squire, Mr. Cross, " who has a noble house, good enough for any nobleman." In this noble house it is arranged that " I should live as he does (which is very well I am sure), that I should have my linen washed by him, and that he should keep my horse (corn excepted) for £21 a year."

In the following January Woodforde becomes curate of Babcary, about six miles from his home at Ansford. In return for free quarters in the parsonage and £20 a year, he agrees to give one service on a Sunday. The principal farmer, Mr. Bowers, objects that this is too little, and Woodforde expresses himself willing to provide two services if his salary is raised to £30. Eventually these terms are agreed upon, and Woodforde rides over on his cream pony to Babcary where he dines upon a sheep's head that he had carried there in his pocket. He was " rung into the parish by Mr. Bowers' orders, who gave the ringers a pail of cyder to ring me into the parish."

Woodforde now begins to describe his famous dinners, which occupy such a large part of the diary. He gives a bachelor party at Babcary and his guests play at Fives afterwards against the churchyard wall.

All through his life Woodforde seems to have been a playgoer. Every country town had its stock company and groups of strolling players performed in the villages. Castle Cary, which had then a population of little more than a thousand persons, was able to support a travelling company, and thither the diarist went, and witnessed, in rather less than two months, the *Beggar's Opera*, *Hamlet* and *Richard III*. There was certainly far more entertainment in the eighteenth-century village than in that of the nineteenth. Few strolling players would have found a living in the hungry forties, nor would a clergyman have patronised the theatre. Woodforde also danced, and he tells us that he went to " a very genteel ball at the ' Bear ' at Wincanton, and danced from ten till four in the morning with a Miss Jordan, the best dancer in the room."

Woodforde's relations with his own family are of the happiest description, though his brother John tries him much.

" After dinner," he writes, " Jack went to Wincanton to a pony race, and he did not return till after ten this evening. I am greatly afraid Jack is rather wild, but I hope not." There could soon be no doubt about brother John's wildness, and stories of his dare-devilry, Mr. Beresford tells us, still linger in the neighbourhood. He caused the diarist and his family much trouble and expense.

Woodforde loses both his father and his mother while he is living in Somersetshire. For them he had evidently the love which lasts through the ages. More than twenty years later he writes, " the loss of my dear parents I feel to this moment. I can never forget it during life." When his mother dies he makes the following entry in his diary :

It pleased Almighty God of his great goodness to take unto himself my dear good mother this morning about nine o'clock out of this sinful world, as easy as it was possible for anyone. I hope she is now eternally happy and in everlasting glory.

In 1771 his father dies and is buried with customary pomp. Crape hat-bands and lamb-wool gloves and half-crowns are given to the underbearers, the clerk and sexton and to the six women wakers, who sat up with the corpse.

Woodforde never married. The lady whom he courted, Betsy White of Shepperton, who apparently returned his affection, suddenly changed her mind and married a gentleman in Devonshire. It was a grievous blow.

In 1773 Woodforde returns to Oxford as a Fellow of New College. He stays there for a year, and is then offered the college living of Weston Longville near Norwich. Early on an April morning in the year 1775, he drives down from London in a post-chaise to inspect his new parish. He arrives at Norwich very late, having driven the hundred and nine

miles in one day, and finds the city gates shut as it
is after ten o'clock.  He spends the night at the
" King's Head " in the market-place, which was to
be his house of call whenever he went to Norwich.
The inn no longer exists, though another hostelry
which he also mentions, the " Maid's Head," is still
famous.

Woodforde now settles down in the village, where
he is to spend the remainder of his pleasant, uneventful life.

Weston Longville was a small country parish,
having then about three hundred and sixty inhabitants.  The church is a fine, perpendicular building
of which any incumbent might have been proud;
but Woodforde tells us very little about it.  His income amounted to little more than £400 a year, and
at that figure it remained.  He never advanced his
tithe, even when farmers at the end of the century
were making huge profits.  He left it to his successor to double it, which he did immediately upon
entering the parish.

On this income of a little more than £400, Woodforde managed, in spite of the heavy taxation of the
war years, to keep a staff of two maid-servants, two
men and a boy, to have three horses in his stables
and also dispense lavish hospitality and great charity
both to his relations and his poorer neighbours.

He is soon on excellent terms with his squire, Mr.
Custance, and his wife, " the best lady I ever knew,"
and he has a pleasant friendship, unbroken throughout his life, with these delightful people.  Such an
intimacy between squire and parson was rare.  Too
often, even if they could meet upon terms of equality,
the parson would quarrel about his tithes, or the

squire would find fault with the church services. Woodforde is constantly entertained at Ringland, the Custances' place, and the squire and his wife pay morning calls, and bring presents of " a shoulder of venison, or a large piece of parmesan cheese." This present giving was not confined to the Custances. Woodforde is continually receiving and bestowing gifts.

" Mr. Priest of Norwich sent a man on foot with a fine fore quarter of London lamb, and two Seville oranges."

The neighbouring clergy are soon Woodforde's friends. They have a pleasant system, modified by moons and weather, of dining at each other's houses every Monday in rotation. There is Mr. Du Quesne and Mr. Priest and Mr. Bodham and Mr. Donne and Mr. James.

Should the host have a carriage, it is usual to send it, if there be ladies of the party who have no means of transport. Mr. Dutton, who keeps a chariot and does not offer it, incurs the diarist's displeasure.

" I think he should have offered it to us, instead of putting us to the expense of hiring," says Woodforde severely. He was so hospitable himself that any failure in open-handedness provoked his censure. When paying a morning call on Mr. Du Quesne he is not pressed to remain for dinner and he notes this in his diary.

" Mem. Not asked to dinner; but should not if so." His brother-in-law had thrown out a vague invitation to come over and help them eat a fawn " but did not mention any particular day." " However they had it last week," says Woodforde bitterly, " and never let me know it."

Of his own wonderful dinner-parties he gives us many menus. The amount of food consumed seems to us to be enormous. For a dinner for four guests he provides " A leg of mutton boiled and capers, a boiled fowl and a tongue, a batter pudding, a fine turkey rosted, fried rabbits, tarts, custard and jellies. Almonds, raisins, oranges and apples after. Port wine, mountain, porter and ale, etc."

On another occasion : " We had for dinner, some pike and fried soals, a nice piece of boiled beef, ham and a couple of fowls, peas and beans, a green goose rosted, gooseberry pies, currant tarts, the charter, hung beef scraped, etc." Then as the company stayed for supper there was another great meal consisting of " fryed soals, a couple of chickens rosted, cold ham, etc., etc., artichokes, tarts, etc. Fruit after dinner and supper, strawberries, cherries, almonds, raisins, etc."

The dinners the Custances gave were even longer and finer, and when they dine with the Bishop, they were given a dinner of two courses with twenty dishes in each course. It is a relief to find that when Woodforde has no company, he dines on a fine piece of boiled beef and a suet pudding or a fine leg of mutton rosted and hot apple pie.

As Woodforde gets older, food seems to become almost an obsession. Not only great feasts, but the everyday dinner is noted down, and such disappointments as " the most miserable dinner " they gave him at an inn, when he had only about two pounds of boiled beef, and an old tame rabbit. When his sister Mrs. Pouncett dies, to whom he seems to have been sincerely attached, he makes the following entry : " It made me very miserable indeed. O tempora quo

modo mutantur !   In his temporibus, quid desdiran-
dum ! [1]   Dinner to-day a fine turkey rosted."

It is not only to his equals that Woodforde dis-
penses kindness and hospitality.   One of his first
actions on entering the parish is to give a " largesse "
to the harvest men, who were cutting wheat at the
bottom of his garden, and largesses are constantly
entered in his accounts.   When his people come to
pay tithe he gives them what he calls a frolic.   They
have a dinner of " beef rosted, a leg of mutton boiled
and plumb pudding in plenty."   On Christmas Day
he entertains various poor men to a dinner of sir-
loin of beef and plum pudding, and gives them 1s.
each.   He sends " the four breasts and hands of my
two piggs, with one of the loins " to his poor neighbours, and " having heard that Thos. Thurston's
wife (who is and has been ill a long while) longed
for some rost veal from my house . . . I sent her
a good plate of it."

" Sent poor Clarke's family a large bushel basket
of apples to make apple dumplings for poor souls "
is another entry, and in the terrible winter of 1794,
when bitter cold and poverty went hand in hand,
he subscribes £10 to the general fund for the poor.
This was a large sum for a man who had little more
than £400 a year and who was continually helping
his neighbours.

" Pray God," he writes, " ever continue to me the
power of doing good."

Woodforde never lives in the great world, but he
throws sidelights on the history and customs of the
age.

[1] " Oh, how times are changing.   What is there now to be
desired ? "

The newspapers come with accounts of battles and victories and defeats. The diarist names one of his horses Rodney after the great admiral of whose victory he reads one day in the *Gazette* at Mr. Du Quesne's, and the servants are given some strong beer and some punch " to drink Lord Nelson's health in."

It is reported at different times that the French have landed in various parts of England. Woodforde's nephew, Samuel, paints a portrait of Frederick, Duke of York, and hopes to be knighted for it. " Sam's news too great to be true," is his uncle's shrewd comment.

On August 4, 1789, " dies memorabilis " he calls it in his diary, Woodforde, when on a visit to his relations in Somersetshire, goes to Lord Digby's place at Sherborne to see the King and Queen who are staying there. " The King," he says, " looked very well and is very tall and erect, the Queen and Princesses rather short, but very pleasing in countenance and fair."

On one of Woodforde's visits to London he goes to see the King pass on his way to open Parliament when

His Majesty was very grossly insulted by some of the mob, and had a very narrow escape of being killed going to the House, a ball passing through the window as he went through old Palace Yard, supposed to be discharged by an air gun; but very fortunately did not strike the King or lords.

The mob which surrounded the coach, and hissed and hooted, was driven to frenzy by the long-continued war with France, and the terribly high prices of which it was the cause.

There are constant allusions in the Diary to out-

breaks of smallpox, which seems to have been en-
demic in the neighbourhood of Weston.   The doctor
from Mattishall comes to Woodforde's house to in-
oculate his servants for which service he is paid 10s.

The diarist is very angry when the maid Molly
puts some eggs into the rice milk which the inocu-
lated people have for supper ; but as he has approved
of their dinner of Norfolk dumplings with vinegar
sauce " of which they ate very hearty " it does not
seem that a small matter of eggs could have hurt
them.   Woodforde had, however, very odd ideas
about illness.   When his garden boy Jack gets a
touch of the ague, he gives him a dram of gin at
the beginning of the fit, and then pushes him head-
long into one of the ponds.   " He was the better
of it," he adds.

Woodforde has " a stiony in his right eyelid " and
has heard

that the eyelid being rubbed by the tail of a black cat would do
it much good, if not entirely cure it, and having a black cat, a
little before dinner I made a trial of it, and very soon after dinner
I found my eyelid much abated of the swelling.   Any other
cat's tail may have the above effect in all probability, but I did
my eyelid with my own black tom cat's tail.

Nancy Woodforde, the diarist's niece, comes to
live with her uncle, an arrangement which seems to
work well for many years, and to afford the worthy
man much comfort and pleasure.   They play backgammon or cribbage together of an evening, and
Nancy wins 1s. 6d.

" Nancy was very entertaining this afternoon," he
notes in his diary, and when she goes away for a
visit, he complains, that it is " very dull for me in
the evening now Nancy is from home."   He gives

his niece ten guineas a year as a dress allowance, five guineas on New Year's Day, and many presents. As the years advance, however, Nancy becomes very restless and " runs out against living in such a dull place."

" Nancy very discontented of late," is her uncle's comment. And yet there seemed to be an endless succession of hospitality and entertaining. There were the rotation dinners, the jaunts to Norwich and Yarmouth, even expeditions to London or to Somersetshire.

" Mrs. Custance and Nancy made the best appearance in the theatre among the ladies," says Woodforde on one occasion when they had gone into Norwich to see Shakespeare or the *School for Scandal*. Nancy's lot, according to eighteenth-century ideas, was an enviable one. She was the mistress of her uncle's house, and she owed him much kindness and generosity. If she found life dull, it was possibly her own fault. One cause of her discontent was the removal of the Custance family from Ringland.

" Our very good and worthy friends Mr. and Mrs. Custance," says Woodforde, " with five of their children with two nurses and Rising the butler, left Weston this morning about 10 o'clock, and gone for Bath. It made us quite low all the whole day."

The reader can turn the pages of the diary and see that the Custances returned eventually to Ringland, and that the intimacy was renewed, but meanwhile Mrs. Custance's unvarying kindness, and her many presents and invitations, were sorely missed by the parson's niece.

Nancy could not complain of being confined like many a countrywoman to one small village for the whole of her life. We may well admire the intrepidity of the eighteenth-century traveller. Woodforde's relations came all the way from Somersetshire to visit him, and though they may complain of fatigue on arrival, they are none the worse after jolting for three or four days in post-chaises or coaches over horrible roads. The diarist and his niece, when they go to the West, generally break the journey in London. For some unexplained reason, they travel by the night coach, which leaves Norwich at nine in the evening and reaches the Bell Sauvage on Ludgate Hill at two o'clock the next afternoon. Woodforde is a great sightseer, even going out before breakfast with Nancy and driving to St. James's Park to see the changing of the Guard. They then go over the state-rooms in the palace, and finally take a hackney coach back to their inn. After breakfast they sally out again to the Tower to see the Horse Armoury, the Small Armoury, the Artillery and the wild beasts.

After their dinner at five o'clock there is a further expedition for shopping, and all this sightseeing and early rising is after a journey of seventeen hours in a night coach.

On another occasion they go from London to Bath in the " baloon coach," so called " on account of its travelling so fast, making it a point to be before the mail coach. We trimmed it off indeed tho' only a pair of horses."

In this rapid vehicle they accomplish the journey from London to Bath in sixteen hours, where they stop at the " White Hart " inn in Stall Street, " kept by one Pickwick, very capital inn, everything in stile."

There are various accounts of such journeys in the Diary, and Woodforde evidently took a keen pleasure in travelling and sightseeing. He was not a great scholar but he makes an occasional note of the books he is reading.

"Busy in reading ' Evelina,' " he writes, " a novel lent Nancy by Mrs. Custance. There are three volumes of it, writ by a Miss Burney. They are very clever and sensible."

" I stayed up till after nine," he says on another occasion, " looking with Mr. Custance over a new set of copper plate prints respecting Captain Cook's voyage to Kamskatsea, very fine they are, cost ten guineas."

Occasionally he buys a book, but not very often. Probably he had inherited a good library from his father. He spends 9*d*. on " a small book with some poems of Goldsmith's " and buys from " a travelling man and woman who sold all kinds of trifling books Robinson Crusoe for 2/6, the life of Bamfield More Carew 2/- Complete Fortune Teller 9*d*. Laugh and Grow Fat 6*d*." It is a curious assortment, but perhaps some of them were for Nancy, and in any case the diarist was a man of simple tastes. He was not a sporting parson, as so many were in those days, but he goes out coursing occasionally.

Had prodigious fine sport with two hares, especially the last, on France Green, but killed neither [he says]. Caught three fine trout, the largest about one pound and a ¼ and 4 fine eels, also very near catching a fine trout about 2 pounds, but in landing it the top of the rod broke and so lost it.

The names of various serving men and maids are to be found scattered through the journal. They seemed to change their places almost as frequently then as they do now, though one or two, such as his man Britton, stay at the Parsonage for years. Woodforde was apparently a kind and considerate master. When his gardener Ben, who had gone to Mattishall to see Mrs. Bodham's hot-house, " did not come home till between 11 and 12, it vexed and fretted me till quite ill."

" She is one of the best maids we ever had," he writes of his young servant-maid, Molly Dade, who " had somewhat of a fever on her."

" We are both most willing to keep her, she is one of the neatest, most modest pretty girls I ever had."

She is finally sent on horseback behind Ben to Mattishall " to see if change of air would do her cough good," and she is provided with a knuckle of veal and a jug of black currant tea. In spite of this nutriment poor Molly remains ill, and the diarist regretfully looks out for another servant.

" As she did not choose to wash dishes," he says of one applicant, " I did not like to take her " ; and of another " don't think she will do, she being rather high, and her late wages £8 per annum."

As the years go on Woodforde evinces a morbid interest in his health, and recounts various symptoms at length.

Poor old man, journeys and rotation dinners and jaunts to Norwich were too much for him now. He was obliged to stay at home and huddle over the fire complaining of the bitter winters which occurred at the end of the century.

" Feel better this morning," he says, " but still very weak and querely at times."

" The gout tho' not very painful, but continually

flying about my constitution, though thanks to Almighty God, my appetite fails me not." This appetite however gives him some anxiety.

"I hope I don't eat too much," he says. "I eat five times a day at breakfast, about noon, dinner, afternoon at tea, and supper."

On October 17, 1803, he writes his last entry, "Very weak this morning, scarce able to put on my clothes, and with great difficulty get downstairs with help. Dinner to-day rost beef, etc."

On New Year's Day, 1804, Parson Woodforde dies, and we feel as we close the last volume of his diary, that we have lost a friend.

This morning [writes his niece, Nancy, in the journal which she also kept] about a quarter after ten o'clock died my ever dear uncle James Woodforde whose loss I shall lament all the days of my life. Mrs. Custance came to me about 12 o'clock.

# CHAPTER V

## THE VILLAGE DOCTOR

NO account of country life would be complete without some mention of the village doctor. A century which produced such men as John and William Hunter, Radcliffe and Erasmus Darwin was not devoid of all medical knowledge and genius.

A young man wishing to study medicine seriously, would be apprenticed to a physician or surgeon, just as any other lad might be apprenticed to a carpenter or a blacksmith. When he was out of his indentures he might perhaps walk a hospital. It was, however, often difficult for a youth to find a good doctor willing to take him as an apprentice; indeed the privilege of being the pupil of a celebrated physician or surgeon was sometimes put up to auction. Hospitals, outside London, were few. Addenbrooke's at Cambridge, which was founded in 1719 and Bristol in 1735 were the first of the country hospitals.

A man could set up as an apothecary with very little or no experience, and no sort of examination. It was not till 1815 that an Act of Parliament obliged men to qualify before setting up as a doctor. Roger Grant, who was Queen Anne's oculist, had been originally a tinker. William Reed, who is described as " mountebank, occulist and sworn operator for the eyes," could not read, his detractors said ; but he managed to get a knighthood, and to keep his own chariot.

Lady Eleanor Butler, who was given to speaking her mind, described their country apothecary as a " dirty little village quack." So, no doubt, the apothecary often was ; but there were men of a very different calibre, men who, if they knew little, as we count knowledge, were the friends of all the country-side. They would ride their rounds on horseback, the tools of their profession in their saddle-bags. They called at the farm or the cottage, they went blooding regularly at the Squire's. These are the men Crabbe describes :

> Helpers of men they're called and we confess
> Theirs the deep study, theirs the lucky guess.
> We own that numbers join with care and skill
> A temperate judgement, a devoted will
> Men who suppress their feeling, but who feel
> The painful symptoms they delight to heal.
> Patient in all their trials they sustain
> The starts of passion, the reproach of pain.
> . . . . . . . .
> To the Physician of the soul and these
> Turn the distressed for safety hope and ease.

As the century advanced, the apothecary discarded the gown and enormous wig, which had marked his profession, and dressed much as other men, though generally in dark clothes. He could not legally charge a fee for his services ; but only for the medicines which he sold, hence the complaint of a poor patient that the doctor had sent a parcel of medicine, as if to a rich man. It was often the custom when the bill was sent in, and the charges had been made for bandages, drugs, leeches, etc., to leave a blank, in which the patient might insert a sum of money sufficient, in his estimation, to recoup the apothecary for his personal attendance.    In many cases, however, the unfortunate practitioner knew better than to trust to the good feeling of his patients.    He had to charge for his drugs.    " Apothecaries' profit is become a bye word," says Adam Smith ;  but he goes on to point out that " the whole drugs which the best employed apothecary in a large market town will sell in a year, may not perhaps cost him above 30 or 40 pounds.    Though he should sell this therefore, for 3 or 4 hundred per cent. profit, this may frequently be no more than the reasonable wages of his labour, charged, in the only way in which he can charge them, upon the price of his drugs."

The following is the bill sent in by a surgeon in the year 1773.

To reducing a dislocated elbow for child or the luxeted Ulna and Radius into the lower parts of O.S. Humeris.

Likewise reducing a fracture on the O.S. Humeri or the upper part of the Arm with splints, plasters, physic and attendance £1 1.

A little medical Latin went a long way, in those days, in impressing the ignorant, and the jargon of the medical profession is ridiculed in the novels of the times.

The surgeon was in a different, though perhaps not much more enviable, position than the apothecary. He could, as we have seen, send in a bill for his attendance ; but he was looked down upon and despised by the medical fraternity, and not even allowed to perform any serious operation except in the presence of " a learned Physician."    The word apothecary comes from a Greek word meaning a

store or repository, and some original characteristics
seem to have clung to the practitioner of the eighteenth century. When Dr. Erasmus Darwin, the
great physician, wrote a letter of advice to a young
acquaintance who was thinking of setting up as a
medical man, he did not tell him to frequent the
hospital, to study medical books or to attend classes
in anatomy. He was to remember that " at first
a parcel of blue and red glasses at the windows
might gain part of the retail business on market
days ! "

" I remember," Darwin continues, " Mr. Green of
Lichfield once told me his retail business, by means
of his show shop, and many coloured windows,
produced him £100 a year."

The medicines given by medical men were often
extraordinary.

" I swallowed 2 ozs. of soap a day for 3 months,"
says an unhappy man who had the gout, " besides
oyster shell or egg shell powder. Thanks to my
constitution," he adds, " I am not killed," and he
comes to the conclusion that it is better to have the
gout.

Lord Egmont fared little better at the hands of
his physicians. " This day," he says, " I visited Mr.
John Temple, who gave me for my rheumatic pains
a bottle of right old verjuice, and advised me to take
a glass of it with a toast in it every morning fasting,
and, going to bed to rub my joints with it."

The unfortunate sufferer from smallpox was given
a black powder which was made from thirty or forty
toads burnt in a new pot and ground into a fine
powder.

" A receipt to cure fitts," seems after this quite

pleasant: " Take of miseltoe berry and leaves, and boyl them in ale, or make tea of them, and drink half a pint of it every morning or oftener if need require. That which grows upon whitethorn if possible."

Lackington quotes, though he does not commend, this prescription for a malignant fever. " A live tench applied to the feet for 12 hours . . . then buried quietly, and the patient will soon recover." This was an unpleasant, clammy remedy ; but not so drastic as Dr. Darwin's cure for hysteria. " To have the back well whipped with a bunch of green nettles." We read that " the patient was the better for it." Probably she never dared have hysteria again.

John Wesley compiled a book which he called *Primitive Physic* or *An Easy and Natural Method of curing most Diseases*. The remedies may well have been primitive, they were certainly peculiar: " To cure the quartan ague, apply to the suture of the Head, when the fit is coming, wall July flowers beating together leaves and flowers with a little salt."

As a remedy for old age the patient is to " take tar water every morning . . . or a decoction of nettles or to be electrified. But remember," Wesley characteristically adds, " the only radical cure is wrought by death."

We shall notice, in the chapter on gardening, that electricity had been used in the cultivation of plants. It is curious to find it advocated in medicine. Wesley afterwards procured a " galvanic apparatus " which was used by thousands of patients.

As late as 1748 Dr. Mead, one of the most celebrated physicians of his day, published a treatise " concerning the influence of the sun and moon upon human bodies, and the diseases thereby produced," showing that the old belief in astrology was by no means abandoned, even by men of education.

William III had declined to touch for the King's evil, saying with his usual pithy common sense, "God give you better health and more sense," but in Queen Anne's reign the service for touching was incorporated into the Prayer Book, and hundreds of people flocked to London to be touched for the evil. The disease, which was then called scrofula, was tuberculous, and it is probable that the cures said to be performed by the sovereign's touch were often genuine.

When so much superstition was countenanced by medical authority, it is not surprising that the country people flocked to white witches and to quacks. Every sort of impostor flourished. " I believe I have seen," says Steele in the *Tatler*, " twenty mountebanks who have given physic to the Czar of Muscovy. The Grand Duke of Tuskany escapes no better. The Elector of Brandenburg is likewise a very good patient."

This is the advertisement from a Lancashire paper of the year 1778 :

Ellen Haythornwaite of Dicklin Green near Whitewell in the forest of Bowland, Lancashire is supposed to be one of the best surgeons in the country. She has performed several amazing cures given up as incurable by the Whitworth doctors and others.

As for asthmas, coughs, fevers and all internal disorders, she will not prescribe a large quantity of drugs, and yet effectually cure if curable ; but as for burns, scalds, fractured skulls, bruises and all external wounds, she will in a very little time, make a perfect cure if they come to her before they are mortified. N.B. She will take nothing in hand if she finds it incurable. Her charges are also very moderate : twelve pence a week if they come to her. She travels none abroad. The following can testify of her excellent remedies with many others too tedious to mention.  John Langton, a lame hand, James Dewhurst, ditto.  James Parker, a fractured skull, his brain was bare. Christopher Martin, lame leg.  Robert Parkinson, ditto.  William Livesey, ditto.  Richard Knowles a lame arm two years standing.

Brigit Bostock, a poor woman who lived at Coppenhall, near Middlearch, as a servant with a wage of 30/- a year cured by touching and prayer.

She was said to have cured eleven hundred in a year, and took no money.  " The poor, rich, lame, blind and deaf all pray for her," we are told, " but the doctors curse her."

The brothers Taylor, after many years as farriers, turned their attention to human beings.  They would say to a patient : " You mon wait a bit, yond hoss has been come a long while.  I mon go to it."

Patients flocked to these men from all over England, till their village became a huge hospital.  They were reputed to have cured every kind of disease, even cancer.  Needless to say, the doctors did not regard them with favour.  " How many patients have you killed this year ? " asked a physician on meeting John Taylor in the streets of Manchester.  " It matters not how many," said Taylor, " I kill them cheaper than you."

Amazing remedies were prescribed for animals as well as men.  Marshall, the writer on agriculture, seriously advised the keeping of a he goat in the stables as a cure for staggers in horses ; and Lackington says that two spoonfuls of common salt was thought to be a perfect cure for a horse that had foundered.

Parson Woodforde writes of " the death of my poor good natured horse, by name Jack," and adds that the farrier had said " that he had died of a fever in the bowels, and that he should have been bled, had a clyster, and some cooling physic also."

In the Verney letters the steward writes to his master, during an epidemic of rabies : " The dogs have been dun with black soape and brandy, according to your honour's order, and the great Dogg in the park is much better. I hope it will cure the rest of 'em." The steward must surely have regretted the waste of good liquor. His efforts were unavailing, and he writes : " The great Dogg in the park went mad yesterday, notwithstanding our dressing his eares with black soap and lathering it in brandy."

The charms which were used to cure illness or accident were innumerable. For a scald or burn nine bramble leaves were to be gathered by the afflicted person, and put into a vessel of spring water. Each leaf was then passed three times over the scald or burn and this charm was repeated three times.

> Three ladies came from the coast,
> One with fire and two with frost.
> Out with the fire and in with the frost
> In the name of the Father and Holy Ghost.

A burning stick was then taken from the fire and passed over and around the burn or scald, and the charm was repeated nine times. The number of cures resulting from these charms seems to have been extraordinary ; but probably they are no more amazing than the cures which are effected by patent medicines. In some cases it was thought possible to transfer an illness from a human being to an animal. A fit of ague could be cured by giving a dog a cake of salted bran. The dog would then get the ague and the person would be cured. The anodyne necklace was another wonderful charm. "After wearing them, but one night," says their advertiser, "children have immediately cut their teeth with safety, who but just before were on the brink of the grave, with their teeth fits, fevers, convulsions, gripes, loosenesses, etc., all proceeding from the teeth and have most miraculously recovered."

Both quacks and doctors must have had their hands full in the eighteenth century. Adam Smith, writing in 1775, declared that half the labouring population died before reaching maturity. There seems to have been an inordinate amount of sickness, and, in addition to this, bleeding and cupping were inflicted regularly upon those in full health, whereby the faculty must have acquired many patients. Plague, after its terrible visitation in the seventeenth century, died out of England. There is indeed mention made of bubonic fever; which was said to have been allied to plague, but may well have been typhoid or even severe influenza.

Smallpox was the disease which above all others claimed its victims. In the year 1710, more than 3,000 persons died of it in London alone, and a fourteenth part of each generation was wiped out by it. The virulence of smallpox seemed to have increased enormously. In the seventeenth century, it was regarded much as measles is looked upon nowadays; almost everyone had it; but, given reasonable care, none need die of it. Whether its greater virulence was due to the increase in drunkenness, or whether it was entering upon a severe phase, we do not know. Very few escaped from it, and many were disfigured for life by it. "Must have had the smallpox" was a very common item in advertisements for servants, and in some cases it was even stipulated in writing, that the servant must instantly leave his place should he sicken with the disease, a sum of money being given as compensation. In 1720 Lady Mary Wortley Montague introduced the practice of inoculation into England, from Constantinople. It was tried first, to their great credit, on the Royal Family, and then on condemned criminals. Doctors were divided as to its merits. Some hailed it as the infallible preventative, others shook their heads, and talked about interfering with the laws of Nature and the will of Providence. There were certainly many objections to the practice. Inoculation produced an attack of genuine smallpox. It was usually a mild attack ; but the patient was infectious, and unless most carefully segregated was a source of widespread infection. An ignorant practitioner, moreover, often made too deep an incision with grave and sometimes fatal results. Although the smallpox patient from whom the matter was taken was almost always a healthy child, there were cases in which serious disease had been carried from one to another by inoculation. Vaccination, which was the offspring of inoculation, was the discovery of Dr. Jenner in 1796, and through the practice of this, and the improvements in cleanliness and sanitation in the nineteenth century, the dreaded disease of smallpox was practically stamped out.

Two other diseases, which are now unknown in England, were typhus and gaol fever. Some authorities held them to be the same, or at least variations of the same illness. They were both caused by dirt, overcrowding and poverty. In 1750, at what is known as the Black Assize at the Old Bailey, between fifty and sixty persons caught gaol fever in court, including two judges, the Lord Mayor, an alderman, an undersheriff and several of the jury.

" The English," says a foreign traveller, " are very much subject to some particular diseases, especially the rickets, the scurvy and the consumption . . . all of them proceeding from the constitution of the air, the rickets from its moistness, the scurvy from its saltness and the consumption from its grossness, and from the fast living of the people."

The intemperate habits of the people, and the imposition of a window tax, with its necessary consequence of a curtailment of light and air, no doubt were the causes of much disease. The damp undrained condition of the country and the heavy fogs which enveloped much of it, caused agues and rheumatism, and were perhaps responsible for an illness known to the faculty as the whirligigousticon, which was a kind of malaria.

The state of medicine before Pasteur, Lister and Simpson can scarcely be imagined by us of this age. Very little progress had been made throughout the eighteenth century, and it was not until the nineteenth that medical science, as we know it, was inaugurated.

## CHAPTER VI

## A COUNTRY DOCTOR

### CLAVER MORRIS OF WELLS

CLAVER MORRIS, the subject of this short biography, was born at Caundle Bishop in Dorsetshire in 1659. His father, William Morris, rector of Manson, had suffered in the King's cause in the civil war, and the son really belongs by birth and upbringing to the seventeenth century. His published diary, however, from which our knowledge of the man is obtained, begins in 1709 and ends in 1726. He lived in Wells and was acquainted with Mr. Woodforde of Yeoviltown, the great-uncle of the diarist. He had the degree of M.D. which meant little enough in those days; but he was much above the ordinary country apothecary both in learning and in social position. His practice was largely in the country, and he was summoned by patients as far afield as Ashton in Devon, and Cottles in Wiltshire.

Morris was married three times, and he seems to have had luck in picking up heiresses, or at any rate women who brought him some property. The last of his wives "my dear Molly Bragge" came from Sadborough in Dorsetshire, and had £3,000 as her portion. It seems to have been one of those arranged marriages, common enough in the eighteenth century, in which a go-between was employed, and Morris notes in his accounts the payment of money to this woman. The wedding took place in August 1703, and at some time after the ceremony the bridegroom seems to have returned home for we read the following extract dated September 18. " I went to Sadborough in my chariot to fetch home my wife, and on September 25 we both came home to Wells, being met by a hundred horsemen who accompanied us."

He had evidently determined to do the thing in style, having bought for the occasion a white camlot coat, which cost £4 11s. He also pays 4s. to " the Fiddlers " though whether they were hired for a dance or came, as the custom was, to serenade the bride, is not stated. The bells of the Cathedral and of the parish church were rung, and also those of Somerton ten miles away.

In spite of the unsentimental courtship, Morris seems to have been very happy with his wife, and she was apparently a kind and sympathetic stepmother to his daughter Betty. They all lived in a house in Mountroy Lane, now known as the East Liberty in Wells, which the diarist had built for himself. It cost £807 14s. 6¾d., and took three years to build. In these days of jerry building, it seems almost incredible that it could have taken so long, but the house remains firm and solid to this day.

His wife bore him two children, Molly who died as an infant from the smallpox, and a son, who though a delicate lad, survived his father. Smallpox seems to have been a scourge in Morris's family : he had previously lost two other children from this dread disease. His son was infected, when he was three years old with the King's Evil, by his nurse. Morris dismissed the woman at once when he discovered the nature of her illness, and gave her a gratuity of £15 ; but the mischief was done. Scrofula, as the disease was then called by medical men, was a form of tuberculosis, and the doctor was in advance of the current opinion of his time in recognizing its infectivity. Though delicate the boy lived to grow up and was able to survive the hard life of an eighteenth-century schoolboy.

When he was four years old he was sent to a Dame's school, where he and his maid were both taught for the absurd sum of 6s. 6d. a quarter. He stayed at this school till he was seven, and was then sent to a Mr. Gravel, who was paid one guinea "for teaching Willy to read." No other studies are mentioned, but the boy must have been well prepared as he had Erasmus's *Colloquies*, Ovid's *Epistles* and Castelios *Dialogues* among his school books when he was twelve years old. He also did well at Sherborne, and when his father went over to see him, the headmaster declared that he would "compare him with any boy in England of his standing" and that he "did not doubt that he would make of him an incomparable scholar."

Perhaps the headmaster thought a little flattery not out of place, for Morris had come over to complain of the excessive chastisement which his son had undergone at the hands of his irascible pedagogue. Few fathers would have thought of complaining of such a thing, which was generally taken as a matter of course ; but Morris was a doctor, and in his experience must have known many cases in which nerves, health and character were ruined by excessive punishment.

His daughter Betty was sent to a day school in Wells, which charged 6*d*. a week, and a pair of gloves to the mistress at Christmas, and for learning singing and the violin her father paid a guinea and two guineas extra. Later on she went to a boarding school at Salisbury which charged £3 a quarter and various fees for French, music, dancing and writing masters. Her father also paid 6*d*. a week to provide fruit, an unusual item in the school expenditure, which shows that the doctor was enlightened in matters of diet.

Morris seems to have been devoted to his daughter, and it was a terrible shock to him when in 1718 she made a clandestine marriage with John Burland of Steyning in Somersetshire, of an old though impoverished family. She was married in the Cathedral, and as she was under age, the marriage, though binding, was, by the ecclesiastical law of the day, irregular. The unfortunate clergyman who performed the ceremony was prohibited from ever holding service in the Cathedral again, and the sacrist who had given the bride away was suspended for a year.

Morris turned his daughter out of the house, and declared that he would never see her again. Her stepmother, however, who had apparently sympathized with the girl, and other members of his household, at length prevailed upon him to forgive his daughter.

My daughter with my wife, Mrs. Evans and all the maid servants came into my chamber while I was putting on my clothes. I refused to see her and ordered her to be had down and going into my closet I shut the door. But she opened it and with abundance of crying and begging she forced me to beg God Almighty to bless her. My wife kept my daughter to dinner.

Before this the stepmother had provided two suits of clothes " to give my daughter for good handsell."

Besides his practice as a physician, of which we shall speak presently, Morris undertook a good deal of public work. He was a Commissioner of the Land Tax, a Commissioner of Sewers, and in 1717 he became a member of the Mercers Company in Wells. For these honours he paid in fees the modest sum of £4 5s. 3d. and expended £3 14s. 3d. in wine and feasting, besides giving alms to the poor.

He was also Commissioner for two Commons near Glastonbury. He had been working for some years towards enclosing these Commons, as he had acquired land in that neighbourhood from one of his wives. Owing to his exertions and the efforts of Mr. Peirs, M.P. for Wells, an Enclosure Bill was passed, and from one Common alone Morris obtained 41 acres. He had to lay out about £35 in making hedges and ditches and levelling 9,600 anthills ; but he had not done badly for himself. It is good to think that his conscience troubled him, and that he finally set aside the sum of £20, which he distributed to these poor commoners, whom he thought should be compensated, at Christmas-time, at the Rose and Crown inn at Glastonbury.

He had a wife and family to maintain and his professional income does not seem to have exceeded £300 a year, and for some time was considerably less. He could not, therefore, emulate that good bachelor Parson Woodforde, and be always distributing largesses. From his epitaph, however, we learn that " he hid his light behind a cloud, when his right hand gave to the poor, gifts of which his left hand knew nothing."

" I gave my Christmas alms," he tells us, " according
to my custom of giving everyone 6*d*."

" To ye French Protestants 5/- " is another item
in his accounts, and " the Scotch persecuted clergy,"
of the episcopal church, are given a guinea.

" The Governor of Libanus in his Turkish habit
with his interpidor and servants (turned out of his
government by the Bashaw) came with the Secretary
of State's pass and a recommendation for charity,
and I gave him half a guinea."

What startling and picturesque mendicants to meet
upon an English road ; but even ex-governors had
to obtain the beggar's pass, before they could ask
for charity.

Morris is constantly sending presents, tokens as he
calls them, of 2*s*. 6*d*. or 5*s*. to his daughter Betty at
school. He seems to have entertained liberally,
having friends to dinner, and even bringing home
guests, to breakfast on beef and ale, after the six o'clock
service at the Cathedral. If he did not go to the
service, he sometimes looked in at a coffee house and
read the newsletters before breakfast. He generally
visited one of these resorts during the morning, where
he would meet his friends and possibly see patients
who had come in from the country to consult him.
He spent his mornings in seeing patients at an inn,
or else in his own home, and in working in his laboratory. After dinner, his time was similarly occupied,
though sometimes he would play at backgammon or
mangola with a friend.

I won three shillings of my brother Farwell at tables [i.e.
backgammon] [he says]. In the evenings we played for two
hours drink, if you please. I had 14*d*. for one glass. Afterwards Mrs. Cherry sung and we all danced eight or ten dances.

Then played some forfeiting plays. We had an excellent bowl of punch, above a gallon, and we went to bed about 3.

Like Woodforde, Morris had his rotation dinners which were known as moonfeasts, mutual entertainments, or sometimes " our weekly meetings," when a party of friends would meet at each other's houses, for supper and entertainment.

I had a great company, both of men and women at mine house, especially men, [Morris says], and some of them stayed with me till 4 o'clock next morning, and seemed very well pleased with their entertainment. Col. Berkeley (my house being full) lodged with me in my bed.

Besides all kinds of social hospitality, Wells had its share of strolling players, jugglers and various mountebanks, including the man who ate fire, so beloved by eighteenth-century spectators. Morris writes of going to bull-baitings and cock fightings, and also to the races at Kingsmoor or Clandon Down. He is not so much interested in his food as was James Woodforde, and one suspects that the parson would have considered his housekeeping to be rather poor. He would dine on three cold trouts and nothing else, and have broiled white herrings for supper. He makes coffee out of horse chestnuts, " horsebean coffee " he calls it, and sets five guests down to a dinner " of stewed rump of beef and a goose."

On one occasion, however, he almost rivals Woodforde's Gargantuan meals. He has eleven guests to supper and gives them " a cold side of mutton, a cold breast of veal, a couple of neats tongues and a gelat." He brews at home a vast quantity of liquor, about 700 or 1,000 gallons in a year. Besides all this beer, he sends as far as Hereford for " sider " although he lives in the apple country, and he buys a bushel of primroses for making wine. He often gets his liquor from his ship-owning relatives, the Bragges, who were fined in 1726 £1,200 for " avoiding to pay custom on goods brought in shippes."

" I upped and let Coggin of Somerson in," Morris says, " about 4 o'clock with one anker of brandy," and he laments when a consignment from the Bragges is seized by custom-house officers at Crewkerne.

Dining, wining and cards were some of Morris's amusements ; but the interest and passion of his life was his music. Wells, like so many other country towns and villages, had its music club, which met every Tuesday in the Vicar's Hall, where they erected a gallery for their instruments. Morris played the organ, the violin, the double bass, the curtile or bassoon, the hautboy and the flute. He also sang. In the lists of composers whose music he possessed, we find Purcell, Byrd, Croft, Scarletti, Handel and many others, some of whom are now entirely forgotten. He is evidently recognized as an authority upon music, and is invited to Shepton Mallet church to report upon the organ there. He has a high standard.

" Mr. Hill's harpsichord being near a note below concert pitch," he tells us, " and no sure hand performing the treble (being only young ladies of Wells and Slopperton), our music was very mean."

He will sit up till " 2 in the morning to hear Schenk's Sonatas for two Viols," which were very excellent, and when he stays with his friends the Harringtons, at Relston near Bath, he has a perfect feast of music. They play all day, and half the night, and go into Bath to hear various musicians and singers, including Florio, whom Morris took back with him to Wells.

He also invents a metal spring jack for the harpsichord to be used instead of a quill.

It would seem that his practice would be crowded out by other interests : but Morris was a man who could do with very little sleep, and his day was very long.   He saw patients every day at his own house, or at some inn or coffee house in the town.   He was sent for to country places miles away, sometimes by the invitation of the local physician or apothecary ; but there did not seem to be any strict etiquette about this.

I went to Sherborne [he says] and saw Mr. Shirley, who was very ill of a jaundice, and his physician Dr. Bull not discerning rightly his disease, and prescribing very languid medecine for what he thought it to be, he (Mr. Shirley) desired mine assistance and I prescribed.

His medicines were certainly not languid.   He prescribed several doses of calomel (6 grains) for an unfortunate infant of 18 months and another babe of 11 months was given 4 grains of calomel " to be joined with 6 grains of rhubarb and made into a paste with syrup of succory.   He was very sinsibly amended," Morris adds.

Prescriptions for such remedies would be written out at great length in the medical Latin of the day, and the doctor carried his travelling ink-pot, often a silver one, and his pen.   Probably more than half the houses which he visited possessed no writing materials whatever.

The doctor of that age spent many hours compounding medicines.   Some of them used the services of an assistant, but Morris apparently did everything himself.   He speaks of his laboratory with its furnace and still, where he compounded many things.   He mentions his arcana, his syrup nervinus, pulv. constip. asentia pacifica.

Besides medicines he apparently made up cosmetics, such as hair butter and face lotion, and he supplied one patient with scented snuff at 2s. 6d. a pound.

"Paid 1/- for sparrow bills for the preparation of a medicine," is one of the entries in the diary. This sounds amazing, and reminds us of Lackington and live tench, but we are told that these sparrow bills were small iron brads used by shoemakers.

Of the illnesses treated ¡smallpox, stone, tertian and quotidian agues seem to be the most common. Morris also speaks of a convulsive cough, which was probably whooping cough, and of a few cases of phthisis. He gives a long account of his own illness, which he calls spotted fever.

> On Aug. 2nd I lay in bed out of order in a cold till near 11.
> 3rd. So sick of a fever with violent pains in my head, stomach and limbs that I could not get out of bed till past two in the afternoon.
> 4th. It being our mutual entertainment at Col. Berkley's though I continued sick I went thither. I eat nothing but a little tench and a glass of a jelly of hartshorn, and drank in the middle of the afternoon half a glass of punch.

It does not surprise us that a patient in a high fever returns home in spite of closed windows on this August afternoon "worse than I came." He continues the diary of his illness.

> 5th. I sweat in the sweating chair, and continued it for three hours after.
> 6th. Was let blood to 16 oz. by Mr. Lucas in the right arm.
> 10th. All doubted my recovery.
> 11th. My disease appeared to be spotted fever.
> 17th. Left off watchers.

18th.   I began to eat flesh.

23rd.   I went to church and first abroad after my sickness. I had Jackson's anthem for my recovery sung by Mr. Wiltshire.

If this were really spotted fever or typhus, the doctor must have had a very mild attack.

The remedies prescribed in all the illnesses Morris mentions were much the same, bleeding, purging, sweating and emetics.

From time to time he is called in by a surgeon to preside at an operation which could not be performed except in the presence of a physician.   He gives some accounts of operations performed in the days when there were no anæsthetics, and the only way to procure partial anæthesia was to give the patient opium, to knock him on the head or to make him very drunk indeed.   The third method was often preferred by the patient though the faculty did not regard it with much favour.

Cutting for the stone is the operation which Morris mentions most frequently.   When a patient has a cancer in the breast, he does not trust the local practitioners, but sends her to London " to Mr. Gay, surgeon of Hatton Gardens."

Mr. Lucas and I visted Mrs. Anne Star [Morris says].   I persuaded Mr. Lucas to push his probe hard into the place made for a seton in Mrs. Star's highly swollen knee and it luckily broke into the pelvis where the abscess had long lain.   To-morrow I advise the making of a larger vent for it.

" I read to my family in the lively oracles."   The doctor of those days must have needed some such distraction, and it is no wonder that surgeons continually confronted with suffering which they could do little or nothing to mitigate often became callous and brutal.

The doctor no doubt did a great deal of work gratuitously, as all doctors have done ; but when he took a fee from the poor it was 2s. 6d. Small trades-men in Wells paid 5s., well-to-do townspeople 10s. 6d., and the gentry a guinea. These charges seem high when we remember the value of money ; but Morris went immense distances into the country and spent forty or fifty hours a week in the saddle.

He gets twelve guineas for going to Ashton in Devon to see Lady Davies, and the same sum for visiting Lord Conway in Gloucestershire. In both cases the journeys to and fro must have taken a week, and he would have to stay at inns on the way. His rate of progress was usually four or four and a half miles an hour, and very much less in hard weather. Six miles an hour is noted as an extraordinary speed.

Morris invented " a machine to be fixed to my calash to count the revolutions of the wheel, and consequently the miles travelled." This taximeter was not the first of its kind, as one had been invented in the previous century.

The trials of a country doctor's life are set forth in the two following extracts.

I visited Mr. Seymour's son Conway at Rudgilbury. I went upon my journey at 5, and intending to go by Compton Martin, missed my way beyond Priddey Numericis, and found myself mistaken when I came to Highdon Lodge. Then I thought of going by Blaidon ; but went to the bogg near Charterhouse-Cupiloe, and had much ado to ride over. Then I went to Blaidon Lodge and so to my journey's end. And between But-combe and Rudgilbury I met with such a storm of rain that I think I was never in a greater.

I went in my calash to Lydbuch . . . the horses were be-mired so that one of them could not stand to draw, and I was forced to send to my cousin Gillingham's for his oxen to pull the calash out.

In 1724 Morris's mother died, and was buried at Manson, next to her husband who had been rector of the parish.   Morris tells how he

borrowed a horse and gambadoes [i.e. riding gaiters] and went out with the horse, the company having eaten of a very large cold rib of beef and of a gammon of bacon and fowls . . . I gave some gloves to those that remained in the parish of my mother's acquaintance.

In the following year his wife dies, and Morris speaks of her with great pity and affection.   The boy Willie was in bed in the next room recovering from the smallpox, and the poor woman had taken it into her head from some chance remark, that she had overheard, that the boy was dying.

To satisfy her fear [Morris says] I was fain to make him get on his clothes, and come to her.   And the sight of him seemed even though delerious to please her, and she looking upon him, being ordered by me to turn himself advantageously to the light of the candle that she perfectly see his face, said she never saw him look better in her life.   Then he kissed her and returned to his bed.

Three days later Morris writes that he is " busied in mulling red wine and the funeral of my dear wife."

The red wine was no doubt prepared for the friends who were expected for the burial.   The amount of cooking and other preparations for funeral guests must have been enormous and a great burden upon the less well to do.

On August 8th, 1726, Morris writes that he still continued ill " from my cold and a rheumatic fever, which was by little every day increased upon me. . . . I perceived myself under a consumption and growing phthisis."   In the days before stethoscopes, X-rays and blood tests many illnesses were termed phthisis which bore no relation to that dreaded scourge. Morris apparently recovered from this attack of illness, whatever it may have been. He lived till the following March, and died, we may be sure, much missed and regretted by many patients and friends.

Remembering perhaps the long weary paraphernalia of grief, which he had so often witnessed, he desires in his will that his funeral

might be with as little show and trouble as possible can be with the office appointed by the Church of England of which I am an affectionate member, and the day of one's death being better than that of one's birth. This carrying us out into a tempestuous ocean. But that bringing us (if we have done well) from a dangerous turbulent voyage into a haven of happiness. My desire is that there might be no appearance of grief and concernment amongst even my nearest relations and friends. But if it might be possible there might be a consort of music of three sonatas at least in the room where my body is placed before it be carried of my house to be interred.

We do not know if this beautiful desire was realized, but Morris's body was buried in the Cathedral which he had loved. A slab with " C. M." upon it marks his resting-place behind the altar. The memorial tablet and bust have been removed to the cloisters, and there the passer-by may read a Latin inscription setting out his many qualities and virtues.

# CHAPTER VII

## THE FARMER

### I

"MY Lords and Gentlemen. It is with much concern that I find myself obliged to open the session of Parliament with acquainting you that the distemper among the horned cattle has lately broke out in this kingdom."

These were the words of Farmer George when he opened his Parliament in 1770, and though they may seem absurd to us, in these days, it would have appeared only natural that such a disaster should be mentioned by the King in Parliament, at a time when misfortune fell upon a staple industry and the wealth of farmers and graziers, and the well-being of the bulk of the nation, was affected.[1] By 1770, the raising of live stock had almost surpassed the growing of wheat in importance, and the size of beasts sold at Smithfield, at the close of the century, was twice as great as those sold in 1710.

The great prosperity of the farmer undoubtedly came with the enclosures. Their effect on the poor was disastrous; but the farmer rose from being a small man, cultivating his strips in the common field,

[1] It must be admitted that "the horned cattle session" was the jest of the clubs; but the Londoner has seldom realized the difficulties of agriculture.

in accordance with custom, to a person of importance and a thousand acres.

Under the manorial system, however ambitious a man might be, he was tied by the rules of the parish. He must sow wheat when he thought he could dispose of oats to better advantage ; and get them in between Lammas and Hallow-e'en. If he was permitted to sow oats, they must be planted between Candlemas (February 2) and Easter, and the time to sow beans was between Hock-day (the second Tuesday after Easter) and Whitsuntide. Mangolds and turnips and potatoes were looked upon unfavourably as foreign crops.

These are some quotations from the Rules for management of open fields agreed upon at a Court Baron held in Shalstone, Bucks, in 1750.

> First it is ordered that no person shall keep or depasture more than two cows or horned beasts, or two horses, or mares, for in respect of one yard land, on pain to forfeit for every offence 3/4. Also that the lot ground in the common fields shall be lotted yearly, on or before the 20th day of May, and that the same shall not be moved, except between Allhallowtide and Candlemas, but flit with horses (i.e. horses should be tethered there). That the cow pasture shall be hained (let up for hay) yearly at Candlemas, and no beasts shall be suffered to go or depasture there (except only the hayward's cow till the 15th April and not longer). That a good and sufficient bull shall be found and provided yearly until the next court is held for the service of the common herd by the occupiers of the farms of the open field land. Also that every cow put or turned into common or cow pasture shall be tipped or nubbed on both horns at or before the age of two years, and if any tip or nubb come off, to be put on again within three days. That no person shall mow his ground, in the open field, above or more than once in any one year. That no horse common shall be let or set to any foreigner or person not inhabitant of Shalstone.

The fieldsmen were to find a mole catcher and, as soon

as corn or grain is ripe, a crow keeper, to shoot and keep the crows and other vermin from destroying the same. "That such person who shall mow or trespass on another's grass or remove stakes or meerstones, or stop up the meteholes, shall forfeit and pay 3/4." This seems to have been the usual fine for any breach of these regulations.

That all the jury or homage residing in Shalstone . . . shall yearly in Easter week or the next week after, go round the open fields and cow pasture and see that all the stakes and meteholes and meerstones be in good repair, and in their right places, and fill up any vacant places where necessary. That the hayward shall be paid 2*d.* for every horse, cow, bull, sheep or swine or other beast he finds or catches trespassing in any of the said fields of Shalstone. And in default of payment thereof such hayward is hereby empowered to impound the same, and give notice and detain the same in the pound till the person injured be satisfied his damage for the trespass and also the hayward the said 2*d.* per head.

Such conditions were the rule in all unenclosed parishes, though they differed in detail.

The farmer in those days may not have known want, but he certainly never reached affluence. Gregory King had computed that at the close of the previous century, there were 150,000 farmers in England with an average income of £44 a year. Knowledge filtered slowly through the countryside, and what improvements there were were effected by the landowner and the yeoman. Without the efforts of those men, prosperity would never have come to the farmer, and Lord Townsend, Coke and Jethro Tull did as much for English agriculture as the whole series of Enclosure Bills which were passed during the eighteenth century.

Jethro Tull has been called " the father of modern

husbandry." In 1733 he published his book on
horse hoeing husbandry, and though its effect was
not immediate, a few enlightened landowners understood its importance, and by the end of the century
the methods which he advocated were almost
universally applied.

The two great authorities on farming towards the
close of the eighteenth century were Arthur Young
and William Marshall.

There has been an attempt of late years to assert
that Young's accounts of rural France just before the
Revolution were inaccurate and exaggerated, and to
prove that the historian of the twentieth century
knows more about that country in the eighteenth
than the man who travelled through it and surveyed
it.   Be that as it may, there is no doubt that Arthur
Young's knowledge of English farming and the condition of agriculture was great.   His books, and those
of Marshall, are mines of information; no detail
seems too small, no rural custom too trivial to be
mentioned.   Young wrote his three English tours
between 1768 and 1771, and Marshall followed a few
years later.   By this time countless enclosure bills
had been passed, and the open field system was
becoming the exception.

As we have said before, the prosperity of the farmer
came with the enclosures, and when Young speaks of
land as fertile and prosperous it is almost always
enclosed.   The keeping of milch cows had become
the rule by the middle of the century, and beasts were
no longer slaughtered in November, and salted for
winter food.   More hay was grown and some turnips
and mangolds for winter needs.

This is a schedule of expenses which Young drew

up of a large farmer in Oxfordshire, who farmed
2,000 acres of arable land. Rent, £1,450. 20
labourers. 40 horses (worth £23 each). 20 cows.
8 young cattle. 700 sheep. 17 men. 5 boys. 5
maids. 10 waggons. 10 carts. 10 ploughs.

In harvest this farmer paid 40s. a month wages
with board; in hay-time 1s. a day and beer, and in
winter the same; which is unusual, winter wages
being generally a penny or two less. He paid his
head men £10 a year, and his other men £8. Boys of
ten to twelve years old were given £1 15s. and £2
a year, but they and the men whose wages are computed by the year would sleep in, and have their
food and drink. The farmer reckoned a man's board,
washing and lodging as costing £10 a year. He pays
his dairy maids £3 10s. a year, and other maids from
£2 to £2 10s. He hires women occasionally in hay-
time, and to pick the stones off the land in the winter,
paying them 6d. a day and beer, and giving 6d. to
1s. 6d. for a load of stones—20 bushels—which seems
cruelly little pay even upon stony soil.

Agricultural wages differed in various parts of the
country. They were as high as 8s. 9d. a week in
parts of the north, and in the south and west as low
sometimes as 4s. 11d. In addition to these wages a
cottage was provided or the sum of £1 10s. or £2
was given for rent. The labourer had the right to
take wood for firing, and if the farm was in a part of
the country where wood was scarce, an allowance
of £1 or 30s. was given instead. Beer or cider was
always allowed, in large quantities, in hay and harvest-
time, and more moderately at other seasons of the
year. Many prosperous farmers gave away such things
as skim milk, and some of the offals after a killing.

None of the farms, which Young mentions, under fifty acres kept more than one labourer, and even farms of one hundred acres did not always have more. Large farms of a thousand acres kept perhaps sixteen or twenty men. As there were no machinery or labour-saving appliances, the work must have been very hard.

De la Rochefoucauld writes of a farm at Castle Acre which paid £1,660 in rent. The farmer there kept fourteen men and three maids in the house, and in addition employed thirty day labourers regularly and seventy in harvest-time.

A small farm in Bedfordshire of 140 acres in all, twenty acres being arable and 120 grass, pays £140 in rent. It has as stock four horses, thirty cows and a hundred and fifty sheep. One labourer is thought sufficient, but Arthur Young considers it to be much undermanned. It was computed that a farm, which was rented at £100 a year, would cost £300 to stock, or, as they put it, took three rents to stock. The annual expense of a horse was reckoned at £10.

The prices paid for animals as compared with the retail price of meat is interesting. In 1739 Mr. Purefoy, a careful man, who knew the price of things to a nicety, gives £3 and £3 5s. for cows, and £9 2s. 6d. for twenty-two sheep, and £1 each for pigs. Beef was then selling at 3d. a pound, mutton at 3½d., and pork at 4d. A farmer could sell his potatoes at 10d. to a shilling the bushel, and milk at a penny a quart, butter at 6d. a pound, and cheese at 4d. If a farmer wanted to build he found that bricks were from 10s. to 18s. per thousand, tiles the same price, and that carpenters and masons charged 1s. 8d. a day and thatchers 1s. 6d. with beer.

Cows were supposed to need from one to two acres of grass and would produce from £4 to £7 in the year. Very little profit was made by dairying, and Young points out the extravagance of feeding cows exclusively on hay, and suggests a mixed diet of cabbages, carrots, parsnips and potatoes—even with potatoes at 1s. a bushel—and other things in proportion. This would seem far more extravagant, and we do not hear that it was adopted.

Sheep made a profit of as much as £1 8s. 6d. each; but this was on Lord Darlington's land, which would be above the average. The ordinary farmer regarded 15s. as a very good profit. The fleece, which generally weighed from 4 pounds to 5 pounds, fetched about 9d. a pound.

In Northumberland flocks of the most wretched sheep were kept which only made a profit of 1s. to 3s. a head, though the ewes were milked, and the milk made into cheese. These must have been akin to the sheep whom Coke saw grazing at Holkham, and, as Young hastens to point out, they were only to be found on unenclosed land. Rent seems to have varied enormously according to climate, soil, and proximity to markets, and also largely in accordance with custom. Young points out that much of the low-rented land produced nearly as large crops as the more highly priced. At Gauton-on-Wolds it was 1s. an acre, and around Temple Newsam 25s. At Barnet land fetched £4 an acre. Rates also varied greatly. At Bendsworth they were 4s. in the pound and in some parishes as low as 2¼d. The average for the whole kingdom seems to have been 1s. 1d.

As the century advanced and agricultural knowledge spread, more labour was needed. Farmers found, for instance, that while unhoed turnips fetched 20*s*., those which had been hoed were worth 35*s*. The number of draught animals may have somewhat decreased. Arthur Young explains that " custom alone has been the guide of the farmers in the number of draught cattle they use," and that the clay land takes a greater force than the loam. " Three and a half," he says, " is more cattle than necessary for any soil in England provided the husbandry be good."

After this advice it may be that farmers eliminated the half animal. The larger the farms the fewer were the draught cattle. On some lands they found it necessary to plough four times over before they could sow a crop of wheat, though for oats they need only plough once. Probably the ploughs were of the old wooden kind.

Farm-houses were generally commodious, and very comfortable, according to eighteenth-century standards. The great kitchen sitting-room had an immense open fireplace, which would have roasted an ox. Here the farmer and his wife sat on the winter evenings, their household around them, sewing, spinning, mending harness, or carving wooden platters and bowls. A great oak table stretched nearly the length of the room at which the family dined with their servants and hinds. In some cases where the farmer was a rich man, his wife insisted upon a parlour and a harpsichord and lived more in the style of the lesser gentry.

The farm-house and buildings frequently formed a square, the house facing the farmyard, with barns, stables, sties and cow-houses at right angles, and there would be a well with a pump, and in some farms a stone cistern for water. In the Midland counties the

yards were often open with mangers round the inside
of the fences. We hear of a Mr. Clark of Bedford
who invented a horse-driven threshing machine.
Whether there was anything in it we do not know,
as he tried to produce it by subscriptions which were
not forthcoming. He had, however, already invented
a draining plough and a turnip-slicing machine which
seem to have been successful.

The following is an extract from his advertisement :

Proposals for making by subscription complete machine for
threshing corn.

### To the Public.

Of all operations of the laudable profession of the husband-
man, it is presumed none are performed less to his satisfaction
and emolument, none more detrimental to the public, and more
oppressive to the poor, than that of threshing corn.

The difficulty of finding people disposed to undertake this
drudgery, the large expense, the unavoidable waste which attends
the present methods of threshing corn. . . . The threshers
themselves, although near a twentieth of all they thresh is allowed
them for their labour, are in general so overburdened with
poverty and distress of body, that they are, of all the honest
labourers in the country, the most miserable. These facts taken
together incontestably prove, beyond the force of custom, ignorance and malice, that the present method of doing this necessary
work is not only prejudicial to individuals ; but also a very great
public grievance. And that, therefore, any contrivance which
would render the labour tolerable, and put it in the power of all
occupiers of corn farms to have their corn separate from the
straw, in such quantities, and at such times, as they may think
proper, at a moderate expense, can not but meet with a candid
reception.

Poor Cuthbert Clark ! His invention did not meet
with that " candid reception " which he anticipated
and threshing with the flail continued into the middle
of the nineteenth century. It was a laborious method ;

but except on large arable farms there was no need
to hire in extra labour for it.   The farm servants did
it in the winter in their spare time.   There was very
little leisure time upon most farms.   The women's
work in particular was never done.   Mrs. How, a
farmer's wife, milked twenty-two cows and made
butter from them with the help of two dairy-maids.
They were up at four o'clock in the summer mornings.
Even on winter evenings, when the stock was bedded
down, and the hard work was done, the farmers'
wives and daughters spun and cut and wove and
made the bed linen, and the garments which the
family wore.   One exasperated woman computed
that there were more than 20,000 stitches in a shirt.
To the inventor of the sewing-machine the women
of England ought surely to erect a statue.   Not only
were all garments made and often spun and woven
at home; but the women also plaited the straw for
horse collars, stuffed and made bags of sheep skin for
the cart saddles and wove stirrups and halters from
hemp and straw.   The men too were not idle.   In
the gleam of the great hearth fire, or by the light
of guttering tallow candles, they carved such things as
wooden bowls, platters and spoons, fitted and riveted
handles into scythes and other tools, made thongs
for flails or repaired the harness.   It was a full, busy,
useful life, the farmer's.   In harvest-time the horn
was sounded at 5 a.m., and anyone who was not in
the field was fined.   Sometimes one of the men was
appointed as a sort of foreman, and called the Lord
or Captain of the reapers, and if he were late, he was
fined double.   Generally the farmer would be out in
the fields himself, superintending matters.   There was
the corn to be cut by scythe or sickle, to be bound

and stooked by hand, and finally carted to the stack-
yard. When the last sheaf was brought home with
its following of men and maidens, singing and sometimes dancing, after it, and the captain of the reapers
with a crown of flowers on his head, he or one
of his fellows would mount upon the corn stack, and
standing up proclaim to the assembled multitude :

> We have ploughed, we have sowed
> We have reaped, we have mowed.
> We have brought home every load.
> Hip, hip, hip, harvest home.

It was the custom to solicit passers-by for " largess,"
a request which was seldom disregarded, and this
retention by the common folk of an old Norman-
French word is a very curious survival. Sometimes
the largess was asked for immediately before the
harvest, when the men retired to an ale-house, to
spend the money on fortifying liquor.

The harvest supper was a great event. The farmer
and his family, his servants and his labourers all sat
down together; neighbours who had helped in the
harvest were kindly welcome, and an immense meal
was prepared. A great joint of beef was always
served, and there were besides, mutton, veal and
bacon, a dish of frumity (wheat boiled in milk and
seasoned) and barrels of beer and cider. Before the
party separated the healths of the master and mistress
were always drunk, sometimes to the accompaniment
of such a song as the following :

Now, supper is over and all things are past,
Here's our mistress's good health in a full flowing glass.
She is a good mistress, she provides us good cheer.
Here's our mistress's good health, boys ! Come drink off your
    beer.

Here's health to our master, the lord of the feast.
God bless his endeavours, and give him increase.
And send him good crops, that we may meet another year.
Here's our master's good health, boys ! Come drink up your
    beer.

The haymaking was 'not such a great affair as the
corn harvest, but owing to variable weather, everyone was pressed into the hay field. As soon as the
dew was off the grass, the farmer would be in the
field, his scythe in his hand, leading the line of
smocked, frocked labourers, keeping time as they
cut the swathes of grass ; often they worked by
moonlight getting in the last load, before an angry
bank of clouds poured down in rain upon them.
No wonder the farming class went to bed at eight
o'clock and spent a large portion of the day of rest
in resting.

The young people had their amusements. Farmer
Flamborough's daughters in the *Vicar of Wakefield*
" were reckoned the best dancers in the parish, and
understood the jig and the roundabout to perfection." They " were totally unacquainted with country dances." These dances—if they were originally
of English origin—had lately been reintroduced from
France, and were danced at polite assemblies in Bath
or London. They had not come back to the English
country village. Lady Eleanor Butler, much later
in the century, tells us that she found a dancing
master in an inn parlour, teaching all the farmers'
sons and daughters French dances, which she adds
" was a melancholy sight."

Farmer Flamborough certainly gave a splendid
party on Michaelmas Eve, even if his stories were
very long and dull. His goose and his dumplings

The Market Woman

The Farm Labourer

were fine ; and his lamb's wool, a drink of roasted apples and spiced ale, was excellent. They played Blind Man's Buff and Hot Cockles, and Questions and Commands and Hunt the Slipper, which was even then described as a primæval pastime. There was often dancing in the winter evenings in the large flagged kitchen, with its gleaming coppers, and its great wood fire on the hearth. In most neighbourhoods there was a fiddler, who went about from house to house, playing at weddings, or at Christmas and Michaelmas parties. The young men sometimes rode to hounds, or engaged in such sports as wrestling or boxing. The older men too often found their pleasure in excessive drinking. The farmers of Holkham might drink port wine ; but the usual liquor of the farm-house was home-brewed ale or mead.

There was generally a rude kind of plenty upon the farmer's table. At a large farm in Norfolk they killed three sheep a day, and two bullocks every week to feed the army of servants and day labourers, who worked there during the harvest. The less wealthy did not have such variety of meat, but they had at least a sufficiency of food, though it may have been monotonous.

I was accustomed [says Richard Parkinson, writing of the last years of the century] to eat what may be termed black bread. . . . Very fat bacon was the chief of our diet, garden stuff not being in such general use at this time, excepting large Windsor beans in summer, and potatoes occasionally, in the winter with pease puddings. I know no greater dainty to me than these beans and fat bacon, or pease pudding to the offal of pigs flesh in the winter or some of the black bread and fat bacon.

The custom of keeping pigeons on a large scale

to kill for food in the winter died out when meat
became more plentiful.

In the earlier years of the century, every manor
house had its dovecote, and the religious orders had
established them on their farms where they still
remained.   At Lady Place, near Great Marlow, there
is still a dovecote which the Benedictine monks had
built.   It is a round stone structure measuring 88 feet
and the walls are 3 feet thick.   It contains 600 nests,
arranged in fifteen tiers; the " potence " or revolving
ladder for inspecting the nests is still in its place.
At Lewis Priory, there was, in the eighteenth century,
a dovecote which had more than 4,000 nests, but it
was pulled down and the stone used for other purposes.   This was the fate of most dovecotes as the
century advanced.   The depredations of the pigeons
on the new crops of swedes and turnips were very
great, and as stall-fed beasts were beginning to supply
winter meat, pigeon pies went out of fashion.

The farmer and his family dressed very much after
the fashion of the squire and his lady, less fashion-
ably perhaps, but with equal comfort.   The farmer
was not above wearing a smock frock in the fields ;
but on Sundays, he might wear, as Lord Ernle suggests, the loose brown coat, scarlet waistcoat, leather
breeches and top boots of the English farmer on the
Staffordshire pottery, a prototype, it may be, of
Punch's immortal John Bull.   The farmer's wife
might wear a riding hood when she went pillion
behind her husband to market, or pattens when
she crossed the stock-yard ; but at church on Sunday
she and her daughters wore much the same clothes
as the ladies in the squire's pew.

As the century advanced the prosperity of the

farmers became, as a rule, very great. There were, of course, exceptions. There were small farmers, men, who in our own day would be called small-holders, who were almost as poor as the day labourers they sometimes employed. The majority, however, enjoyed great prosperity.

Young computes agricultural profits at from 16 to 20 millions a year. Some of this increase in wealth was no doubt passed on to the landlord in the shape of rent. There was, however, a large class of men who owned their own land and paid no rent to anyone. These were the yeomen, of whom, at the beginning of the eighteenth century, there were computed to be 160,000. They were often very prosperous. Marshall speaks of a yeoman farmer in the Midlands who had £2,000 a year.

This class of occupier [he says] have many advantages over the lower order of husbandmen. They travel much about the country, especially those whose principal object is live stock. They are led to distant markets, and perhaps to the metropolis, and mix in various companies, consisting not merely of men of their own rank or life. Men of fortune and science have of late years admitted them to their company, to their mutual advantage.

If the tenant farmer was not always so prosperous as the yeoman, he did not do badly. His landlord undertook his improvements for him, and often helped him when times were bad.

De la Rochefoucauld was astounded at the pros-perity of the farmers. That they should have the means and inclination to go for long tours through England in search of agricultural knowledge seemed to him amazing. De la Rochefoucauld met the grazier Robert Bakewell, who taught Coke farming.

He was about to return home, after a tour of three or four hundred miles, through the best cultivated districts in England, with the sole object of gaining knowledge about the various methods employed by other cultivators, who are always willing to give the fullest information about them. . . . This farmer was accompanied by another, one of his friends, who was making the same trip with the same object. They generally spend two or three months in making a tour, with a view to gaining fresh knowledge ; they travel on horseback with good mounts, and spend a guinea a day.

De la Rochefoucauld admits that Bakewell was exceptionally prosperous, and he was describing conditions at the end of the century, that heyday of English farming.

" A particular class," says Thorold Rogers, " engaged in supplying the necessaries of life, throve on the misery of the people and, in course of time, came to think that it had a right to thrive on this misery."

This very well describes the attitude of the farmer to the starving labourer at the close of the century. If he refused, out of his abundance, to raise their miserable wages, he was only acting as the political economy of the day taught him to act. He was generally a kindly, hospitable, open-handed man ; but he was quite convinced that an extra crown added to the wages of a hind would bring the whole farming industry tottering to its ruin. Nemesis, that capricious female, never visited him ; but she has laid a heavy hand upon his posterity.

## ROBERT BAKEWELL OF DISHLEY

ROBERT BAKEWELL, the most celebrated farmer and cattle breeder of the eighteenth century, was born at Dishley in Leicestershire in 1725. His father and grandfather had rented the farm before him, and Bakewell's childhood and youth were passed in country pursuits, and in learning the business of agriculture. The elder Bakewell was a good farmer, and, according to the standards of those days, he was prosperous. His health failed, however, while his son was still a young man, and the latter then took charge of the farm of 440 acres, a large estate as holdings were reckoned in the middle of the century.

He was a man of original mind, and of great determination, and he resolved to improve his farm and produce such cattle and sheep and horses as had never been thought of before.

When Bakewell began his experiments, cattle were bred for their size, for largeness of bone, length of horn or other trifling peculiarities. They were valued as draught animals or for their milk. He realized that profits were to be made on smaller beasts, as they were fatted at less expense, and that in the case of sheep as well as cattle animals should be bred which would produce the most weight in the smallest joints with the least possible amount of coarse flesh and offal.

"You can get beasts," he declared, "to weigh where you want them to weigh, in the roasting pieces and not in the boiling pieces." To select suitable animals he would travel immense distances.

His motto was : " Small in size and great in value." To attain this end he started several experiments in breeding. Instead of crossing two entirely different breeds, as was then the custom, Bakewell selected the finest animals of the same good strain, and even the same family. His system of in-breeding seems to have produced the most extraordinary results. In fifty years his breeds of cattle and sheep had been spread all over England, into Europe, and as far as America. In the year 1760, when he had just taken over the farm, on his father's death, he was letting out his rams for breeding purposes at 15*s.* or a guinea each, and it is recorded that, before his death, he had let a ram at the immense sum of 400 guineas. A celebrated animal called Two Pounder brought him in £800 in a season. The sheep he bred, and indeed all his stock, were strong and hardy. Arthur Young declared " that he gains a breed much hardier and easier fed than any others."

He chose his stock from the Leicestershire and Warwickshire long wools, and very strange animals they must have been when Bakewell first took them up.

"The true old Warwickshire ram, according to Marshall, had

a large frame remarkably loose. His bone throughout was heavy, his legs long and thick, terminating in large splay feet. His chine as well as his rump was as sharp as a hatchet, and his skin might be said to rattle upon his ribs like a skeleton wrapped in parchment.

"A ram of the true old Leicestershire sort" was, according to Marshall, equally odd. "A naturalist would have found some difficulty in classing him, and seeing him upon a mountain, might have deemed him a nondescript, something between a sheep and a goat."

Out of these curious animals Bakewell evolved his celebrated breed of New Leicesters. These sheep could be prepared for the market in two years, whereas other kinds took three or even four years to come to maturity. The breed has not lasted, it is true, like the Southdowns which John Ellman of Glynde brought to such perfection, but there were many men ready to step upon Bakewell's shoulders, and imitate his methods, as far as they could. The new Leicesters, moreover, were most suited to the enclosed arable land of the county after which they were named, and for mountainous country or the Downs, other breeds were gradually evolved.

Early in his career, Bakewell turned his attention to carthorses. These had been, for the most part, neglected and despised, and had become poor, small animals. In the midland counties, however, there was a breed known as the Black Horse which had been crossed a few years previously with some mares from Zeeland. Bakewell began to breed from these animals. Marshall, who visited Dishley in 1784, speaks with great admiration of Bakewell's stallion K.

"He was," he says, "in reality the fancied war horse of the German painters, who in the luxuriance of imagination, never perhaps excelled the grandeur of this horse."

Stallions such as this were let for the season for a hundred guineas or more, and one of them was brought to London, and exhibited to the King in the courtyard of St. James's Palace.

In the breeding of cattle, Bakewell was less successful; though his bull Two-Penny was celebrated throughout England.

His beasts were " as fat as bears," Arthur Young declared, and it is true that he specialized in the breeding of fat beasts for the butcher. In a dairy country such as Leicestershire, where the Stilton cheese industry was prospering, good milch cows were in great demand. The Durham shorthorns, or the Hereford cattle, were preferred as milkers and beef producers to Bakewell's Longhorns. His farm was managed on the most approved methods. No expense was spared in buying the best stock, the newest implements and in drainage and irrigation. He had cisterns of water in his farmyard. His hay and corn were stacked on brick bottoms. He had movable racks for feeding horses. His fishponds were filled with water from his canal, and his blacksmith's shop on the estate employed two men all the year round.

So lavish was he that he is said to have become bankrupt in 1776. Be this as it may, no suggestion of bankruptcy is given in any of the accounts of his farming operations which have come down to us. The neatness of his hedgerows and the cleanness of his ground are as much remarked upon as the great size and beauty of his stock.

With immense labour he diverted water from the river Soar, which flowed through the parish, and made a canal. With this water he irrigated his land,

and brought manure in boats from his stockyard to distant fields. Turnips were thrown into the same stream and floated down to the wharf he had constructed where they were collected.

" We throw them in," Bakewell said, " and bid them meet us at the barn end."

His sheep were said to be kept as clean as race-horses, and he had a system of double floors in his cow sheds, whereby the stall was kept clean and the manure easily collected. By this manuring and watering his fields, Bakewell raised the land to such a state of fertility, that he always obtained from it two and sometimes as many as four hay crops in a season. He had his seed sown broadcast, and in drills, in order to demonstrate the superiority of the latter method. He grew willow trees by the stream which were cut down every ten years or so, and the wood used as handles for rakes and pitchforks. A large stack of peeled willows stood in the yard, the bark being tied up neatly in bundles.

Visitors came to see him from all parts of the world, and, as there was no inn in the neighbourhood, Bakewell entertained them hospitably at his farm. In the great farm kitchen would be found Russian princes, German nobles, English lords and every kind of sightseer. The table groaned under the weight of Bakewell's meats, and on the walls hung skeletons of his most celebrated animals, and even joints preserved in pickle. There were pieces of beef there, relics of " Old Comely " the first mother of his stock who had lived to be twenty-six.

Bakewell maintained the simplicity of his life no matter who might be his guests. Princes and Grand dukes had their breakfast at eight o'clock, and went to bed when their host knocked out his pipe at ten-thirty.

For dinner he gave them good ale, and the finest meat, and a bottle of good wine after the meal was ended.

He never married : an energetic sister looked after his house, and saw to the comfort of his guests ; which must have been a heavy task for any woman.

Bakewell was a tall, broad set man, with genial, pleasing manners, much respected in the neighbour-hood, and a pillar of the neighbouring Nonconformist chapel, popular with everyone and given to unbounded hospitality. The one thing, however, which he did not give away were the secrets of his trade. Men might come to him from the ends of the earth, and they were welcome to stay as long as they pleased, to go round the farm, and see the famous stallion which the King had admired, to look at the bull Two-Penny and the celebrated ram Two-Pounder.

To none of them, however, did Bakewell give away his secrets. Coke of Holkham might come, and the farmer showed him how to judge cattle, Mr. Bakewell's cattle, and to appreciate their many merits ; but to only one man did he ever impart the secrets of his trade. This was his old shep-herd, William Peet, who was with him for more than forty years. He was so careful to keep all knowledge in his own possession as far as this was possible, that he would only let his stallions, rams and bulls for one season, and when he sold his sheep to the butcher, it is said that he deliber-ately infected them with foot rot, a disease from which his flocks were free, so that they could not be used for breeding purposes. So says Arthur

Young; but Bakewell was essentially a kind master, and the practice seems foreign to his nature. In an age of cruelty, he was continually protesting against the brutality of butchers and drovers. His own animals were treated with the utmost kindness. His bull Comely, a son of the Old Comely whose anatomy was exhibited in a glass case in the hall, " affection- ately licks the hand of his feeder " and is described as having " all the gentleness of a lamb in his looks and in his actions."

No bulls of his were ever tied up or confined for long periods. They ran with the herds, and a boy with a small hazel switch could control them. " All this gentleness," says Arthur Young, " is merely the effect of management, and the mischief often done by bulls is undoubtedly owing to practices very contrary, or else total neglect."

Robert Bakewell died in 1795. His farm passed to his nephew, who for many years had helped in its management. The *Gentlemen's Magazine* in its obituary notice declared that " his vices were few and without name, his virtue such as most men ought to imitate, and his utility was of such extensive consequence as to be a proper object of emulation to all men."

## CHAPTER VIII

## THE VILLAGE TRADESMAN

### I

THE eighteenth century marked the descent of the tradesman. In the early days the sons of good families went into trade. The son of George Corydon, a wheelwright of Plymouth in 1748, described himself as a gentleman, as he had every right to do; for he was one of the Corydons of Bratton-Clovelly. In 1717, a certain Jack Baker, who is established as a linen draper in London, sends his uncle and aunt, Lord and Lady Fermanagh, the present of a gallon of madeira. The Fullers, who had made their money in iron works, were so far from being ashamed of it that their coat of arms displayed a pair of tongs, and their motto was " *carbon et forcipibus.*"

It was not until the middle of the century that the absurd idea that trade was degrading, began to creep into England. It is said that the notion came from Germany with the Georges. Be this as it may, the status of the tradesman certainly declined, and by the close of the century, he had sunk low indeed in the social scale. Money was not then the lever that it afterwards became, and there was a great outcry when plain Mr. Smith, the banker of no particular family, and with no connections, was made Lord

Carrington. His is the only example of a business man being so honoured. Tradesmen, even in the country, made very fair fortunes. The general dealer at East Hoathley in Sussex, at the close of the century, had the enormous turnover of £5,000. Money has, of course, decreased very greatly in value.

Parson Woodforde regarded the squire with £1,000 a year as living in a very handsome manner. To-day he would be starving in a corner of his house if he attempted to live there at all. The parson pays £6 1s. for a gown for his niece Nancy, and dress seems to have been very expensive. Cambric was 10s. a yard, damask 5s. or 6s. a yard, and the village tailor, who, according to Lady Fermanagh, " spoils all he makes," sent in a bill for 18s. 6d. for the making of a " collrd cloth suit " with the extra charge of 10s. for such things as ribbon at knee, silk puffs, stays and " dimity to lyne the body of vest."

On the other hand a horse could be bought for 6 or 7 guineas, and John Byrom loses a valuable mare that is worth £14. The Purefoys pay 6 guineas for 6 worked chairs, and two dressing chairs, and six flag-bottomed chairs are only £1 7s.

Defoe says that £400 a year was considered a very ordinary income for a tradesman, and as the century advanced he became far richer.

" Walked to the joiner," says Lady Eleanor Butler, " and found him at dinner, a comfortable dish of boiled meat and new cabbage, large loaf of household bread, jug of beer."

This good cheer was a sign of considerable prosperity, at a time when the labouring man hardly ever tasted meat.

Many tradesmen in the villages and country towns

lived most comfortably, joining, in spite of Defoe's advice to the contrary, in the social life and conviviality around them. Sometimes they were men of education, like Crabbe's father, who took in the *Philosophical Magazine*, or like the tailor's widow whom Pastor Moritz met, who read Milton.

The village tradesman might complain of the fairs and of the pedlars, who brought their wares to every door; but they had not to face, like their successors of to-day, the competition of the towns.

Thomas Turner, as we shall presently see, in the biographical sketch of him, supplied every kind of commodity to everybody in and around East Hoathley. He was a general dealer, and we do not hear that in East Hoathley there were other shops.

In a large village, however, there was likely to be quite a number of tradesmen. The market town was often far away, and transport was difficult and dangerous. There would be the miller and the blacksmith, the tailor and the mantua maker; the grocer, the barber, and, in the south, the butcher and the baker.

The smith did not confine himself to shoeing horses or reblading scythes. He could turn his hand as a locksmith, and could make stair rails and torch extinguishers, lamp irons and window bars. Some men could make the fine wrought iron gates, and the beautiful scrolls that supported the signs outside inns and shops.

When few could read, a painted sign was a necessity. In country towns they often arched the street. The oldest of these signs was the Bush, really a bundle of ivy and vine leaves, the symbol of Bacchus. The barber's pole is still sometimes seen.

It represents a limb swathed in bandages, and

reminds us that the barber of old days was also the surgeon. The golden arm holding a mallet, which denoted the goldsmith, the grocer's sugar loaf, the chemist's purple jars are sometimes found in old established shops. The three golden balls is no longer the banker's sign; but there was a time when banking and a kind of superior pawn-broking were carried on by the same firm. These painted signs must have added greatly to the beauty of a town or a village; but when they arched the street and swayed, creaking in the wind, they were often the cause of accidents. Horses shied at them, gales blew them down, the outside passengers on coaches hit their heads against them. They were taken down and Parson Woodforde remarks upon the improvement to the streets of Oxford when the signs were removed and set up against the houses. He did not regret the loss of the beautiful ironwork, but the destruction of beauty was a thing which the eighteenth century regarded with as much equanimity as the twentieth.

One of the oldest of the village trades was the miller's. Whether the windmill was introduced into England by the Crusaders or still earlier by the Northmen is a matter for antiquarians' dispute. Bury St. Edmunds had a windmill in 1191, and it is thought that in flat wind-swept Lincolnshire they may have been known even earlier. It is said there was a water mill at Buttermere at the time of the Norman Conquest.

In the eighteenth century most villages of any size had a mill. The corn grown in the parish would be ground at the mill, the miller usually taking a portion of the flour in return for his labour.

Hours in all trades were long in those days. In the towns the shops were open from 7 a.m. till 9 in the evening ; in the country from six till dusk. There was no weekly half-holiday ; but all the shops shut upon a Sunday. The act of Charles II which ordained that only " macarel and milk " might be sold upon the Lord's day, was generally observed, though towards the end of the century practices became more lax. There were, besides the Sunday, various other days that were kept as holidays.

January 30th, the anniversary of Charles I's execution, was made a public holiday in the reign of Anne. Oak Apple Day and Guy Fawkes Day were holidays, when apprentices put up the shutters and disported themselves appropriately. The village feast days were holidays, but Christmas Day and Good Friday were not always or so generally observed in the eighteenth century.

One annoyance to which the country tradesman of those days was exposed and to which his descendant of to-day is not subject, was the shortage of small change. Copper coins were exceedingly rare, and even small silver money was difficult to come by in the country. In some cases employers of labour, having workmen earning a few shillings a week, were compelled to pay several together with a guinea or half-guinea piece.

To remedy this state of things the issue of token money had been general since much earlier times. Merchants, innkeepers, corporations, tradesmen in the towns and even the small village shopkeepers issued these tokens. They were used in the general business of buying and selling, but only in the neighbourhood of their place of issue, and they were honoured by those who issued them just as a bank honoured its notes. Some of these tokens had very curious mottoes. They were made of copper, lead or brass, and one of the latter metal has the following inscription.

" Although but brass let me pass."

" Remember the poor," says another, and, " Remember the poor in goal " (*sic*) and " For change and charity " are other mottoes.

Among English industries the weaving of woollen goods easily took the first place. It was regarded favourably by the legislature, which had decreed that every corpse must be buried in wool, and had forbidden the importation of the raw material into England.

In Yorkshire and Lancashire, in Norfolk and Suffolk, and Essex, in Kent and Surrey, Wiltshire and Dorset, and as far west as Devon, the industry flourished. Broadcloth and serges, friezes and flannels, stockings and kerseys, druggets and calimancoes, these and many more were the products of the loom.

Dyer, when he wrote his verses on the fleece, was not harking back, like most poetasters of the eighteenth century, to ancient Greece. He was not chanting the praises of Jason; he was extolling English wool. It was largely a village industry. If Halifax, Norwich, Frome or Exeter were centres where the wool was taken, and where it was fulled, teazled and finally sold to the wool merchants, every adjacent village produced it. The weaver had his loom in his kitchen, the whole family assisting. The wife and daughters spun the wool, the boys carded it, the father worked the shuttle of the loom. A loom could provide work for five or six spinners;

and several girls and women would be employed at spinning in their own homes. Some weavers washed their cloth in the village stream and dyed it in tubs outside their houses; but it was more usual to take the stuff to the nearest market town where it was fulled and dyed.

Besides, the weaving of wool, linen and, later in the century, cotton, occupied a number of workers, and there were such cottage industries as straw plaiting and lace making. These were not as a rule whole-time occupations. The father of the family attended to his own plot of land, or worked for a farmer, the women had domestic duties. The small farmer, especially in the north, where the winters were hard and long, was not above working at the loom, while his wife and daughters spun wool or flax. High wages, as they were considered in those days, could be earned by weaving; a man and his wife in 1757 could earn from 13*s.* to 18*s.* a week, and later in the century, when wages had fallen, about 11*s.*

Among village industries must be included that of charcoal burning. Early in the century Abraham Darly of Coalbrookdale discovered the possibility of smelting iron ore with coal. This invention gradually put an end to the use of charcoal for smelting iron, and transferred the industry from Sussex, Kent, Hampshire, the Forest of Dean and other wooded parts of England, to the north and midlands. For some time, however, the old method prevailed, and charcoal burning was a considerable industry. Kent and Sussex became denuded of timber early in the century, and Sherwood Forest had been laid so bare that the deer lacking shelter wandered away into

meadows and cornfields " to the insupportable injury
of the landholders."

Fears were expressed that the naval dockyards
might run short of timber, and the wooden walls
of England be sacrificed to iron. An immense
quantity of foreign wood was imported from the
Baltic ports, and the iron-smelting industry moved
from the south of England to Shropshire and the
Forest of Dean. In these counties there was still
wood to be had.

Country gentlemen read Evelyn's *Sylva* and grew
timber as a matter of course. The great difficulty
was transport. Quantities of timber were floated
down the Thames to the London dockyards ; but
in the wooded inland counties far from seas and
rivers, it was often sent to the iron forge.

Large quantities of charcoal were used in these
forges, and the charcoal burner's huts were to be
found in many a forest clearing. In winter the
woods rang with the clang of their axes, and in the
summer their fires glowed through the short nights.

The fairs were events of importance at a time
when the country was divided into regional markets,
and the small trader went no farther afield than the
county town. These fairs were attended by the
travelling merchant, a wholesaler, who went to them
to buy his goods, loaded a string of packhorses
with his purchases, and then set off through the
country towns and villages to sell his wares to the
shopkeepers. This man travelled on horseback the
greater part of the year, and had often a string of
thirty or forty packhorses, the leader with a bell on
him to warn approaching wayfarers in the narrow
twisting roads of the approach of such a cavalcade.

These packhorses were very strong, patient animals, and each would carry two bales or baskets slung across his back. Towards the end of the century, when roads had improved, carriers' waggons took the place of packhorses, and the commercial traveller with his samples travelled by the stage or in his own chaise. In out of the way parts, however, where the roads were bad, the packhorse was still to be seen, and the fairs in all their glory lasted into the nineteenth century.

The social side of these fairs, with their strolling players, dancing bears, and bouts of single stick and wrestling will be dealt with in another chapter.

It must be remembered, however, that their chief purpose was commercial. At Stourbridge the fair ground was three miles in circumference, and a trader did not think a turnover of £200 during the three weeks or so of the fair, anything unusual. Horses, cattle, sheep and pigs were sold, besides fruit trees, cheeses, and all kinds of manufactured goods, woollen cloths, linens, earthenware, clothing, pots and pans and children's toys and sweets. People flocked to the fairs from the surrounding country, and though the shopkeepers might dislike them, as competitors, they would, without them, have found it difficult to replenish their stock.

The corn factor and the wholesale cattle dealer were other features of the country-side. These men travelled into the remotest districts buying up the farmers' grain crop as it stood in the field, or as men threshed it with the flail on the barn floor, bargaining for lean cattle on the Welsh hills or the Yorkshire wolds, and driving them to finer pastures near their markets.

We are accustomed to think of the apprenticeship system as peculiar to towns, but in the country villages the children were apprenticed ; parishioners, from the squire down to the tradesman and small farmer, being obliged to take them.   The apprentice was bound to remain with his or her employer for a period of years, and in some trades, till the age of twenty-one or till marriage in the case of a girl.

" The said apprentice," the old indentures declare, " his master faithfully shall serve, in all lawful business, according to his power and ability, and honestly, orderly and obediently behave himself towards his master."

The employer had also his duties.   He was to " find, provide and allow unto the said apprentice meet, competent and sufficient meat, drink, apparel, lodging, washing and all other things necessary and fit for an apprentice."

Parliament was very slow in passing humane laws, and Peel's factory act of 1802 is a commentary upon the wretchedness of pauper children bound to iron-hearted masters in the factory towns.   There were horrible cases of cruelty towards helpless apprentices. In 1767 a howling mob surged round the scaffold where Elizabeth Brownrig was executed for the murder and revolting torture of the unfortunate children in her power.   In large towns such things could be carried on for years without anyone being the wiser, and no doubt in lonely outlying farms and cottages there was often terrible cruelty to weak and helpless creatures.   In the villages a strong public opinion such as had actuated the mob which had howled round Mrs. Brownrig, would prevent such odious crimes, though it was powerless to soften the hearts of masters and mistresses. There was also a wholesome fear of the justices. Magistrates would order his indentures to be cancelled if an apprentice could prove that he was starved or ill-used. Defoe, indeed, complains that "the state of our apprenticeship is not a state of servitude now, and hardly of subjection, and their behaviour is more like gentlemen than tradesmen, more like companions to their masters than servants."

The overseers of the parish of Bleasley in Nottinghamshire certainly showed much care and forethought in apprenticing a girl.

> Paid for stuff to cure the lass of itch 1/1*d*.
> For stuff to make her two gowns and a petecote and making 12/5.
> Pd. for indentures to bind the lass 5/–.
> Pd. for 3 yds of cloth to make her two shifts.
> For keeping the lass for ten days before she went to George Belshaws 3/–.
> Pd. to make the lass capps 5/1.
> For two pairs of stockings 1/2.

The most common evil of the apprenticeship system was not the ill-treatment of the children, but that they were not taught a trade. When apprentices were foisted upon people who did not want them, the natural tendency, especially among the poor, was to get as much out of them as possible. They were set to hard drudgery, and often to work far beyond their strength, and learnt little that would help them on in the world. When the master did his duty to his apprentice, however, and really taught him a trade, the system worked well. If the end of the virtuous apprentice was not quite so prosperous as that depicted in Hogarth's plates, he could, in normal times, earn a fair living, when he was out of his indentures, and often rise to a position in which many apprentices and journeymen worked under him.

## THOMAS TURNER OF EAST HOATHLEY, SUSSEX

THE journal of this small tradesman of the eighteenth century is one of the most interesting on record. He was born in 1728, and was probably of an old Sussex family, the Turners of Tablehurst. This is the less surprising as it was still the custom in the earlier days of the century for people of good family to engage in trade. The custom, it is true, was going out by the time Turner reached manhood; but Sussex was a backward county despite its trade in iron.

The roads were so bad that, early in the century, the judges at the spring assizes could not get farther than Horsham or East Grinstead, and a large part of the country was a swamp. Old customs good and bad linger where communications are slow and difficult, and thus we find Thomas Turner established as a mercer and general dealer in the village of East Hoathley. The business seems to have been comprehensive and surprisingly lucrative. Turner supplied the parson's wife with a gown and also with lace for liveries and "some shagg for a pair of breeches for Mr. Porter."

On another occasion he orders "pandles" (the Sussex name for shrimps), and 1,100 herrings for which he pays 33s. He complains, as all tradesmen are apt to do, of slackness of trade and dearness of provisions, beef being 2s. a stone and mutton as much as 3d. a pound.

"Luxury," he complains, " increases so fast in this part of the nation, that people have little or no money to spare to buy what is really necessary," the " really necessary " being sold in Mr. Turner's shop.

"The exhorbitant practice of tea drinking has corrupted the morals of the people of almost every rank."

Great is his anger when an interloper makes his appearance—an itinerant merchant, who sets up a stall in the village.

This day came a man with a cart load of millenary, mercery linen drapery, silver etc. to keep a sale for two days, which must undoubtedly be some hurt to trade for the novelty of the thing will catch the ignorant multitude and perhaps not them only, but people of sense, who are not judges of goods and trade, as indeed very few are ; but however as it is, it must pass.

In spite of these drawbacks Turner was able to bequeath such a flourishing business that his son reckoned his turnover at £5,000, an amazing sum in these days, still more in those.

Turner, however, was no ordinary man. He is amusing, very well read, hospitable and neighbourly. His vice was the vice of his times. No wonder men came into his shop and lingering there, talked and drank, and there was Halland close by, the seat of the Duke of Newcastle, who entertained, we are told, people of all denominations, from a duke to a beggar.

We have said that Turner was an educated man. He reads, he tells us, in five or six weeks, Gray's *Poems*; Stewart on *The Supreme Being*; *The Whole*

*Duty of Man ; Paradise Lost* and *Paradise Regained ; Othello ; The Universal Magazine ;* Thompson's *Seasons ;* Young's *Night Thoughts ;* Tournefort's *Voyage to the Levant* and *Peregrine Pickle.*

He reads the last book of *Paradise Lost* twice and comments : " It exceeds anything I ever read for sublimity of language and beauty of similes."

Having perused what he calls Homer's *Odysseyss* he comments thus : " I think the character which Menelaus gives Telemachus of Ulysses when he is speaking of the war-like virtues, of the first book very good."

" My wife read to me that moving scene of the funeral of Miss Clarissa Harlow, that divine being," is an example of the extraordinary effect which Richardson's novel had upon all sorts and conditions of men. His reading, however, is not usually of so light a nature.

" Thos. Davey at our house in the evening to whom I read 5 of Tillotson's Sermons." And yet the man came again, for we find a few months later :

" Tho. Davey at our house in the evening to whom I read *The Christian's Triumph against the Fear of Death.*"

Death seems to have attracted him, for he also reads *Sherlock on Death,* and Drelincourt on the same, and exclaims with unction : " Oh, let Mankind consider that no voyager is exempt from death," a sentiment which might possibly have occurred to mankind before.

The eighteenth century was much addicted to lessons in morality : the pity is they were too often left adorning tales, and were not brought into the everyday practice of life.

" Came home drunk," is the frequent entry in Turner's journal.

" Not quite sober, at home all day, and know I behaved like an ass . . . not like one who calls himself a Christian.  Oh, how unworthy I am of that name."

" What can I say in my own behalf for getting drunk ?   Sure I am a direct fool."

" I cannot say I came home sober," he says upon another occasion, but adds complacently, " was far from being bad company."   There lay poor Turner's temptation.  He was a jovial fellow, a good companion, an interesting man, of more education than his neighbours.  They liked his company, and to be in company meant to drink.  The parson of the parish, a drunken fellow of the name of Porter, sought him out.  He describes how the clergyman and his wife with a party of friends turned up at the shop at six in the morning, and

drew me out of bed, as the common phrase, is topsy turvy ; but however, at the intercession of Mr. Porter, they permitted me to put on my breeches, and instead of my upper cloaths they gave me time to put on my wife's petticoats, and in this manner they made me dance about without shoes or stockings till they had emptied the bottle of wine and also a bottle of beer.

On another occasion the parson of the parish " was among the mixed multitude."

" After ten we went to supper on 4 boiled chickens, 4 boiled ducks, minced veal, cold rost goose, chicken, pasty and ham."   This Gargantuan meal might have conduced to somnolence, but the time for that was not yet.

After supper our behaviour was far from that of serious, harmless mirth, it was downright obstreperius.  Our diversion was dancing and jumping about without a violin or any music, singing of foolish healths and drinking all the time as fast as it could be well poured down. . . . I am always very uneasy at such behaviour, thinking it not like the behaviour of the primitive Christians. Though I was very far from sober I came home, thank God, very safe and well, without even tumbling.

Turner naïvely adds, " The precepts delivered from the pulpit with so much ardour must lose a great deal of their efficacy by such examples."

He makes various good resolutions.

" If," he says, " I am at home or in company abroad I will never drink more than 3 glasses of strong beer, one to drink the King's health, the second the Royal Family, and the third to the pleasure of the company."

Could loyalty and politeness desire more ?

The whole of the diary is not concerned with drinking and moralizing. We have seen that Turner was a lover of books. He was also a man of an independent mind.

In the even [he writes] read several political papers called the *North Briton*, which are wrote by John Wilks, for the writing of which he has been committed to the Tower, and procured his release by a writ of Habeas Corpus. I really think they breathe forth such a spirit of liberty that it is an extreme good paper.

For a village tradesman who lived close to Halland, and so was dependent on the Duke of Newcastle for countenance and custom, to dare to take in the *North Briton* showed an independence and courage rare in those days.

He was undoubtedly patriotic ; though like many another man who loves his country, quite convinced that she is going to the dogs. After the loss of Minorca, he exclaims, " oh my country, oh Albian ! Albian ! I doubt thou art tottering on the brink of ruin and desolation this day. The nation is all in a foment upon account of losing dear Minorca."

Turner's married life does not seem to have been harmonious. His wife might reasonably have complained of his drunken habits; but wives in this age were tolerant of drunkenness and infidelity, and his " dear Peggy," as he calls her, only too often shared in his insobriety.

Oh, what happiness there must be [he writes] in the married state when there is a sincere regard on both sides, and each party is truly satisfied with each other's merits. But it is impossible for tongue or pen to express the uneasiness that attende the contrary. Were I endued with the patience of a Socrates, then might I be happy; but as I am not, I must pacify myself with the cheerful reflection that I have done my utmost to render our union happy, good and comfortable to ourselves and progeny.

Poor Turner! He was afflicted with a mother-in-law, " a very Xantippe, having a very great volubility of tongue for invective, especially where I am the subject."

His wife apparently sought relief in such harmless distractions as came in her way.

We played at bragg in the evening [is a not uncommon entry]; my wife won 19d. In the afternoon my wife walked to White-smith, to see a mountebank perform wonders, who has a stage built there, and comes once a week to cuzen poor deluded creatures out of their money, by selling his packets which are to cure people of more distempers than they ever had in their lives for 1/– each, by which means he takes sometimes £8 or £9 a day.

This mountebank was no doubt half comedian, half quack doctor, and poor Mrs. Turner seems by this time to have been seriously ill. When she died Turner, in spite of former " anemosities and dissentions," appears to have sincerely lamented her.

" I have lost," he says, " a sincere friend, a virtuous wife, a prudent good economist in her family, and a very valuable companion. I may justly say with the incomparable Mr. Young, ' Let them whoever lost an angel pity me.' "

For some time after his wife's death he seems to have lamented her loss.

How do I lament my present and very irregular way of life for what I used to lead in my dear Peggy's time. I know not the comfort of an agreeable friend and a virtuous fair ; no, I have not spent an agreeable hour in the company of a woman since I lost my wife, for really there seem very few whoes education and way of thinking is agreeable and suitable with my own.

After a time, he, however, bethought him of another virtuous fair whom he considered might suit him.

Jenner and I walked to Lewis in order to see a girl which I had long since had thoughts of paying my addresses to. I was not so happy, shall I say, as to see her, or was I unfortunate in having only my walk for my pains, which perhaps was as well ?

Apparently the Lewes lady would have none of him and he eventually becomes affianced to Molly Hicks of Chiddingly, " a most clever girl."

In the afternoon rode over to Chiddingly to pay my charmer, or intended wife, or sweetheart, or whatever other name may be more proper, a visit at her father's, where I drank tea. I supped there on some rashers of bacon. It being an excessive wet and windy night I had the opportunity, sure I should say the pleasure, or perhaps some might say the unspeakable happiness, to sit up with Molly Hicks, or my charmer, all night. I came home at forty minutes past five in the morning, I must not say fatigued ; no, no, that could not be ; it could only be a little sleepy for want of rest.

After another night spent in a similar manner, he

says, " This courting does not agree with my constitution and perhaps it may be only taking pains to create more pain."

In another entry he sums up the character and disposition of his future wife with the cold-blooded apprisal characteristic of the countryman of that age.

The girl, I believe, as far as I can discover, is a very industrious, sober woman, and seemingly endued with prudence and good nature, with a serious and sedate turn of mind.   She comes of reputable parents and may perhaps one time or another have some fortune.   As to her person, I know 'tis plain (so is my own) but she is cleanly in her person and dress, which I will say is something more, than at first sight it may appear to be, towards happiness.   She is, I think, a well-made woman.   As to her education, I own it is not liberal but she has good sense, and a desire to improve her mind, and has always behaved to me with the strictest honour and good manners, her behaviour being far from the affected formality of the prude on one hand ; and on the other of that foolish fondness so often found in the more light part of her sex.

Thomas Turner and Molly Hicks were married on the 19th of June 1765, and on Wednesday, July 3rd, he continues his diary.

I have been so embarrassed with a multiplicity of business that I was not able to continue my journal, being on the 19th day of June married at our church to Mary Hicks, servant to Luke Spence Esq. of South Malling, by the Rev. Mr. Porter, and for about 14 days was very ill with a tertian ague, or rather an intermittent fever ; then the ceremony of receiving visitors and the returning of them has, with the business of my trade, taken up so much of my time that I was obliged to omit that which would have given me the greatest pleasure imaginable to have continued, but however, thank God, I begin once more to be a little settled and am happy in my choice.

This is almost the last entry in the diary.   There is one other describing the funeral of the Duke of

Newcastle, who was laid to rest at Laughton in November 1768, and Turner, who, in his trade of general dealer, included also that of funeral furnisher describes the trappings with much gusto.

"Atchievements very large embellished and emblazoned," were placed on Newcastle House and Clearmont House; two more of smaller size on Halland House and Bishopstone House; the four mourning coaches were drawn "by six full tailed horses" and the hearse was "finely dressed with escutcheons, pendants, shields, starrs and garters and banners."

At this the journal abruptly ends though Turner lived on till 1789. With the exception of Pepys', no diary is more valuable as a picture of the times and the man. We can see the friendly, jovial, country shopkeeper with his love of books, his naïve simplicity and his hearty desire to do what is right, if only his importunate friends would have let him.

No other document can tell us so much of the daily life of a village tradesman.

# CHAPTER IX

## THE VILLAGE SCHOOLMASTER

### I

#### EDUCATION

IN education, as in other things, the eighteenth century was a century of contrasts. There were country gentlemen, who could hardly read, and there were scholars, like Porson and Bentley. Defoe describes the squire as almost illiterate and declares that nothing on his estate was neglected except the heir. Defoe, as we know, often wrote with exaggeration and bitterness; and he could not have known the class, which he condemns, with any intimacy. Education depended upon means and opportunity. Many of the smaller country gentlemen had never been to school in their lives, or journeyed outside their own county. The library of one of these men consisted of Baker's *Chronicles*, Fox's *Book of Martyrs*, Glanvil on *Apparitions*, Quincey's *Dispensatory*, the *Complete Justice*, and a book on farriery. This was, indeed, quite a good library for the small squire, who, according to Leslie Stephen "was more than usually cultivated if Baker's Chronicle and Gwyllin's Heraldry lay on the window seat of his parlour."

" Zur, ples to zen me ax relatting to Agustus pax "

is the letter quoted by Blackmore as written by a
Devonshire squire to his bookseller. There were
exceptions. Henry Purefoy, who was of the lesser
gentry, and by no means rich, had a library of 376
books, and a man of great wealth like Coke of Holkham, would fill his house with books, pictures and
statuary.

Arthur Young visited many such houses, and
wrote in his journals long catalogues of their contents.

Boys from the larger country houses went to Eton
and Westminster, and to the Universities. Country
gentlemen sat in the House of Commons, and made
speeches, which rang with quotations from Horace
and Terence. It was, however, very difficult for men
of small means, living in remote country places, to
educate their children. There were the great public
schools of Eton and Westminster, and a large number
of grammar schools, some good, and many very bad,
and there were private schools.

Arthur Young speaks of a school in Yorkshire,
where "the method of teaching is the same as at
Eton. Boys are boarded in a very handsome manner
for ten guineas a year. The tutorage is two guineas
more, and all expenses do not rise to thirteen guineas."
Was the headmaster the father of our old friend
Wackford Squeers? Probably not. Mr. Squeers
would never have left that Eton touch out of his
prospectus.

The preparatory school was almost entirely a product of the nineteenth century, and boys were, therefore, educated at home, which meant running more
or less wild, with perhaps some smattering of the
humanities from a neighbouring parson; or else
being sent at a very tender age long journeys by

coach or on horseback to some distant school. A boy of twelve, one Thomas Thackeray, is sent all the way from the Yorkshire village of Hampsthwaite to Eton and this in the year 1705 when the journey must have occupied many days. It is true that " halves " were halves then at Eton, and there were only two in the year; but the parents must have been enthusiastic for education before they would send a boy so far over such roads in winter weather.

A kinsman of this Thomas Thackeray went to Eton when he was six, which was then the age of entry for boys on the foundation. It is pleasant to read that the little fellow was made the pet of the whole school, and returned home each holiday well and happy. His home was, however, near the school, and he had many opportunities of visiting it.

De Quincey gives a sad picture of the miseries of these little children.

Children torn away from mother and sisters at that age not infrequently die of grief. I speak of what I know. The complaint is not entered by the register as grief; but that it is grief of that sort and at that age, has killed more than have ever been counted among its martyrs.

It was usual for the girls of the family to be taught at home by a governess or the aunt or other spinster relation who was quartered upon the family. In the days when gentlewomen could not work for a living, they were obliged perforce to dwell in the houses of their relatives and make themselves useful in the household or in teaching the children.

There were, indeed, girls' schools. Catherine Hutton went to one at the age of seven, where she was taught spelling and reading in the Bible, with needlework, useful and ornamental, for 6d. a week.

She also went to a writing school for an hour a day, where she copied the printed letters of a battledore or horn book; but this was apparently all the school education which Catherine, the daughter of a man of letters, ever enjoyed.

There were, no doubt, better schools, the More sisters kept a famous one at Bristol, but in the country they were generally poor and pretentious. This is the advertisement of a country school in 1703:

Taught by a gentlewoman from London the following works: viz.—Waxworks of all sorts, as one's picture to the life. Figures in shadow glasses, fruits upon trees, or in dishes, all manner of confections, fish, flesh, fowl or anything that can be made in wax. Philigrim work of any sort, whether hollow or flat. Japanese work upon timber or glass, Painting upon glass. Sashes for windows upon sarsnet, or transparent paper, straw work of any sort, as, houses, birds or beasts. Shell work in sconces, rocks or flowers, twill work, gum work, transparent work, puff work, paper work. Platework on timber, glass or brass. Tortoise shell work. Mould work, boxes and baskets. Silver landskips, gimpwork, Buglework. A sort of work in imitation of Japan very cheap. Embroidering, stitching and quilting Truepoint or tapelace. Cutting glass. Washing gazes or Flanders point and lace. Pastry of all sorts with the finest cuts and shapes that's now used in London. Boning fowls without cutting the back. Butter work, Preserving, conserving, and candying. Pickling and colouring. All sorts of English wines. Writing and arithmetic. Music, and the great art of dancing, which is a good carriage and several other things too tedious to mention.

One might think they had mentioned enough; and it was all taught by one unfortunate lady from London.

The modern educationalist would suggest that too much attention was paid to handwork, and that writing and arithemetic must have been crowded out; and the same criticism might also be applied to a school mentioned in the Verney Letters, where the boys were taught to ride, fence, dance, vault, and to perform exercises of pike and musket. Geography and mathematics are the only other things included in the curriculum. " Them that will learn Latin might have a master att his own charges att twenty shillings a month." Adam Smith would probably have approved of these schools.

There are no public institutions [he says] for the education of women, and there is, accordingly, nothing useless and fantastic and absurd in the common course of their education. They are taught what their parents or guardians judge necessary for, or useful for them to learn. . . . Were there no public institutions for education, a gentleman could not come into the world completely ignorant of everything, which is the common subject of conversation among gentlemen and men of the world.

Adam Smith is, of course, alluding to the very narrow classical education which was given at the public schools and grammar schools. Little but Latin and some Greek was taught in them or at the Universities. The Senior Wrangler did not have to attain as far as the Differential Calculus.

Schools were often terribly brutal and cruel, the scholars were half fed, bullied and constantly flogged, the rule of the rod applying to girls as well as boys. Lamb's account of the Blue Coat School has come down to us, and stories of Keate's rule at Eton, and we are therefore inclined to think that all schools were like this and that all children were kicked and cuffed, flogged, starved and generally ill-treated. There is, however, a delightful school mentioned in the *Spectator* where the master ruled his boys by kindness, and their greatest punishment was his refusal to speak to them. The love of children lives in all the ages. No modern parent, writing to his boy, could pen a more charming letter than that of John Byrom.

DEAR TEDDY,

I had thy letter last post, which I liked very well. Pray write again, for by thy writing, thou wilt learn to write. The Prince of Wales is married to be sure. I saw him and his lady the other day, in a cloud of dust, that hindered me from asking them any questions ; and as she could not talk English neither, I thought it best to let her stay in the dust. And so you have had bon fires and bells and shooting and drinking ; for such is the custom of the world on such occasions. Pray, Teddy, tell me, do you think that if a man by drinking another's health should lose his own, that other man would get it ? Observe, Teddy, how simple and foolish men make themselves, when they drink strong drink, and say to thyself : " I will not be like these men nor put anything into my body that will take away understanding from my mind." Yes, I have sold North. I believe the gentleman, that has him, does not speak so much in his favour as you do. The eating his head off means that he would eat so much hay and corn as he is worth, and that they call eating his head off, which is indeed an odd expression, for how can he eat his own head ? He might sooner eat his legs if he was disposed to feed upon himself, which he hardly will. In France, it is a common saying of a man that has spent his estate, that he has eaten his estate up, though the ground be still there ; but with respect to him who has then no use of it, it might as well have been eaten away.

As for the price of him I made no bargain because

I sold him to a friend. Now, friends do not or should not, differ much about money in such cases. I desire no more than what he is esteemed worth, and my friend desired to give no less. Pray give my service to Mr. High Sheriff and thank him. If I must keep the gaol I must have you for under gaoler and we will use the poor prisoners very well. Pray return my service to Ellen Nelson, and when you write let me know how she does, for I reckon her amongst you always. I thought to have writ to Mamma and my paper is ended and it is late so give my dear love to her, and tell her I'll write to her next. Deus benedicat vobis, omnibus. Amen.

No modern parent, as we have said, could write a more charming letter. Few indeed in the rush and hurry of modern life would write at such length; and fewer still would go to the lengths of Charles James Fox's father. The boy had been promised that, if a certain garden wall were blown up, he should see it. By some inadvertence, the operation was carried out while he was away; but his father had the wall set up, and then blown down again. This, he said, was a valuable example to a youth on the propriety of keeping his word.

The father, Henry Fox, was a thorough-paced reprobate, and had never kept his word to anyone in his life; but he resolved to set the boy at least one example of good faith.

Children in the eighteenth century had often a rough time; but this had been characteristic of England down the centuries. Foreigners had noted, with horrified surprise, the cruelty of the English towards their children. In all ages brutal men will wreak their will upon the weak; but some, at least, of the harshness towards children was due to the idea, re-enforced in the eighteenth century by Wesley, that the hearts of infants are desperately wicked, and that they can only be driven into the way of salvation by many beatings.

Child suffering is the most painful of subjects, and it is pleasant to turn to the brighter side. In the large country places, with woods to run wild and to shoot in, streams to fish, horses to ride, the village feasts and fairs, the harvest merry making, the mummers at Christmas; it must have been a poor heart, and a much bullied youngster, who could not rejoice.

If education was difficult for gentlepeople of means and leisure, it was often impossible for the farmer. Marshall, indeed, speaks of the farmers who have had a regular school education, and " whose sons are fit to follow the professions," but his mention of this shows that it was some new and rare thing, which was coming in when Marshall wrote at the close of the century. For the most part, the farmer's boys and girls went to the dame's school in the village, and in some cases, if they were near a town, the sons might ride in to a grammar school. These grammar schools had often greatly deteriorated, and there were many complaints that they merely taught piety and the three R's, and the latter not too successfully. The mayor of Great Yarmouth in 1745 could not write his name, Pastor Moritz met two farmers who could not read; and to such technical education as was offered, the argiculturist turned a deaf ear. Various societies were founded for his benefit, but they existed in a more or less languishing condition, and the *Agricultural Magazine* was oftener read by the landowners than by farmers, who have ever had a rooted objection to being told how to mind their own business. The labourer had a greater choice of schools than the farmer. In 1698 Dr. Bray, and four friends, founded the Society for Promoting Christian Knowledge, and proceeded to set up charity schools all over the kingdom. In 1740 nearly 2,000 schools had been provided by this society, and there were others, where poor boys were admitted free. It was computed that about 20,000 children were educated in rural charity schools, which were all built, and for the most maintained, by charitable subscription.

It was an effort of which the eighteenth century might be proud, and it was carried through in the face of much opposition.

"Going to school," says Mandeville, "in comparison to working is idleness, and the longer boys continue in this easy sort of life, the more unfit they will be when grown up for downright labour." They are words which echo down the ages, and may be heard even in our own day.

Sir Alan Gardiner went so far as to attribute the Mutiny of the Nore to the spread of education and complained that "Sunday schools have done much harm by giving education disproportionate to situation." "Sailors," he added in disgust, "were able to read newspapers." It might have soothed these extremists to know, that in many schools, the children learnt very little. When they could earn a few pence, they were taken away, and even in those schools which fed and clothed the scholars, more attention was paid to teaching a trade than to book learning. Some of these establishments became veritable factories. We hear of a school at Attleborough

where the children earned from 1*s.* to 2*s.* 6*d.* a week
spinning yarn, and the poor little creatures worked
from five or six in the morning till eight or nine at
night, with very little time for a meal. The masters
and mistresses of such schools took over all the
proceeds of the children's labour, and after paying expenses pocketed the surplus. No wonder the
scholars were sweated and underfed. Child labour
was not a product of the industrial revolution. Defoe
found children of four and five labouring all day
for their bread, and in *Moll Flanders* a little girl of
eight prays that she may not be sent into service in a
great house, where all the upper servants will thrust
their work upon her, and beat her if she does not
do it.

In many cases, however, the schools were admirably
run, and the children were happy. Over the door
of Sir Thomas Parkyn's school, at Bunny in Nottinghamshire, was the motto " Disce vel Discede " and
so much trigonometry was taught there as related to
the mechanical and useful parts of mathematics. This
was an unusually good school, a more normal specimen was the school at Oswestry. There twenty were
" set to strive against 20 for shoes, and the 20 that
get most of the exposition and other books by heart
get shoes. Then there remain ten against 10 and so
on till they are all shod all round." " A shift was
given as a prize to the best spinner, a headdress for
the best sewer, a pair of stockings for the best knitter,
a Bible for the best reader, a copy book for the best
writer." At another school the bribe was in money,
each child being given 6*d.* a week, and there was a
fine of 1*d.* if a child were absent. " By such means,"
we read, " the school is kept pretty full without much

trouble." School teachers who could really teach were not easily obtained. Some trustees of country schools took their responsibilities seriously and sent their teachers to London, or to some local centre to be instructed. Others looked about for someone who would answer the purpose and would not be too dear. At a time when the University would accept a Regius Professor of Greek who did not know a word of the language, though he expressed willingness to learn it, country schools were not very particular. A clergyman's widow, a broken-down journeyman, a bankrupt shopkeeper, these too often were chosen, without much regard for suitability. It is true, they had to be approved of by the parish clergyman, and be of humble behaviour, able to write a good hand, and to understand arithmetic. They must be content with ten or twelve pounds a year salary, and if they could teach the children anything, why so much the better.

In 1780 Robert Raikes started a Sunday school in Gloucester, and it was from his impetus and example that thousands of such schools were established all over England. He was not, however, the earliest founder. In 1769 Hannah Ball, a Wesleyan, started a school at High Wycombe, and a clergyman, Theophilus Lindsay, with a woman helper, Catherine Capp, founded one at Catterick in 1763. There had always been catechizing in church; but the Sunday school found itself obliged to give secular instruction, as many of their scholars had no other schooling, and it was necessary to teach them at least to read the Bible. The influence that these schools had on the poor and ignorant was enormous. The most famous example was that of Hannah and Martha More, whose teaching and influence christianized and civilized the wild, barbarous people of Cheddar, and Adam Smith was probably not exaggerating, when he suggested that " no plan has promised to effect a change of manners with equal ease and simplicity since the days of the Apostles."

Madame d'Arblay notes in her diary how she went with Lady Spencer in 1791 to see a Sunday school.

It was [she says] a most interesting sight. Such a number of poor innocent children all put in a way of right; most taken immediately from every way of wrong, lifting their little hands in these prayers and supplications for mercy and grace, which, even if they understood not, must at least impress them with a general idea of religion, a dread of evil, and a love of good.

The music schools which had fostered the love of good music in England, were, with the exception of one at Newark, either abolished, or set to teach other subjects. Many villages had, however, their music clubs; the fiddler who played at weddings and feasts was a well-known figure, and the band, who performed in the gallery of the village church, kept alive a love of music, which has never died out.

We must now consider the education which men found for themselves, the teaching of books. Learned writers wrote countless volumes on many subjects; but these are not the books to which the ordinary men and women who " could just about read," as was said of an eighteenth-century lady, turned for pleasure and solace. Some of them read poetry no doubt. Pope and his imitators were immensely popular; Collins and Akenside and Shenstone were much read, and so was Gray, though his great fame came later.

Cowper's Sofa furnished many a parlour, nor did

his *Task* remain in the schoolroom.   There were people of culture and refinement who loved poetry and who read French and Italian authors.   Crabbe's father, who was of the lower middle class, took in the *Philosophical Magazine*.   Pastor Moritz found a tailor's widow who read Milton, and James Lackington tells us in his diary how he picked up odd volumes of Shakespeare and the poets for 1*d*. or 2*d*. on book-stalls.   He finally collected quite a number of books. The two classes of literature to which the reading public in the country most often turned were the newspapers and the novels.   The former could be very good and very bad.   The best included the *Spectator* ; the *Tatler* ; the *Examiner* ; the *Gentlemen's Magazine*.   Addison and Steel, Swift and Boling-broke wrote for them, and the household who took them in was indeed fortunate.   In 1711 there were 44,000 newspapers sold every week in London.   The tax which was then imposed upon them killed the *Spectator* ; but many worthless and disreputable journals held out against it.

In the country the squire, if he were a cultivated man, might have the *Spectator* or the *Gentlemen's Magazine* sent to him every week, or arrange for the *Public Advertiser* or the *Morning Post* to be brought down every day by the London stage.   Most men, however, contented themselves with the country paper, and not all of them took it in.   It was often possible to obtain a paper at an inn.   Parson Wood-forde goes over to the Ansford Inn where he pays 4½*d*. "to read the news."   These country papers were printed in the country town, and sent out to the villages by the coach or the market people.   There was the *Norwich Postman*, a quarto sheet, for which a halfpenny was charged, but according to the advertisement " a penny would not be refused." There was the *Salisbury Postman* which, as it contained " the whole week's news, cannot be afforded under 2*d*." At the close of the century, ninety country papers were published every week.

Of the eighteenth-century novel volumes have been written. Fielding and Richardson, Smollett and Sterne, Miss Burney and Daniel Defoe lie upon our modern bookshelves ready for us to read. Lackington speaks of the country people reading *Tom Jones* and *Roderick Random*.

When John [he says] goes to town with a load of hay, he is charged to be sure not to forget to bring home *Peregrine Pickles' Adventures*, and when Dolly is sent to market with eggs, she is commissioned to bring the history of *Pamela Andrews*.

The great novelist then wrote for all the world, and all the reading world read him. There were no highbrow writers who could not be understood ; but, ast he century advanced, the demand for books became greater. There was not enough good literature to go round. An enormous amount of reading matter, it cannot be called anything else by the utmost stretch of courtesy, has practically disappeared, and the names of most of the novelists of the eighteenth century are now only known to scholars.

The circulating library, although it was abused even by novelists themselves, which was surely ungrateful, had become a feature of country life. Clara Reeve, who wrote romances, might abuse it as " one source of the vices and follies of the present time." Mrs. Griffith, the novelist, might talk about " the slop shops of literature " ; but most women agreed with a writer in the *Critical Review* in June 1771 that " it was no less necessary for a lady to unbend her mind, than to unlace her stays."

When the squire's lady drove into the market town, she stopped her chariot outside the circulating library, paid a subscription which might be the crown a quarter that Lydia Melcombe paid at Bath, or even less, and looked round the shelves. The number of books to be found there, we should think amazingly small. In 1771, which was called by the *Critical Review* "this prolific scribblerians' year," scarcely more than sixty novels were reviewed, and some of these were reprints and translations. Fortunately, books were longer than they are now. Richardson runs to inordinate lengths. Henry Brooks' *Fool of Quality*, the curious religious novel, which was at last finished in 1770, ran to five volumes. The country lady in the middle of the century, who cast searching eyes round the shelves in the circulating library, would find there the great novelists, and a host of their imitators.

Richardson was the most popular, at least with the women, who were, and are, the chief novel readers. They did not consider the epistolary methods of story-telling tedious, they loved the author's moralizing, wept over the death of Clarissa and even rejoiced when the wretched Pamela cajoled her master into marriage. There were a hundred imitators of Richardson, who were as moral and verbose and epistolary as their master; but who, for the most part, lacked his power to make those dry bones of didactic propriety live and move. Fielding had his imitators, but they were far fewer than Richardson's. Not many women, Thackeray tells us, cared for

Fielding, and he suggested that it is from a lack of the sense of humour. It may also have been, in some cases, from a dislike of his coarseness. The eighteenth century was not squeamish ; but in those days, as in these, there were a few people who disliked dirt. Dr. Johnson informed Mrs. Thrale, who had just confessed to a liking for it, that no modest woman would read *Tom Jones*. The picaresque novel, however, founded upon Fielding and Smollett, had its readers. The sentimental works of Sterne were immensely popular, in spite of their unpleasantness, and he had a host of imitators. " Come hither, honest gravedigger," says the *Monthly Review* in a fit of exasperation at having so much Sterne and water to review, " and cover up Yorick's skull. The flies have blown on it." The novel of mystery and horror, satirized by Jane Austen in Northanger Abbey, began with Walpole's *Castle of Otranto*, and continued in many forms and shapes through the century. Mrs. Radcliffe and "Monk Lewis" were its chief exponents. For children, and such of the labouring people who could read, there were the chap books. They were paper books embellished with woodcuts and engravings.

" My uncle Toby " as a boy at school purchased *Guy, Earl of Warwick, Valentine and Orson* and the *Seven Champions of Christendom*, and no doubt many other children read them. The pedlar brought them in his pack, together with the ballads, and the broadsides so beloved by the people. Of other children's books there was a spate from the middle of the century onwards, the Newberrys and a number of other less-known booksellers turned out dozens of books for the young.

declines to sit in church with them, although a new
gallery had recently been provided for their accom-
modation.

"Began my school at noon," is the first reference
to his duties, surely a scandalously late hour in days
when schools commonly began at six-thirty or earlier.
The trustees, like many sweating employers, did not
approve of short hours and scamped work.

A certain John Kent was their spokesman and he
seems to have had some reason for his complaints.

"He treated me with a mugg of fivepenny."   "He
treated me with a quartern of gin."   He "sat down
with the alderman and drank raisin wine, very good";
entries such as these are numerous in Gale's diary.
One evening, coming home in the dark after imbibing
a quartern of brandy, a pint of halfpenny and a mug
of mild beer, Gale fell off a bank.   This coming to
his ears, John Kent

loaded me with opprobrious language, and told me the report
of the town was that I was a drunken, saucy, covetious fellow
and concluded with his opinion that I had neither good breeding
nor honesty.   In answer I disallowed the report, the old man
charged upon the town.   I allowed there might be a little truth
in my being covetious, but as to drunkenness and sauciness, it
was utterly false.

Foreseeing trouble, Gale went round the parish and
prudently got up a testimonial to himself, certifying
his attachment to Church and State, his sober life and
conversation.

John Kent, however, was not taking much stock in
testimonials.

The old man [Gale wrote] entered the school with George
Wilinhurst and Eliz. Hook, and insisted that they should be
taught free.   I asked him how many I was to teach free; with-

out any further ado he fell into a violent passion. Among other abusive and scurrilous language he said I was an upstart, runagate, beggarly dog, that I picked his pocket, and that I never knew how to teach school in my life. He again called me upstart, runagate, beggarly dog, clinched his fist in my face and made a motion to strike me and declared he would break my head. He did not strike me but withdrew in a wonderful heat, and ended all with his general maxim " the greater scholler the greater rogue " [which does not seem, at least as regards scholarship, exactly applicable to poor Gale].

Left off school at 2 o'clock having heard the spellers and readers a lesson apiece, to attend a cricket match of the gamesters of Mayfield against those of Lindfield and Chailey.

This is another typical entry, and it is not surprising that old Kent complained again " that the children did not improve, and said that he would get an old woman for 2*d.* a week to teach them better."

To this Gale replied that the boys were " extremely dull, and that I would defie any person that should undertake it, to teach them better." Kent also complained that the schoolmaster spent his time " in reading printed papers to the neglect of the children " and it is interesting to see what he read.

Mr. Rogers came to the school and brought with him 4 volumes of *Pamela* for which I paed him 4/6 and bespoke Duck's poems for Mr. Kine and a *Caution to Swearers* for myself. He wanted to borrow of me the three volumes of *Philander and Silvia*, which I promised to lend him. . . . Left at Mr. Rogers the three volumes of *Love Letters of a nobleman to his sister.*

Fearing perhaps that he might be dismissed from his post, Gale made some attempt to procure other employment.

I set out for Brighthelstone and came at noon to Mallingstreet and went to the Dolphin. Kennard told that Burton's successor had had a great many scholars, but their number began to decrease, by reason of his sottishness, and he offered if their dislike of him much increase, to let me know of it. . . .

Gale remained at his post, however, till 1774 when it was resolved by the Vicar and four parishioners

that he be removed from the school for neglecting the duties thereof, and further that he be not paid his salary due, till he has absolutely put the school house in such a condition, as to the form of it, as it was time of his entering upon such house.

There were many eminent and efficient school-masters in the eighteenth century, but in country villages such as Mayfield they were rare. Gale was typical of his age and profession; perhaps no better, certainly no worse than many, and Mayfield was only singular in having a John Kent to concern himself with the interests of the scholars. In another parish the master of the grammar school

having grown lusty, not having for some time had any scholars who might afford him exercise, employed himself upon a rainy day in rolling up and down the school room a butt of Madeira for the purpose of ripening the wine and keeping himself in good condition.

# CHAPTER X

## THE LABOURER

IN another chapter some account has been given of the Enclosure Acts, and of the very great harm these inflicted on the rural poor. At the beginning of the century the agricultural labourer was prosperous. He did not indeed approach the affluence of his prototype in the days after the Black Death, that piping time for English labourers; but his wages were higher than in any other country in Europe. There was, as Defoe said, "in England more labour than hands to perform it."

In Yorkshire and Durham wages were 4s. a week, in Kent 7s. 9d. and 10s., and there were cases where men earned as much as 15s. a week or even a pound. When he earned less, the man would have his strip of common land, his right to cut wood and peat, his pig or cow. The value of these to a cottager cannot be estimated.

"I kept four cows before the parish was enclosed," said a cottager, "and now I don't keep so much as a goose."

The labourer was often only a labourer on a few days in the week or at hay- and harvest-time. For the rest of the time he lived upon his own property, upon the grain which he grew on his strip in the arable field, on the produce of cows and pigs, with the fuel he had the right to cut upon the waste. His sons helped him in his work, or more often hired themselves out as farm servants in the neighbourhood. In some cases, tempted by the good prices offered for land, the small man sold his rights to the Lord of the Manor, but when this had been done, he usually continued to live upon his holding as a tenant.

After the enclosures large farms became the rule. The small man was squeezed out, and sank down into the rank of labourer. His house was often a miserable building, sometimes erected by his own hands or bought by money he had saved.

The good old cottages which have come down to this day, dwellings of comfort and beauty, did not usually belong to the agricultural labourer. They were small farms, dwellings inhabited by the village tradesman, or, if by a peasant, one who had saved money. The cottage of the labourer had seldom more than two rooms in it, with perhaps an outhouse or a stable. It was built of wood, cob or clay, thatched with reed or straw. The good solidly built cottage of stone or brick was an exception, erected by the big landowner who took a pride in his estate.

" In most towns and villages," says the Rev. Wm. Jones, " the poor and indigent class, I fear, have very wretched accommodations. They are usually crowded together in dark courts and narrow alleys, in cellars or in garrets, where damp stagnated air and accumulated filthiness injure their healths and facilitate the progress of contagious diseases."

Bad housing was, and is, the curse of the country-side. It took its toll of life and health in typhus, ague and smallpox; but the men and women who survived were of great health and hardihood.

> Probably no workmen in Europe [says Lecky] could equal the Englishman in physical strength, in sustained power and energy of work, and few, if any, could surpass him in thoroughness and fidelity in the performance of his task, in general rectitude and honesty of character.

The historian is speaking of the earlier part of the century before enclosures, war, unemployment, and starvation wages had sapped the vitality of the British labourer.

"How much," says Adam Smith, "the lowest class of people in the country, is really superior to those of the towns is well known to every man whom either business or curiosity has led to converse with each."

It was a fine stock, and it took years of poor living in insanitary dwellings to rob it of its robustness. Indeed, Dr. Heberden, writing in 1801, gives statistics showing the improvement in health and the lowering of the death rate which had occurred during the latter years of the eighteenth century. Statistics in those days were most unreliable and proved even less than they do in these. Plague which had occurred early in the century disappeared and the government had taken steps to check the indiscriminate gin-drinking.

The rents, to our ideas, were absurdly small, a guinea, £1 10s. or £2 were the rents nominally charged, or a cottage would be given, as it still is, as part of the labourer's wage.

£2 5s. was paid by the overseers of Finchinfield to one "Widdy ffrench for the furniture."

It purchased " a table, a forme, a press cupboard, 2 kettles, 2 scellets, 2 pewter dishes, a kneading trough, 3 barrels, 2 tubs, a porridge pot, a trammell, a pair of tongs, two bedsteads, a flock bed, a coverlayd, and a pillow."

The barrels strike us as unnecessary, but they were doubtless for beer. The poorest would have refused water.

Prudence Wallaker, who is described " as a poor thing " and who is constantly being relieved by the parish, possessed the following, when the overseers, perhaps thinking, after the manner of their kind, that she was too well off, ordered an inventory of her goods.

A red steadle, a fether Bed, and two Bolsters, one pillow, two coverlets, one long table, one Forme, one Kneading trough, a press cobberd, a hutch, a brass porrish pott, one scellet, a warming pan, a pair of cob irons, two fine sheets, two pillow boards, one Towell, one Table cloathe, two linen Aprons, three handkerchiefs, two quoines, about 3 ells newe Lining Cloathe and Mortor and Pestle and other Implements and a red waiscoate.

In some cottages there were settles with lift-up seats in which the baby was deposited. During the earlier years of the century in spite of bad housing and gross overcrowding the poor were prosperous. They were used to these conditions and expected nothing better. Dr. Johnson said, " £6 a year will fill your belly, shelter you from the weather, and even get you a strong lasting coat supposing it to be made of good bull's hide."

Rich men lived in a way we should now think intolerable.

There was plenty to eat and drink and a good

variety of food. The hours were long, twelve in
summer and till dusk in winter. The labourer was
on the farm by six o'clock in the summer. He dined
at eleven or twelve, having had his nuncheon or
beavor about nine o'clock. He supped at five or
six, and was in bed by sundown, except when hay
or harvest claimed him. Then the farmer and his
men worked as long as the light lasted. Extra money
was of course earned during hay and harvest. 1*s*. 8*d*.
a day and board was given for harvest work, and
1*s*. 4*d*. for hay, though in some parts of the country
it was as low as 9*d*.

The labourer generally reckoned to earn more in
harvest than was necessary to cover his rent. His
ordinary wages in the early days of the century
covered the necessities of life, and his holding of
common land gave him a few simple luxuries. He
could afford mutton and veal at 2*d*. a pound, and
even beef at 2½*d*.

Bread varied in price as wheat rose or fell. In
1715 it was 32*s*. a quarter and the cottager could have
afforded wheaten bread had he so desired. If he ate
it at all, it was generally what we call brown bread
and frequently the wheaten flour was mixed with
pease or rye. In the north oaten bread was eaten.
1*d*. a pound was an average price for bread in the
early days of the century; but it was generally made
at home, from the grain which the cottager had
grown upon his strip of arable. A round bulge in
the walls of some old cottages shows where the oven
has been. It would have been filled with brush wood
and bracken cut from the waste, which was set on
fire, and burnt till the oven was red-hot. The ashes
were then raked out and the bread put in to bake.

It was only necessary to bake once a week, bread baked in this way keeping moist and fresh. As the century progressed, the habit of eating pure white bread increased among the poor though the price of it was raised enormously.

Even a common washerwoman [says a writer] thinks she has not had a proper breakfast without tea and hot buttered bread. I could not forbear looking earnestly and with some degree of indignation at a queasy and ragged creature who came into a shop with two children and asked for a pennyworth of tea and a half-pennyworth of sugar, and said she could not live without drinking it every day.

When bread was 1s. 3d. a quartern loaf the poor man insisted upon buying it. Loud were the out-cries against his folly and extravagance. Davies, however, in his book on the *Case of Labour in Husbandry* points out one reason which may well have been true. In the earlier years of the century there was plenty of other food. The poor man could eat meat and milk, cheese and butter, besides poultry and garden produce. He grew these things for himself. The unfortunate labourer, at the close of the century, with a wage that had not greatly increased since the reign of Anne, and a rise in the cost of all provisions, had to eat what gave him the most sustenance at the price, and this he found to be wheaten bread. It is true that in the north the poor ate oatmeal; but in the north milk could still be obtained. In the south, the man who farmed on a large scale, would not trouble to sell driblets of milk. He poured it into the pig trough, or sent it to the nearest town to be sold in bulk. Eden quotes the instance of a Cumberland labourer who only spent £7 9s. upon meal, but drank 1,300 quarts of milk in the year. A labourer in Berkshire thought himself lucky if he got 2 quarts a week.  He did not often eat oatmeal.  Porridge without milk is a horrible food akin to the skilly of workhouses and prisons.  Moreover, it requires long cooking, and fuel was very dear.

The Berkshire labourer spent £36 a year on wheaten bread and washed it down with tea.

The following are some samples of the budgets collected by Eden at the close of the century, and they illustrate with a miserable clearness the plight of the unfortunate labourer.  This is the budget of an Oxfordshire man, a widower, with three children earning nothing.

```
4½ peck loaves a week at 1/2 each    £13    13 p.a.
Tea and sugar £2  10
Butter and lard £1  10
Beer and milk £1
Bacon and other meat £1  10
Soap, candles, etc. about 15/–
House rent £3
Coats £2  10
Shoes and shirts £3
Other clothes £2                Total expenses £31   8   0
```

This man earned 8s. a week at carting and digging and 9s. during one week in the summer.  His expenditure exceeded his income by £5.  The parish gave him 2s. a week for his children and one of them was clothed, though not fed, by the charity school where she was educated.  The man confessed to being between £3 and £4 in debt, and he was well off compared to many who had large families and smaller earnings.  He lived near Banbury and it is interesting to look at the table of diet which was given in the workhouse of that town.

|           | Breakfast.            | Dinner.                |
|-----------|-----------------------|------------------------|
| Sunday    | Bread and Broth       | Meat, Vegetables.      |
| Monday    | ,,   ,,   ,,          | Cold Meat.             |
| Tuesday   | Bread and Cheese      | Meat, Vegetables.      |
| Wednesday | ,,   ,, Broth         | Cold Meat.             |
| Thursday  | ,, Cheese and Beer    | Bread, cheese, beer.   |
| Friday    | Bread and Broth       | Meat, vegetables.      |
| Saturday  | ,,   ,,   ,,          | Cold meat.             |

The supper was always bread and cheese and beer. This diet was monotonous; but as Eden points out such food could not be afforded by any agricultural labourer in the kingdom.

Here is the budget of another labourer living at Buckden in Huntingdonshire. This man earned only 7s. 3d. a week. He had four young children who earned nothing. His wife made 1s. 2d. a week. For rent he paid £2 7s. a year. For shoes, clothes and furniture for six people £4 6s., and for births, burials and sickness £1 1s.

They divided a miserable income of 7s. 2¾d. a week as follows:

| | |
|---|---|
| Flour (in this case chiefly barley meal) | 4/10½ |
| Yeast and salt | 3 |
| Tea, sugar and butter | 1/- |
| Soap and blue | 3¾ |
| Candles | 3 |
| Potatoes | 6 |
| Thread and worsted | 1½ |

There was no meat, cheese or milk in this dietary.

"During the last year," says Eden, "they received a shilling a week from the parish; but never received a farthing before. Notwithstanding their scanty fare this family is getting into debt."

The misery of life lived under these circumstances

can be imagined.  A woman of Cumberland, aged sixty-one, furnished Eden with an example of marvellous frugality.  She was employed for fifteen weeks of the year at spinning wool for 4*d*. a day and her keep.  For the rest of the year she earned 1*s*. 1½*d*. a week by spinning lint in her own home.  Her house rent was covered by the interest on a sum of money which had been left her by her father, a small farmer.  She lived upon £4 1*s*. a year and apportioned it as follows :

| | | |
|---|---|---|
| House rent | | 12/– |
| Peat and turf | | 7/– |
| Barley 2½ bushels | @ 5/– | 12/2¼ |
| Oatmeal 6 stone | @ 2/4 | 14/– |
| Butter | @ 8 | 5/4 |
| Milk | 120 quarts | 1*d*. 10/– |

She gets three pecks of potatoes planted for her. Her turf ashes produce about 9 bushels; and the balance of expenses is about £1 9*s*.

| | | |
|---|---|---|
| Sugar and treacle | 4 | 0 |
| Soap, salt, candles, etc. etc. | 4 | 0 |
| Clogs (1 pair in two years) | | 6 |
| Butcher's meat | 1 | 6 |
| Wheaten bread | 1 | |
| Shifts | 2 | 9 |
| Other clothes | 10 | |

She seems [remarks Eden] perfectly happy, content and cheerful and always takes care to avoid debt.  When she is able to reap in harvest, she earns a little more money; yet, notwithstanding her present scanty income, she has no thoughts of applying to the parish.  Her common diet is hasty pudding, milk, butter and potatoes.  She never had a tea pot in her house in her life.

Eden apparently admires the woman's courage and

cheerfulness, as well he may; but it never seems to have occurred to him that there was anything wrong in a state of society which permitted a woman to live thus. The hasty pudding, of which Eden speaks, was a kind of porridge—it was a Cumberland dish. The farm labourer there had it for breakfast with milk and sometimes butter; for dinner, potatoes cooked with butter or a little bacon, with milk and barley bread. On Sunday there was meat and pudding and sometimes during the week as well, especially during the harvest, when the work was heavier and the wages higher. Supper in these households consisted of porridge made with milk and barley bread.

This dietary is far better than the southern labourer's bread and tea. In the north there were fewer enclosures, and a man could often grow his own corn. He could get milk, and fuel was easy to procure. It could generally be had for the cutting. In the south the cottager was forced to send his Sunday dinner to be cooked at the baker's, and for the rest of the week to live on bread and cheese. Fuel was too dear to buy, and the fireplaces in cottages were seldom adapted for cooking.

As these budgets show us, there was very little left over when the food had been provided. In the north all clothing was spun at home; in the south it was bought. Many labourers were so poor that they could not even afford to purchase the raw material necessary to spin thread or yarn at home. Clothes could be bought cheaper in shops; but homespun lasted much longer. There was no regular peasant dress, though in some parts of the country the women wore red cloaks.

The following are some of the prices charged for clothes :

| | |
|---|---:|
| A good foul weather coat (will last very well two years) | 13/– |
| A common waistcoat | 6/6 |
| A pair of stout breeches (one year) | 3/9 |
| Stockings the pair | 1/10 |
| A dowlas shirt | 4/6 |
| A pair of strong shoes | 7/– |
| A hat (will last three years) | 2/6 |

Women

| | |
|---|---:|
| A common stuff gown | 6/6 |
| Linsey wolsy petticoat | 4/6 |
| A shift | 3/8 |
| A pair of shoes | 3/9 |
| A coarse apron | 1/– |
| Check apron | 2/– |
| A pair of stockings 1/6 | 1/6 |
| A hat (the cheapest sort will last 2 years) | 1/8 |
| A coloured neckerchief | 1/– |
| A common cap | 10d. |
| Cheapest kind of cloak (will last 2 years) | 4/6 |
| Pair of stays (will last 6 years) | 6/– |

These prices were in the neighbourhood of London. In country districts clothes would be considerably cheaper.

The overseers of the parish of Morwenstow paid as follows for an outfit for a man :

| | | |
|---|---:|---:|
| 2½ yds. of cloth | 7 | 1d. |
| ½ yd. canvas & 5 oz. thread | | 7 |
| 1 doz. buttons | | 3 |
| 1 pair shoes & tapping | 5 | 8 |
| 4½ yds. of kersey | 15 | 9 |
| 4 yds. of canvas | 3 | 4 |
| 2 skins for breeches | 2 | 6 |
| Buttons, thread and canvas | | 7½ |
| For making coat and breeches · | | 6d. |

The poor could not have afforded such prices. They bought second-hand clothes, or had them given to them. Eden speaks constantly of the wretchedness of the poor.

"This family never tastes meat." "They are much in debt." "No labourer can at present maintain himself, wife and two children. Many poor families are said to subsist entirely on bread and tea." These are some of his entries; but no one seemed to think that higher wages might assist matters. The educated classes were bound up in the Political Economy of their time; which taught that wages must be kept at their lowest, or the whole structure of industry and commerce would totter to the ground. Many suggestions were put forth. The poor were adjured to eat less; to eat barley or oats or rye, to give up tea and beer. They were told that "the French lived prudently upon roots, cabbage or other herbage," and they were recommended to do the same. They were to be fed with the crumbs which fell from the rich man's table.

A Mrs. Shore furnished an account of how fifty-two persons might be fed on stewed ox-head with household scraps at a cost of 2s. 6d. "The power of giving an increased effect to Christian benevolence by these soups" was not appreciated by the poor, who have always hated soup, in which prejudice they are now upheld by medical opinion.

To Marshall, the writer upon rural economy, it appeared "incomprehensible how a common farm labourer, who perhaps does not earn more than six or seven shillings a week rears a large family as many a one does without assistance." He turned to "old George Barnwell, who had brought up 5 children, to clear up the mystery." This old labourer admitted that he had frequently " been hard put to it." There had often been bread enough for the children only and he himself had made a dinner of raw hog peas. " He had taken," he said, a handful of peas, and ate them with as much satisfaction as, in general, he has eaten better dinners, adding that they agreed with him very well, and that he was as able to work upon them as upon other food ; closing his remarks with the trite maxim—breathed out with an involuntary sigh, " Ay, no man knows what he can do till he's put to it."

This brave old man died at the age of seventy-three, and even in his delirium he talked about his work. He had amassed the astonishing sum of £100, and was troubled on his death-bed by his only debt, that of 6d., which he kept on entreating his children to pay. In such lives there could have been no scope for the smallest indulgence. In most cases the poor had but one luxury, that of tea. Beer or cider would have been considered almost a necessity. They were always given in hay- or harvest-time and frequently at other seasons. Marshall indeed mentions one wretched employer, who hired an old man at eighteen-pence a quarter and board, and who only gave him water to drink." He speaks of such meanness, however, with reprobation.

In the south of England nearly every poor family drank tea. In 1741 750,000 pounds of tea entered the country, and paid a tax of 5s. in the pound. Such tea was naturally out of the question for the poor. It would be sold in the shops at 12s. or 16s. the pound. What the poor bought was generally stuff that had been smuggled in, and freely adulterated with sloe leaves, gooseberry leaves, and pieces of stick. In the houses of the gentry, the used tea-leaves were the cook's perquisite, and they could often be bought at the back door for a penny or two. Such being the tea the poor drank, it is not surprising that they were told it was deleterious; but they continued to drink it.

In most parishes some attempts were made to relieve the poor. Ancient endowed charities distributed food and clothing, or put boys and girls to school. A kindly farmer did not rake his fields too bare, and the poor gleaned enough corn to keep them for a year in bread, and enough beans to feed a pig. The squire and his family generally realized that they had a duty to their tenants. Coals and blankets, bread and beef were distributed at Christmas; help was given in sickness.

Lady Byron writes:

Amongst the many interests that engaged the zealous good offices of my parents, I never saw any preferred to the comfort of the labouring poor. It then seemed to me a mere matter of course that the best horse should be sent many miles for the best doctor to attend on rustics, who are usually consigned to the Parish Medical officer, that the finest claret should be taken out of the cellar to be applied to the exhausted patients in a tenant's house.

There were other landowners equally good and charitable. Some encouraged allotments, and where these were available the lot of the poor was happier and more prosperous.

One of the few labouring men who have written an account of themselves is William Huntingdon, who afterwards became a Methodist preacher. He writes thus of his childhood:

My father was a day labouring man, who worked for 7 or 8 shillings in the winter, and in the summer for 9 shillings a week,

which is but a small pittance to keep a family. My mother
bore 11 children, of which number I am the tenth. My parents
being very poor, and receiving no support from the parish,
we children fared very hard, and indeed seldom knew what it
was to have a belly-full of victuals, above once in the week,
which was on the Sabbath day, when we were allowed to know
what a bit of meat was. But it often happened that rent or
some other debt was to be discharged, and on such accounts
no meat could be procured. These barren Sabbaths were
mourning days indeed to us young ones, but to our sorrow they
frequently came. Suffering with hunger, cold and almost
nakedness so embittered my life in my childhood, that I often
wished secretly that I had been a brute, for then I could have
filled my belly in the fields.

From Henry Fielding downwards men wrote
pamphlets on the subject of poverty and the poor
laws, with suggestions for amelioration and relief. A
Devonshire parson, John Acland, actually anticipated
Lloyd George and advocated a system of insurance
" for rendering the poor independent of public
contributions." He was one of that great band of
men who were before their time. The remedy usually
suggested was the workhouse or outdoor relief.

The latter had been the general method since the
reign of Elizabeth till the middle of the eighteenth
century. An act of 1722 authorized vestries to build
workhouses ; before this date the erection of each
new one required special legislation. Workhouses
accordingly began to spring up like poisonous fungi
all over the country. Some vestries granted outdoor
relief ; others forced the indigent into " the House."
A workhouse dietary from *Eden's State of the Poor* has
been quoted. He gives many others in his book.
They are on much the same scale, and they look pretty
well on paper. There was, however, a most pernicious
system in the latter part of the century of farming the

workhouse out to contractors, who made what they
could of them. The plight of the inmates may be
imagined ; it may also be learned in Crabbe's poem
of " The Village."

> Theirs is yon house that holds the Parish Poor,
> Whose walls of mud scarce bear the broken door ;
> There, where the putrid vapours, flagging, play,
> And the dull wheel hums doleful through the day ;
> There children dwell who know no parents' care ;
> Parents, who know no children's love dwell there.
> Heartbroken Matrons on their joyless bed,
> Forsaken wives, and mothers never wed ;
> Dejected Widows, with unheeded tears,
> And crippled Age, with more than childish fears ;
> The Lame, the Blind, and far the happiest they
> The moping idiot and the Madman gay.
> Here, too, the sick their doom receive,
> Here brought, amid the scenes of grief, to grieve,
> Where the loud groans from some sad chamber flow,
> Mixt with the clamours of the crowd below ;
> Here sorrowing, they each kindred sorrow scan,
> And the cold charities of man to man.
> Whose laws indeed, for ruined Age provide,
> And strong compulsion plucks the scrap from pride ;
> But still that scrap is bought with many a sigh,
> And pride embitters what it can't deny.

One hopes that some of this is overdrawn, but
Eden's remarks upon workhouses seem rather to
confirm the description.

> A fever prevails now in the Workhouse [he says, speaking
> of the workhouse at Sunderland] and has done so for some time
> back. Mr. Howlett informs us that in 1774 126 persons in this
> house died of that disorder (putrid fever) out of an average of
> about 220.

It is needless to say that the workhouse was cordi-
ally detested. Men starved rather than enter it.

An army of sturdy beggars overran the country-side. Defoe writes in great wrath of the men who refused honest work, saying that they could make more by begging. Parish relief was looked upon by the respectable poor with almost as much horror as the House. It was certainly made as odious as possible.

By an act passed in 1697

> Anyone, who shall be upon the collection and receive relief of any parish or place, shall upon the shoulder of the right sleeve of the uppermost garment . . . wear such badge or mark as is herein mentioned and expressed: that is to say a large Roman P. together with the first letter of the name of the parish, or place whereof the poor person is an inhabitant.

If any refused to wear this badge their relief was taken away and they were sent to the House of Correction and whipped. Sometimes the parish would contract with individuals to take a pauper or two for some months and board and lodge him. Mary Briggs was paid £4 18*s*. 8*d*. by the overseers of East Bridgeford in Nottinghamshire for keeping Robert Hourtt for thirty-two weeks.

Another great grievance from which the poor suffered was the difficulty of moving from one parish to another. A man, living in one parish and out of work, might hear that in another a brick-field or silk manufacture had been set up, and that labour was wanted. He could not move from his home and take up his abode in the other parish without a certificate. Unless there was a great outcry from employers, who were in urgent need of labour, those certificates were seldom granted. No parish wanted a man who might become a charge upon it.

A poor man [says a Mr. Hay, who vainly championed his cause in the House of Commons] is no sooner got into a neighbour-hood, habitation and employment that he likes, but upon humour or caprice of the parish he is sent to another place, where he can find none of these conveniences. Not certain long to con-tinue there ; for perhaps after appeal, he is sent back again, and then hurried to a third place . . . 'tis no wonder if by this treatment he is very much impoverished.

Overseers would go to almost any lengths in order to shift a pauper to another parish. In 1780 Mary Mann, who had, a fortnight before, given birth to an illegitimate child, was " barbarously and unnatur-ally " dragged for 7 miles in bitter winter weather, that a justice might inquire into the paternity of her child, and so shift it and her into another parish. During the examination before the magis-trate, the poor creature had to be held up by two persons, " for which hard usage, Mary Mann died."

The magistrate, Sir Francis Molyneux, finding that the overseers and constables had done it " of their own heads," and not upon a justice's order as they pretended, bound them over to good be-haviour. They had perhaps a little overstepped the limits of propriety, and showed rather too much zeal.

Parishes were continually wrangling about the poor and attempting to thrust them upon other parishes. The enormous expense of these settlement cases is exemplified in the records of the parish of Morwen-stowe. A certain Wm. Heines, being dissatisfied with his treatment by the overseers of the parish, who had once allowed him half a bushel and half a peck of wheat valued at 5s. and after that refused him any-thing, appealed, as his right was, to the justices. By them he was awarded 2*s.* in money, 2 yards of canvas for a shirt and a pair of shoes. He had done well, too well the vestry thought. They applied for a justice's order to remove Heines to Milton Abbot, near Tavistock, where he had originally dwelt. The overseer wasted several days in taking Heines and his sons to the justices, and then to the court at Stratten, and this is the bill he sent in to the vestry.

|  |  |
|---|---|
| Paid the first day when went to get the justices to sit to grant an order for removal | 2/8 |
| Pd the second day for mee and hors. | 2/– |
| Pd the third  „   „   „   „   „ | 1/8 |
| Pd the fourth  „  to put forth | 6 |
| Pd for three horses and for feeding ye horses | 4/1 |
| Pd for ye order | 5/– |
| Pd at Tamerton by Mr. Phillips' order for meat, drink and firing for ourselves and poppars (paupers) | 3/6 |
| At Stratton by Dto. | 3/6 |
| Pd ye poppars 6*d.* apiece and my labour | 1/6 |

This was only the beginning of the charges. The parish constable and one of the churchwardens, with a justice's order in their hands, proceed to evict William Heines and his family and take them to Milton Abbot. There are further expenses " for mee and hors," and the whole bill comes to £2 2*s.* 10½*d.* This is followed by another bill " ye charge at Setions."

Apparently the parish of Milton Abbot objected to receiving the " Poppers "—parishes always did—and carried the matter to the quarter sessions. The expenses there came to £2 11*s.* and on the top of this there is a big bill from the attorney, Mr. Phillips, of over £15.

In some cases vagrants were licensed beggars. If a man had suffered a great misfortune, if his house had been burnt, his cattle died of the plague, if he had suffered shipwreck, or had all his goods stolen, he might apply to the magistrates, who could, if they saw fit, give him his licence to beg through the county. Some such form as this would be made out.

To all whom these presents shall come Bordolphs Wasteneys, Bart, Isaac Knight, and Jonathan Ocklom Esqs, send greeting. We have upon the petition of our neighbours upon it appearing to us upon oath that Thomas Wake, the bearer hereof, hath by the great losse he hath lately sustained by the losse of his cattle is become an object of charity and compelled to implore the relief of charitable people. Wee have therefore as much as in us lyeth given leave unto him to go from place to place within the said county to ask, receive and take the charity and benevolence of all well-disposed people towards the recovery of said losses.

Some labourers made what were often abortive attempts to help themselves. They formed friendly societies or box clubs which gave help in times of sickness. Trade Unions, whether of masters or men, were forbidden by various statutes; but in spite of this working men were known to form combinations to raise wages. The largest of these was the wool combers, who formed a society in the year 1700 in Tiverton which spread over England. The wool combers decreed that no wool was to be combed for less than 2s. per dozen, and that non-union men were not to be employed. The weavers were not slow in following their example; the journeyman tailors and others also formed combinations, and from time to time strikes broke out. The silk weavers were so far successful that they forced

Parliament to pass laws regulating the wages in their trade.

The rude boisterousness of village life is illustrated by an extract from Read's journal in 1721.

On Wed. the 13th at Windsor a piece of plate is to be fought for, at cudgels by ten men on a side from Berks and Middlesex. The next day a hat and feather to be fought for by ten men on a side from the counties aforesaid. 10 bargemen are to eat 10 quarts of hasty pudding, well buttered but infernally hot. He that is done first to have a silver spoon of 10s. value, and the second 5s. And as they have anciently had the title of Merry Wives of Windsor, 6 old women of Windsor town challenge any 6 old women in the universe (we need not, however, go further than our own county) to outscold them ; the best in three heats to have a suit of clothes, and (what old women generally want) a pair of nutcrackers.

It is difficult for us to look back from an England of ordered civilized life, with newspapers, libraries, schools and women's institutes and drama leagues, all at the service of the country labourer, and to picture an England where men rushed to see a half-naked woman whipped, or a wretched bull driven mad by crackers and fire-balls and baited to death by dogs. Whether the country was in any real degree less civilized than the towns is very doubtful. Possibly there was more drinking in the country. Life was monotonous, and if the ale-house was far away there was always home-made mead and spirituous liquors to fall back upon. In 1735 there were reckoned to be over 5 million distilleries in England, and the ale-houses put out a notice : " Drunk for a penny. Dead drunk for 2d."

These accursed spirituous liquors [says Bishop Benson, writing about the middle of the century], which to the shame

of our government are so easily to be had, and in such
quantities drunk, have changed the very nature of our people.
There is not only no safety in living in towns, but very little
in the country, now robbery and murder are grown so
frequent.

Eden computed that in one rural parish of 1,671
persons £3,840 was spent annually in drink in the
sixteen public-houses, mostly by the inhabitants, for
few travellers passed that way. Six gallons per head
of the population was the estimated consumption of
spirits in the early years of the century.

Two causes of much crime and disregard of human
life were poaching and smuggling. To the average
countryman there was nothing inherently wrong in
either. He had a right, he considered, to the wild
creatures which lived in the woods and on the moors
and stubble fields. His ancestors had shot and snared
them, unreproved and unpunished. In the reign of
Charles II an act had been passed which gave shooting
rights to those persons only who possessed a freehold estate of £100 a year or a leasehold of £150.
This act, as Blackstone pointed out, raised up a little
Nimrod in every manor, and Fielding has described
the activities of those Nimrods in punishing the
poacher. In 1770 an act was passed whereby the
poacher could be imprisoned, and for a second
offence publicly whipped, between the hours of
twelve and one. Not content with this act, and
others of an even fiercer nature, some landowners
went so far as to plant man traps and spring guns
in their woods and coppices. These horrible in-
ventions caught and maimed and even killed many
an unfortunate creature. Sometimes it was not a
poacher who was trapped, but a harmless farm

labourer or even a gamekeeper. Yet these " dia-
bolical engines," as Lord Holland termed them, were
not prohibited by the Legislature till 1827. In spite
of these pains and penalties, man traps, whippings
and imprisonment, poaching flourished. Sport is
in the Englishman's blood, whether it be the sport
of lurking in the woods after dark to snare a
pheasant when the gamekeeper's back is turned,
or the sport of kicking a football before him into
battle. The creatures were wild, the countryman
argued, though the landowner might talk of the
expenses of preserving. They made a tasty addition
to a man's dinner, and as times became harder and
food dearer, game was often the only meat which
the labourer tasted. Though poaching was an
offence and the selling of game illegal, it could
always be bought. Rich men in towns always had
it. It appeared on the Lord Mayor's table, at the
judge's dinners, at the barristers' mess. No one
inquired how it had been got, though everyone knew
it was poached. Landowners in those days sold
nothing except the advowson of a living, or a seat in
Parliament. They certainly never dealt in game.
The pheasants and partridges and hares, which hung
up outside the shops, or were sold at Leadenhall or
Newgate Market, were bought from poachers. It
was an organized business. Poulterers had their
agents in the country, who organized gangs of men
to shoot or snare what they wanted. In one village
the whole small population, including the constable,
lived by poaching. No one except the landowner
and the magistrates thought a penny the worse of
them. The tradesman encouraged them, the farmer
turned a blind eye, and a common jury found

them not guilty on any evidence or no evidence at all.

If poaching was a source of corruption, smuggling was another and an even greater. That the Government should put a tax on the necessaries, or even the luxuries of life, was thought by the common people to be iniquitous. They did not know, and it would have been useless to point out to them, how much better off England was as regards taxes and imports than most continental nations. There was no taille or octroi, as in France, no tax on bread, as in Holland, no duty on all sales, as in Spain. There were no Government monopolies, no farming out of the taxes. The Englishman, however, wanted his tea and tobacco, his French wines and his brandy, without paying a large tax to the Government. The women wanted their cambrics from France, their Mechlin laces, and India muslins. It was calculated that over £2,000,000 worth of goods was smuggled into the country, including over 7,000,000 pounds of tea.

The most spirited and enterprising of the men, like those who took to poaching, threw in their lot with the smugglers. On the south and the south-east coast every village had its gang, or at least its receivers of smuggled goods; nor did the enterprise confine itself to the sea coast. In the wilder inland districts, such as the Weald and the New Forest, store places were made, and regular lines of communications established with the coast. Both poaching and smuggling, however they may have been regarded by the common people, led to the commission of serious crime. The poachers fought with the game-keepers, the smugglers with the preventive men. A band of smugglers, known as the Hawkhurst gang, perpetrated the most horrible cruelties and even murder on two unhappy men whom they suspected of informing against them. The Owlers, another gang, were actually in league with the magistrates and the neighbouring gentry to outwit the customs officers.

The " free trader " thought himself well repaid if he saved one cargo out of three. He sometimes had to fight for it; but there were quiet beaches where a ship might be safely unloaded, and from whence a score of waggons, or strings of packhorses, carried the stuff away to secret hiding-places. It was computed, though the figures cannot be very reliable, that during six months 1,835 horse loads of tea were borne away from the Suffolk coasts, and that about 2,000 hogsheads of spirits were landed every year on the southern shores of England.

Almost everyone shared in smuggled goods. The squire was not above accepting a keg of brandy, the parson was glad to get his tobacco cheap, the farmer's wife wanted her cambric and her India muslins. That peaceable, law-abiding parson James Woodforde stays up till midnight as he expects " Richard Andrews the honest smuggler with some gin."

Even Adam Smith wrote apologetically of the smuggler as

a person, who no doubt highly blamable for violating the laws of his country, is frequently incapable of violating those of natural justice, and would have been in every respect an excellent citizen had not the laws of his country made that a crime, which nature never meant to be so.

If the labourer fell foul of the law he was haled by

the constable into the village lock-up or round-house. This was a very small, dark, stone building, having sometimes only a grating for light and ventilation. One of these existed till quite recently at Purton in Wiltshire, and through the grating, it was said, the prisoner's friends would insert a pipe and so convey liquid refreshment. The lock-up was only intended for use until the prisoner could be brought before the magistrates. When sentenced by them to imprisonment he was conveyed to gaol in the nearest town. What the horrors of these gaols were, especially to the poor, we know from the reports of such reformers as Howard and Oglethorpe. They were generally farmed out to monsters who battened upon the luckless prisoners, loading them, quite illegally, with chains and fetters, so that they might gain money by taking them off, starving, flogging and torturing them. Happy the prisoner who was not imprisoned, or transported as a slave to the American plantations. It was better to be whipped, far better to be set in the stocks or the pillory.

There was yet another way of dealing with a man who had made himself obnoxious to the authorities. Perhaps the evidence was not sufficient to convict him, and juries at assizes were often lenient, but a word to the lieutenant of the press gang and the man was carried away on board a king's ship, and it would be years before he returned to his native village, if he ever returned at all. In all seaport towns, the sight of the press gang charging down the streets was only too common. There was perhaps a struggle. There might be some doughty shipowner like old William Hurry of Great Yarmouth, of whom the lieutenant of the press said that he would rather meet the devil incarnate than Mr. Hurry if he had pressed one of his men. In general, however, in these seaport towns the press gang was looked upon as a necessary nuisance. The king's ships must be manned, and it was not to be supposed that any man, unless he had escaped from the gaol or from Bedlam, would voluntarily ship in a man-of-war. The conditions in most of these vessels were horrible, even according to eighteenth-century standards. The press gang seemed to be a necessity, and the seaport towns were accustomed to its activities. When, owing to continuous warfare and many casualties, more men were needed, and the press gang went out into distant towns and villages, it was received with horror and consternation, and often with armed resistance. It was not now the merchant seaman who was taken, a man inured to the hardships of the sea, nor was it the offscourings of the gaols and the hulks who would never be missed. They were pressing honest, decent men, the fathers of families, who knew that they might never see their wives and homes again. No wonder that men fought for their liberty, and that such proceedings as those described in a news sheet published in London in 1706 were not uncommon.

The Newberry Skirmish. Being a true relation of a fight that happened at Newberry in Barkshire on Friday last between the townsmen and soldiers, about pressing men, and how one serjeant and seven or eight others were killed and wounded. With an account of their apprehending and examination before the Worshipful Justice Kingsmill of Newberry and their commitment to the common gaol. Also an account of one Lieughtenant Blake, who was barbarously murdered on the same account by a butcher of Market Drayton in Shropshire, who clove the Lieughtenant's head with his cleaver for having listed his brother. For which he was apprehended and committed to gaol.

Impressing for the army was illegal, but it was winked at, and many a man was forced or cajoled into becoming a soldier. When we consider what manner of men they often were, and how they were enlisted, it is remarkable that the soldiers and sailors of eighteenth-century England fought for her so gallantly.

No account of the labourer would be complete without some mention of domestic servants. These did not always spring from the labouring classes. In a day when domestic service was far pleasanter and easier than life in shop or factory, the farmers' sons and daughters often went in for it. It was not disdained by the parson's family. Among the Verney letters are many from servants which are often better spelt and expressed than those of their betters. Defoe declared that the English were too independent to make good servants, and that instead of being content with 30_s_. or £2 a year, as had been the case formerly, they were demanding £6 and £8. Defoe would have liked to see wages fixed at not more than £5 " otherwise, without doubt," he says, " they will soon be asking £20."

Probably money wages rose very little, and real wages did not rise at all, during the century.

Parson Woodforde pays his servants as follows :

| | | |
|---|---|---|
| To Betty, 1 years wages, due this day and for tea also | Paid £5 | 15 6 |
| To Lizzie  Do  Do  Do | Paid £2 | 12 6 |
| To Will Coleman for years wages | 5 | 5 |
| To Ben Leggatt 1 years wages | 10 | |
| To Jack Wharton | 1 | 1 |

Lord Fermanagh, when corresponding about a butler who has the audacity to ask for £10 a year, says, "I would have a sightly fellow and one that has had the smallpox, and an honest man, for he is entrusted with store of plate, and can shave, but I will give no such wages as this." The English servant had certainly preserved something of his independence. In the Purefoy letters we hear of a servant who, on being struck by his master, turned on him with a pitchfork and killed him. It amazed foreigners, to whom servants were nothing more than slaves, that a nobleman like Lord Ferrers should have been hanged for the murder of his steward. The scarcity of women servants, which Defoe also deplores, certainly did not exist in the later years of starvation and unemployment. There is a record of a lady who let it be known that she would consider taking another housemaid, and who had 200 applications for the post. If money wages were low, the servants in big houses could always supplement them with vails. A foreigner, travelling in England, describes how, after dining with a friend, "you'll find all the servants drawn up in the passage like a file of musqueteers from the house steward, down to the lowest liveried servant, and each of them holds out his hand to you in as deliberate a manner as the servants in our inns on the like occasion."

It was said that when a clergyman dined with his Bishop, he spent more in vails than would have fed his family for a week ; and the Duke of Ormonde on inviting a poor relative to dinner always sent him a guinea for the vails. When Parson Woodforde departs from a friend's house after a week's visit, he

The Dairymaid

The Drover

leaves 10s. 6d. in his bed chamber for the chamber-maid and gives the coachman and servant boy 10s. These would be very large tips if reckoned in our present money value.

A movement which came, it was said, from Scotland, was set on foot to abolish vails. The gentlemen on the grand juries in Northumberland and Wiltshire declared that they ought to be done away with; but no grand jury in any county or any century has been able to abolish vails. They are still with us; but the fine old name has gone, and we are left with the tip. There are complaints of servants all down the century. Some employers expected a great deal. Mrs. Purefoy advertises for a coachman who can not only " drive 4 horses in a coach," but " understands husbandry business and cattle, for shall have some ploughing to do." She also wanted a footman who could "work in the garden, lay the cloth, wait at table, go to the cart with Thomas, and do any other business that he is ordered to do and not too large sized a man, that he may not be too great a load for the horse when he rides."

The servants were said to be lazy and selfish, to leave their places to get higher wages and larger vails, to be so insolent that they could not be spoken to, in fact the complaints were much the same as those we listen to nowadays. Sometimes, however, in some memoir or in a packet of old letters we read of a servant who has become the loved and honoured friend of the family. Perhaps it is the children's nurse, to whom John Byrom sent messages in his letter to his son, " for I reckon her amongst you always," or the old coachman to Richard Bampfylde

who has the following epitaph on his tombstone at
Poltimore in Devon.

> Coachman the foe to drink of heart sincere
> Of manners gentle and of judgement clear
> Safe through the chequered track of life he drove
> And gained the treasure of his master's love.
> Upright his carriage, now with wondrous skill
> Nor stopped but when the wheels of life stood still,
> Here now he lies, expecting that reward
> The faithful servant meeteth from his Lord.

## CHAPTER XI

## A LABOURER GENIUS

THE agricultural labourer could seldom, as we have said, either read or write, so that few records have come down to us of a most valuable and highly skilled class of men.

Arthur Young has, however, left us the description of a perfect marvel among men, a collier named James Croft, with such a passion for agriculture that he did wonders upon the acre of moorland which he cultivated. The account is best given in Young's own words.

Thirteen years ago, he began his husbandry, by taking an acre of moor, which he pared and burnt, spread three chaldrons of lime among the ashes, and sowed it with oats, of which he got but an indifferent crop. He threw in three more chaldrons, planted half of it with potatoes, and sowed the other half with barley, the crops middling. He then limed it again, sowed it with oats, and gained 50 bushels. Next he limed it again, and sowed half of it with barley and planted the other half with potatoes, the crops but indifferent. He then limed it again and sowed oats once more, of which he got 40 bushels; with these oats he sowed hay seeds all he could get together and procure, which was 36 bushels. After the oats were off, he mixed some lime and earth together, and spread it over the land. The grass came very finely, and has been exceedingly good ever since, and improving every year; it is now worth 20/– an acre. I viewed it attentively, and I think it well worth the rent. This first essay was very spirited; but not carried on upon principles which can altogether be approved of. Indeed, it could not be expected that a poor collier should strike at once and without any experience, into an accurate and correct husbandry. His next effort was upon an addition of 8 acres, which however was too much for him to improve at once ; but he effected it by degrees. These acres were certainly stony, so that, after a division of walls built out of them, many remained. One acre cost him two months to clear, and fill up the holes. Some single stones require near a week. Laborious as the work was, he completed it by degrees and pared and burnt the soil. He threw these lands into a better husbandry (though not totally defensible) than what he used before. His method was to sow turnips upon the pared and burnt land, after liming two chaldrons per acre. It costs, by the time it is on the land, 14/6 per chaldron. The turnips are generally worth from 20/- to 30/- an acre. He draws and scatters them on his grass for his cows and his young cattle. After the turnips, he ploughs four times, lays on two chaldrons per acre more of lime, and sows oats 8 bushels per acre ; the crop varies from 40 to 60 bushels. After these oats, he sows four more successive crops of them for each of which he ploughs three or four times, and also limes at the rate of two chaldrons per acre.

The average of these crops is forty bushels per acre. With the best he lays down to grass, by sowing plenty of hay seeds. This has been his general course ; but sometimes he has sown rye, of which he generally gets 32 bushels per acre. Potatoes he has regularly cultivated ; sets them in rows two feet asunder and one foot in the rows ; in which manner 13 bushels plant an acre ; the mean produce is 158 bushels.

Two years ago he took in eight acres more on which he is now hard at work. It is astonishing with what perseverance he attacks the most enormous stones, cutting them in pieces, carrying them away, and then bringing mould to fill the holes up ; and he has such an idea of neatness that he will not pass one.

He has five acres of grass ; his management of which is very good. He lays all the dung, he can raise, upon it, mixed well with lime ; and sometimes with good earth. And this dressing he repeats every third year without ever failing. His stock of cattle is three milch cows, a heifer and his gallway. Their winter food hay, turnips and straw. Two acres of commonly improved grass, from moors he reckons sufficient to summer feed a cow ; but an acre and a half of his will do. He makes

6 lbs. of butter per cow per week, 24 ozs. to the lb. for three months, and 4 lbs. for the rest of the summer. And each of his cows eats an acre of hay in the winter. He has not yet had enough of his own for them, buying some ; but hopes soon to effect that. Besides the mere husbandry of his fields, he has done something in the ornamental way, having almost sur-rounded two of his closes with a young plantation of firs and other trees which thrive extremely well.

Attentive to every object that can render his little farm either profitable or agreeable, he has, with no slight trouble, directed a little rill of water from the moor through his fields ; by which means he not only has water in every field for his cattle, but can also water some of his grass and thereby fertilize it much. Were I to dwell upon every circumstance of this collier's hus-bandry, I should be afraid of tediousness ; but I shall not con-clude without attempting to give you some idea of the man as well as his farm. I have shown you how he has managed, for several years, above nine acres of land, much of it always in tillage, and some constantly fresh breaking up and improving —we found him cropping his land several years successively (a practice, though bad, yet of increasing labour) never sowing any without a previous ample liming and three or four ploughings ;—adding to his cultivated land, by perfectly clearing the fresh soil from all stones, some of them an enormous size, and of many tons weight ; and by paring and burning in the most spirited and laborious manner. When you consider these circumstances, and that at the same time he has had the courage to attack eight acres more—will you not conclude he has received much assistance, either money or labour ; or that many favourable circumstances hitherto unrelated have enabled him to make such advances in so spirited a conduct ? But the very contrary of all this is the case. His work in the colliery has been regular, equal in every respect to the other men, and in some superior. His hour of going to the mine is twelve o'clock at night, the work is over at noon the next day. The remainder is all the time he had had to perform what I can scarcely call less than wonders.

Nor has he ever received the least assistance of any kind or ever expended 1/- in hiring the labour of another man. The quantity of lime he has laid upon the land is very great, and much more than what is commonly used by the neighbouring farmers ;

the number of ploughings he has given his fields is equally superior; and yet all this labour has been performed with a single gallway : the lime brought six miles.  It is astonishing what a spirit of perseverance must have animated this extraordinary man, to execute with such slight engines, work that will put many farmers, with teams, to the blush.  Some assistance in weeding potatoes etc. in harvest he has had from his family; but you may suppose it is not considerable, when I tell you, that of four or five children, he has only one son about fourteen years of age, who works with him constantly in the colliery.  From the time of leaving off work in the mine till that of sleeping, he regularly spent in unremitting labour on his farm.  Since his beginning he has never had more than four hours sleep, and of bright star light or moon light nights seldom so much.  The regular severe fatigue of twelve hours labour in the colliery has not been sufficient to bow down the spirit of this poor fellow; he applies the remainder of the day, and even steals from the night, to prosecute his favourite works of husbandry—that is, to make up his hours of work twenty out of the twenty-four.

Such conduct requires a genius of a peculiar cast.  Daring in his courage and spirited in his ideas, the most extensive plans are neither too vast nor too complicated to be embraced with facility by his bold and comprehensive imagination. . . . I asked him what he would do if he had his whole time to apply to his farm.

" I would perform something," said he, " at present I do nothing."

Hinting that I would mention to Mr. Danby the releasing him from the colliery, that all his time might be applied to farming, his countenance was animated at the very idea—his eye sparkled with pleasure.  Upon my asking him further, if he thought he could improve a larger tract, than was within the power of one pair of hands, by having other men, horses and carts put under his direction, " Aye sure," he replied, " for it is nothing more than extending the proportion of ten acres to a greater number.  It would be hard indeed, sir, if a man that had improved ten acres with his own hands, could not direct the improvement of a hundred or a thousand."

" What would you do if any unthought-for accident gave you £100 ? "

" Lay it all out in the improving of the land."

The view of this remarkable man's little farm and the conversation I had with him upon the improvement of moors, a point of such vast importance in this country, prejudiced me so much in his favour as to make me wish it were possible to enable him, not only to add greatly to his farm, but to conduct the culture of it upon a more spirited plan.

I mentioned it to Mr. Danby (who had first introduced me to him as an extraordinary fellow) and he agreed with me that his being a collier spoilt a good farmer, adding that he had thoughts of giving him more land, and also releasing him from the coal mine. This gave me much pleasure, not doubting but so spirited a mind with a body so active and vigorous would alone do wonders.

One is glad to think that Young opened a public subscription for this agricultural genius, heading the list with a guinea from himself, and one hopes that the poor man was set free from his twelve hours' drudgery in the mine, in which colliers were then prisoners without any power to remove themselves.

It is an extraordinary account of almost superhuman effort and the triumph of courage and genius over circumstances.

# CHAPTER XII

## VILLAGE AMUSEMENTS

THE tradition of a Merry England has come down to us from a remote past, though, as Dr. Coulton points out, it is so remote and untraceable that it probably originated in some mythical golden age.[1] In spite, however, of every discouragement and animadversion from Church and State, the Englishman insisted upon having his sports and pastimes. The Maypole in the Strand was hewn down by the Puritans; in 1661 another, 134 feet high, was set up by twelve sailors under the supervision of the Duke of York himself. The popular festival of May Day had its origins far back in pagan Britain, but the necessity for welcoming the spring, and rejoicing that the hated winter was past, was felt by everyone. If the celebrations gradually died out, and we do not now go forth with songs and garlands to welcome in the spring, it may be because the full rigours of winter, such as our forefathers endured, are quite unknown to us. The average farm labourer to-day has warmth, housing, comforts and amusements, even through the coldest winter months, of which his betters in the eighteenth century had never dreamed. Be that as it may, all classes of people went out at early dawn, on May morning, and brought

[1] *Chaucer and his England*, G. G. Coulton.

238

back branches and garlands of the spring flowers, all glistening with the dew. In the villages where there would be no permanent maypole, as in the large towns, they carried home a young birch tree, tied ribbons and streamers and garlands to its graceful gleaming stem, and danced around it in the market-place, or on the village green.

" Give them as formerly used to be, ten shillings for a maypole," says Sir John Verney, writing to his steward. " The East Claydon young men," he adds, " desire a maypole also."

May Day customs and celebrations will be mentioned more fully in another chapter. We are at present enumerating the various sports and amusements of the eighteenth century. The twelve days of holiday feasting at Christmas-time were no longer kept, but Christmas itself was observed with feasting, hospitality, and dancing.[1] Beef and plum pudding or plum pottage were eaten in many parts, though in the north, a goose pie, made with a crust of barley meal, was the Christmas dish. The Mummers came round, and acted in the farm-house kitchens, and there were besides the waits, the wassailers and the hand-bell ringers. These are now almost extinct, though in some villages attempts have been made to preserve or revive the old Christmas plays. In the eighteenth century nearly every village had its troop of Mummers. Christmas was the chief season for Mumming ; but, in many parts of the country, a play was also acted on Plough Monday, and at Easter, the latter being known as the Peace egg play. The Mummers would go round the village to the principal houses and there

[1] There were places where Puritan influences still lingered, and Christmas was not much observed.

perform, being regaled with beer and given some money reward for their entertainment. In the Christmas and Easter plays St. George and his dragon were the principal performers; there was also a fool, a doctor, the Prince of Paradine, the King of Egypt, Hector, Beelzebub and the devil Doubt. Sword dancing was generally introduced, and there was a good deal of rough horse-play. Plough Monday was another festival. In mediæval times, and even later, this day marked the end of the ten days of Christmas holiday, and money was then collected for the plough light which the villages kept burning in the parish church. The eighteenth century, however, would have no such waste of time, and men and women came back to work on Boxing Day. They still insisted upon keeping Plough Monday, and in the north, where work on the land, at that season, is not great, the custom lingered into the following century. Long ropes were attached to the plough, and it was dragged through the village by the labourers, in white smocks adorned with ribbons. They were accompanied by an old woman, dressed up in bright clothes who was called the Betsy and sometimes by a fool attired in skins and a long tail. This creature collected money from the spectators, and he was followed by the parish band, and Morris dancers, if they could be procured. In some villages if the ploughman had been to work on Plough Monday, he would come to the kitchen window and call "Cock in the pot." The cook, who had been waiting for him, would try to get her phrase in first and call out "Cock on the dunghill." If she succeeded, the ploughman would give her a cock to be thrown at on Shrove Tuesday, and if he was the winner, the cook presented him with a cock. The money which had formerly been given to the church was now used for feasting and dancing. In some villages the Mummers acted their Christmas play once more or gave a version of the trial of Sir John Barleycorn.

The custom of wassailing at Christmas-time was of very great antiquity. The wassail bowl was filled with spiced ale, and carried about by a company of young men and women to the various houses in the neighbourhood. The drink was offered and this song or some variant of it was sung, the recipients returning a small gift of money.

> Wassail, Wassail, Over the town.
> Our toast is white, and our ale is brown.
> Our bowl is made of the maplin tree
> We be good fellows all, I drink to thee.
>
> Here's to the Master, and to his right ear
> God send the Master a Happy New Year
> And a good Christmas pie as e'er I did see
> With my wassail bowl I drink to thee.
>
> Here's to the Mistress and to her right eye
> God send the Mistress a good Christmas pie
> A good Christmas pie, as e'er I did see,
> With my wassail bowl I drink to thee.

" Wassail the trees, that they may bear," says Herrick, and in the west of England it was the custom to go out into the orchard at Christmas-time and drink the health of the apple trees in a wassail bowl of cider. Some such song as this was sung and in between the words charges of shot were fired into the trees.

> Here's to thee, old apple tree,
> For we are come to wassail thee.
> Long may ye live and long may ye bear,
> Hatsfull, capsfull, five bushel bags full
> Barnsfull, floorsfull, stables full, tallats full
> Hip, hip hurrah, shout we.

Many villages had their feasts, or wakes, a custom which still happily lingers in East Anglia and the north. They were generally held on the patronal festival of their church, though they heeded it not, and would have considered such observance to be popish.

There was the great Harvest Home; there was dancing and merry-making at Michaelmas, and a fair on the green or at a neighbouring town or village at least once a year. There were the "Church Ales" too, which, according to Lady Fermanagh, brought "A Bundance of rabble, and the worst sort of company round us."

The original idea of a Church Ale was that the churchwardens should raise funds for church expenses, by selling liquor. They had been held several times in the year; but in the eighteenth century only the Whitsun ale was celebrated, and the affair was a speculation on the part of the local innkeeper.

Towards the close of the century, friendly societies or box clubs were established in many villages. They paid out money to their members for sickness and accidents, and in some cases in old age. Once a year they held their feasts, perambulating the village, their officers adorned with scarves and badges, holding a service in church and ending up with a great meal at the village inn.

"All this for liquor" is the indignant comment in the account book of one of these societies. They had spent £4 6s. it appears on drink, and only a little more than £1 on victuals. In their sober moments, the members of this society in the Devonshire village of Broad Clyst, seemed to think the amounts disproportionate, and they added a note to the effect that Stewards getting drunk in future would be suspended.

" Every fair," said Coke, " is a market, but not
every market is a fair." The country fair was a
great event. It generally combined business with
pleasure. There was buying and selling of stock and
produce, woollen goods and household gear ; servants
came there to be hired, the travelling bagman brought
samples of his wares. We are speaking now of the
fair in the village or small country town. A great
fair like Stourbridge was a commercial event of the
first magnitude. At the same time it was an opportunity for pleasure and amusement. In some cases,
indeed, it was like Bartholomew's Fair, entirely given
over to diversion, and, in any case, the villagers could
find enough excitement and pleasure in their memories
till fair time came round again. For weeks before
the people had been talking and thinking of nothing
else. The boys had run about the village blowing
on cows' horns ; there had been bonfires on Fair
Eve. Then early in the morning of the day the
people had left the farms and cottages, the men in
their clean white smocks, the women in Sunday
bonnets and gowns, and had walked or driven in farm
carts all decorated with ribbons and branches to the
fair ground. The gipsies were before them ; the
gipsies went from fair to fair as they do at present ;
but in those days their itinerary was much greater.
They would tell fortunes, sell baskets, and clothes-
pegs, and set up games of skill and chance.

There would be booths and stalls selling mead
bowls, and caudle cups, brandy balls and ginger-
breads, white whip or syllabub glasses, laces and
ribbons, hog's pudding and Dutch snuff. Every
young man bought his young woman a fairing.
There were puppet shows and Punch and Judy shows,

at which the countrymen gaped, and said that there must be some life in them, they supposed, as they talked and danced.   The master of the puppet show in *Tom Jones* declared that

The present age was not improving in anything so much as in their puppet shows, which by throwing out Punch and his wife Joan, and such idle trumpery, were at last brought to be a rational entertainment.

I remember [said he] when I first took to the business, there was a great deal of low stuff that did very well to make folks laugh, but was never calculated to improve the morals of young people, which certainly ought to be principally aimed at in every puppet show.

Tom Jones, as may be supposed, was not attracted by austere morality.   The entertainment had been " without anything which could provoke a laugh," and though " an attorney's clerk and an exciseman both declared that the characters of Lord and Lady Townley were well preserved and highly in nature, Tom put in a plea for his old acquaintance, Master Punch."

The landlady of the inn, however, whose maid, having seen it " on the pictures," or, in this case, at the puppet show, emulated the heroine and fell into disgrace, sighed for the good old days " when puppet shows were made of good scripture stories, as Jephthah's rash vow, and such good things and when wicked people were carried away by the devil."   These puppet shows that the landlady remembered, must have resembled those held in Crawley's booth at Bartholomew's Fair, where there was

presented a little opera, called *The Old Creation of the World*, yet newly revived ; with the addition of Noah's flood, also several fountains playing during the time of the play.   The last scene does present Noah and his family coming out of the ark, with all the beasts two and two, and all the fowls of the air, seen in a prospect sitting upon trees, likewise over the ark is seen the sun rising in a most glorious manner, moreover a multitude of angels will be seen in a double rank, which presents a double prospect, one for the sun, the other for a palace where will be seen six angels ringing of bells. Likewise machines descend from above, double and treble, with Dives rising out of Hell.

Every kind of quack frequented the fair, as they do now ; there were giants and mountebanks and fat women and dwarfs. Backswording or singlestick was a game often played at fairs, and there were besides such sports as wrestling, climbing the greasy pole, jumping in sacks, hunting a pig with a soapy tail and grinning through horse collars. Old women would drink scalding hot tea for a prize of snuff, girls would run races for a smock. There were tumblers and mountebanks. The fair generally ended in a dance at a neighbouring ale-house. It was the talk of the country-side for months and was looked forward to with a keenness of anticipation which this age with its cinemas, its dances and its dog races, cannot hope to experience.

A wedding was the occasion of much general festivity. If the squire married, or his eldest son, an ox was roasted whole, and gallons of beer and cider were broached. The farmer on such an occasion feasted his hinds, there was dancing and often such sports as wrestling and running races on the village green. In the north, which was more prosperous than the south, the festivities were kept up for several days. It was the custom for the brides to give ribbons as prizes for the winning of a race, and it was said that a young man who was fleet of foot, and who attended many weddings, could accumulate enough ribbon to fill the pack of an itinerant haberdasher.

The prolonged feasting, which took place after a funeral, should not, we suppose, be included in a chapter upon village amusements. That it was the cause of great satisfaction, and even pleasure to many, cannot be gainsaid; but besides this funeral feasting there was, as we have pointed out, so much of the old gaiety and holidaying still lingering into the eighteenth century, that in the first half of it at least, the country may have been termed a Merry England.

# CHAPTER XIII

## SPORT

A S the eighteenth century advanced the sports and amusements of the upper classes became less brutal.

Bear and bull baiting, which in the early years of the century were patronized by everyone, were later only attended by the lower orders.

Sport among the gentry consisted chiefly of hunting and shooting. Cockfighting, indeed, continued to be most popular, and many country houses had cocking courts.

" I have just got back from a cock match, where I have won £40," writes Rigby to George Selwyn.

Hogarth's picture of the Cockpit is too well known to need description. The man in it, who is depicted as turning away in disgust, is a Frenchman, a commentary, if one were needed, upon the brutality of English sports. Steele, in the *Tatler*, laments that some French writers should have imputed this barbarity to " natural fierceness and cruelty of temper." The reproach, though justified, does not come well from a nation which considered the spectacle of a criminal being broken on the wheel to be a public entertainment.

Among the upper classes, however, field sports were by far the most popular and were given the first place in life. Walpole always opened the letters of his gamekeeper, even before those of his sovereign. Hawking, which all gentlemen had practised down through the centuries until the eighteenth, was dying out.

Still a few sallied out in May with hawks upon their wrists and made sport upon woodcock or plover. Round Bridport in Dorset, hawks were trained, until well into the nineteenth century, to prey upon the landrails in the hemp and flax fields, which were then found in the neighbourhood ; but for the most part hawking had given place to hunting. This was not always organized as it afterwards became. Often a mixed pack would ride out with dogs of various breeds, and whether they fell in with a deer or a fox, a hare or an otter, they hunted it, and were equally pleased.

" In coming from hare hunting," writes Sir Thomas Cave to John Verney,

just by the parke, we spyed a sorel out of bounds, and the esquire and I resolved to kill it. In short we uncoupled the beagles and laid out on him. He held hard running, I believe near an hour and a half; the dogs ran like staunch hounds and never changed, though several hares started up before 'em, which I wondered at. The deer took the pales after so hard running and we killed him afterwards.

Very soon, however, the various hunts sorted themselves out and the chief field sport became what it is now, fox-hunting, which was continued almost all the year through. It was not until the reign of George III that it was prohibited until after the harvest, and the country gentlemen no longer passed like a blast over the fields of corn, as Sir Andrew Freeport picturesquely remarked to Sir Roger de Coverley.

Sir Roger was a mighty hunter, and had, we are told,

a remarkable enmity against foxes, having destroyed more of these vermin in one year than it was thought the whole country could have produced. Indeed, the good knight does not scruple to own among his intimate friends that in order to establish his reputation this way, he has recently sent for great numbers of them out of other counties which he used to turn loose about the country by night, that he might the better signalize himself in their destruction the next day.

Sir Roger [Addison continues, with that fine confusion concerning the sport, which we have just noticed], being at present too old for fox hunting, to keep himself in action, has disposed of all his beagles and got a pack of stop hounds. . . . Sir Roger is so keen on this sport, that he has been out almost every day since I came down ; and upon the chaplain's offering to lend me his easy Pad, I was prevailed upon yesterday morning to make one of the company. After we had rid about a mile from home, we came upon a large heath and the sportsmen began to beat. They had done so for some time when, as I was at a little distance from the rest of the company, I saw a hare pop out of a small furze brake almost under my horse's feet. I marked the way she took which I endeavoured to make the company sensible of by extending my arms, but to no purpose, till Sir Roger, who knows that none of my extraordinary motions are insignificant, rode up to me and asked if Puss was gone that way. Upon my answering yes, he immediately called in the Dogs and put them upon the scent. As they were going off I heard one of the country fellows muttering to his companion that " t'was a wonder they had not lost all their sport for want of the silent gentleman crying ' stole away.' "

The description of the close of the hunt is the pleasantest of all.

The poor hare was now quite spent and almost within reach of her enemies, when the huntsman getting forward, threw down his pole before the dogs. They were now within eight yards of their game, which they had been pursuing for almost as many hours, yet on the signal before mentioned, they all made a sudden stand, and though they continued opening as much as before, durst not once attempt to pass beyond the pole. At the same time Sir Roger rode forward and alighting took up the hare in his arms, which he soon delivered up to one of his servants, with an order that, if she could be kept alive, to let her go in his great orchard, where it seems he has several of these prisoners of war, who live together in very comfortable captivity.

This charming account of the hares living together in peace in the great orchard, reminds us of the poet Cowper and his solicitude for his pet hares.  It is a hunt in which we should have liked to join, as much as we should have enjoyed the great course in Mr. Townshend's plantation, where as Parson Woodforde tells us, "there were 12 greyhounds, and 12 beaters on horseback, playing the violin ! "

One of the first packs of real foxhounds was started in 1730 in Dorsetshire by Thomas Fownes of Stapleton.  The Duke of Rutland founded the Belvoir about 1740, and the Cottesmore and Pytchley followed a few years later.  Sport is never what it was, and a century ago some praiser of former times wrote a song about the old English hunting squire as he had remembered him fifty years before.

About fifty years ago when George the Third was King,
And the Prince, the Star of Fashion, shone in Pleasure's
    ring,
The old English country Squire was a man of great renown.
He'd an old house in the country, and a modern house in
    town.
A Justice of the Peace he was, also an M.P.
But was fettered to no party ; his principles were free.
He courted not the Premier, though his son was in the
    Guards.
With Fox he sometimes voted ; but much oftener played at
    cards.

He kept a stud of racers, 'twas a joy to see them run.
And his sideboard was well covered with the gold cups they
    had won.
To the town he represented every year he gave a plate;
And to the course, in coach and six, he always came in state.
Six goodly nags they were indeed, though rather fat and slow;
Their manes were decked with ribbons, and their flowing tails
    also.
His lady sat beside him, tall and upright as a wand,
And the people loudly cheered them on alighting at the stand.
He kept a pack of foxhounds too, of pure old English breed,
Most musical and staunch they were, but not much famed for
    speed.
His hunters were enduring and could go a decent pace;
To suit his hounds he bred them, not to ride a steeple chase.
He boldly went at hedge and gate, nor stopped at ditch or
    brook,
And many a Melton Mowbray swell might shy the leaps he
    took.
'Twas a pleasant sight to see him through a bullfinch make a
    gap,
With his pigtail, like a drumstick cocking out behind his cap.
On the first day of September, as the season still came round,
With his pointers to the stubble he was certain to be found.
Though his gun was like a musket, an old-fashioned flint and
    steel,
Wide muzzled and a kicker, she was heavy in the heel,
Yet birds, there being a plenty, he brought down many a brace,
And if he found them sitting, why, he showed them little grace.
Few thought of shooting, flying about, fifty years ago.
Kill when you can, was then the word and surest shooting
    low.

Women were seldom seen in the hunting field.
Before the introduction of the riding habit, it would
have been almost impossible for them to do more
than ride pillion, or amble along on a quiet palfrey;
though some intrepid ladies of Bury in Suffolk adopted
a modern fashion. " The Bury ladies," we are told,
" that used hawking and hunting, were once in a

great vaine of wearing breeches." The indelicacy of
such conduct was, however, brought home to them;
and even when the riding habit made hunting possible it was considered an unfeminine sport. The
prejudice against women in the field lasted on till the
days of Surtees; and perhaps even later. There were,
however, intrepid women who rode to hounds, like
the old Lady Salisbury, who became Master of the
Hertfordshire, then called the Hatfield Hounds, in
1793. She continued as Master until she was
seventy-eight, when she relinquished her post; and
ceased to hunt with the Foxhounds, contending,
however, that she was still good enough for the
harriers.

At the beginning of the century game was very
plentiful. Preserving was scarcely known, for if
pheasants and partridges were not so numerous as
they became later, there were flocks of other birds,
snipe, woodcock, plovers, landrails, wild duck and
geese, grouse, teal and bustards. There were hares
and rabbits in plenty. The sportsman was, no
doubt, contented with smaller bags. Gilbert White
speaks of " parties of unreasonable sportsmen " who
killed as many as twenty and sometimes thirty
brace of partridges a day.

No one was allowed to shoot game who had not a
freehold estate of at least £100 a year, or a leasehold
estate of £200, and the Lord of the Manor had the
right to shoot over the waste as well as over his own
property. Game was legally the monopoly of the
well-to-do; but the poor never regarded it as such.
To them, the creatures were wild, and down through
history from the days of the Norman Conquest, the
English peasants had shot and snared game, and varied

a monotonous diet with hare and wild duck, grouse
and partridge.   When game was so plentiful, the
practice, though frowned upon, was seldom punished.
As the century advanced, the pheasant and the partridge gradually diminished in numbers, and it became
the custom for rich men to preserve.   Game being
now their own property as much as their poultry or
their cows, they took measures to protect it.   The
squire who discovers that Tom Jones has shot a bird
on his land, " complained of the trespass upon his
manor in as high terms as if his house had been broken
open and the most valuable furniture stole out of it."
" And," says he, " we have found only this partridge but the Lord knows what mischief they have
done."

If there was plenty of game in the woods, there
was also plenty of fish in the rivers and ponds.
The lordly salmon still came up the Thames, and was
to be found in many another river where nothing is
now to be fished but perch or eels.

Sea fish were sent up to London by men on horseback from as far afield as King's Lynn; but many
country towns and villages were dependent upon a
fresh-water supply.   It was a valuable food, especially
in the winter, when only salt meat was to be had.
In the early years of the century it was still eaten in
Lent, and we hear of many curious fish being caught
and eaten.

Pennant speaks of a " Burbot," a fish of disgusting
appearance, the mouth large, armed with small teeth;
the nose furnished with two beards; the chin with
one; on the back are two fins, the skin smooth and
slippery of a disagreeable green colour spotted with
yellow.   Timothy Burrell speaks of his tench and

carp, and classifies them as "small fish, sizable, middling, large, noble and vast."

"The bounteous Trent that in himself enseams both thirty sorts of fish and thirty sundry streams," was the home of this creature and we hear of tench and shad and bream and pike and shell-fish. The descendants of Isaak Walton found lakes and rivers and even ponds teeming with fish. The eighteenth-century country-side was indeed the sportsman's own kingdom.

Horse racing, which had begun in friendly rivalry between the owners of various horses, who generally rode them themselves, was in the eighteenth century attracting enormous crowds to the accompaniment of betting and bookmakers. The prize, which had formerly been a silver bell, now became a piece of plate, and large sums were lost upon the Turf. Charles II had been a great patron of racing, and even rode his own horses at Newmarket. Queen Anne kept a racing stud. On July 30th, 1714, her horse Star won a plate of £40 at the York races, and a day or two later during a race for the gold cup, a messenger arrived, riding hard from London, to announce the news of the Queen's death. Those who were then described as the "nobility and gentry" left the race-course, in haste, to join with the Lord Mayor of York, and the Archbishop, in proclaiming George of Hanover as King.

The *Spectator* quotes a curious advertisement,

on the 9th of October next will be run for on Coleshill Heath in Warwickshire a plate of 6 guineas value, three heats by any horse, mare or gelding that hath not won above the value of 5 pounds : the winning horse to be sold for £10 to carry 10 stone weight if 14 hands high : if above or under, to carry, or

be allowed weight for inches, and to be entered on Friday the
5th at the Swan in Coleshill by six in the evening.    Also a plate
of less value to be run for by asses.

In 1740 an act was passed for regulating race
meetings.    The stakes were raised whereby many
small country meetings were abolished ; the weights
which horses had to carry were also settled, five-year-
olds carrying ten stone, six-year-olds eleven stone and
and seven-year-olds twelve stone.    The owner of any
horse carrying less than the proper weights was to
be fined £200, and his horse confiscated.    The
races were over a distance of four miles, which
made it impossible for two-year-olds to be entered.
Parliament was not, however, the only or the best
authority upon racing.    About 1750 the Jockey
Club was founded, to supervise at first the racing
at Newmarket ; but gradually its authority spread
over every race-course in England, its honour and
integrity being as unquestioned then as they are
now.

At the end of the seventeenth, or the beginning of
the eighteenth century, there were brought into
England three Eastern horses, and these are the
ancestors of all the thoroughbreds, not only in England but throughout the world.    The first of these,
the Byerly Turk, was the property of a Captain Byerly
who had ridden him throughout King William's wars
in Ireland.    The Darley Arabian was imported early
in the century, by Mr. Darley of Buttercramb in Yorkshire, and the great-grandson of this horse was the
celebrated Eclipse, whose name, and the saying,
" Eclipse first and the rest nowhere," are remembered
still.    The third of these famous horses was the
Godolphin, which was discovered by Coke of Holk-

ham drawing a water-cart in the streets of Paris.   He
was either an Arabian or a Barb, and afterwards
became the property of the Earl of Godolphin.   That
racing was fairly general throughout the country,
and very much the sport of the people, we may gather
from the fact that it took place at seventy-two
different places in England, and that many race
meetings, including the Derby, the Oaks, and the
St. Leger were inaugurated.

Of football, another sport, which to-day draws its
thousands of spectators, little can be said.  Joseph
Strutt, writing in 1801, dismisses it in a few words.
" It was formerly much in vogue among the common
people ;  though of late years it seems to have fallen
into disrepute, and is little practised."

Probably it was a game played by boys on village
greens and in town streets and alleys, just as bat trap
and ball, and fives against the church tower were
played.   Its immense popularity did not arise till the
middle of the nineteenth century.   Of cricket more
can be said, though a knowledge of the game does
not seem to have been widespread, when Dr. Johnson
could describe it in his dictionary as " a sport at
which the contenders drive a ball with sticks in
opposition to one another."   " Pure ignorance," the
doctor might have urged in excuse, as on another
occasion.

The Hambleden Cricket Club, which was founded
in 1755, could have taught him better.   They beat the
All-England eleven on Broad Halfpenny Down in 1777
by an innings and 168 runs.   In 1744, on the Artillery
Ground at Finsbury, where the H.A.C. still play, the
landlord of the Pyed Horse Inn raised his gate money
from 2*d.* to 6*d.* on the strength of the great match

between Kent and All England, which James Love
celebrated in a copy of verses.

> Hail Cricket! Glorious manly British game!
> First of all sports, be first alike in fame!

Lord Chesterfield writes to his son: "If you have a
right ambition you will desire to excell all boys of
your age at cricket," and, according to Horace
Walpole and Gray, it was played at Eton early in the
century. Girls sometimes played as is shown in a
curious print entitled "Miss Wickett and Miss
Trigger." Beneath the picture are the lines:

> Miss Trigger, you see, is an excellent shot,
> And forty-five notches Miss Wickett's just got.

This reminds us that the scoring apparatus was simple,
the runs being notched on a stick or a piece of wood.
The stumps, which were sometimes only two, were
placed at the same distance apart as at present. They
were twenty-two inches in height, and there was but
one bat. The crease was not painted on the turf,
but was cut into the ground, and the bat was curved,
something like a wide hockey stick. John Small,
who was a member of the Hambleden Cricket Club,
was the first man to bring a straight bat on to the
field. He had some peculiar stroke of his own,
which could not be executed by a curved bat. After
this, for some years, cricket bats might be of any size;
but an ingenious gentleman, a Mr. White of Reigate,
having covered his wicket with a monstrously wide
bat, it was thought well to fix the width at four and
a half inches. With the old curved bat, it was hardly
possible to block; the player must have run out and
hit everything, and the bowler, who always bowled

underhand, sent down quiet, gentlemanly balls that were easily played with the new straight bat. A race of bowlers arose who bowled length balls; and blocking, stone walling, and the other less-exciting features of play became general.

Golf had been known in Scotland in the fifteenth century or earlier. There is a tradition that James I brought the game to England; but nothing is certainly known beyond the fact that there was a golf club at Blackheath in 1745. Alexander Carlyle speaks of playing a match at Hampton in 1758 with Garrick, the Duke of Cumberland and others. As they passed through the village of Kensington, the Coldstream Guards at the Palace caught sight of their clubs " and gave us three cheers," Carlyle says, " in honour of a diversion peculiar to Scotland."

Bowls, that ancient English game, was played in private gardens and on many a green behind an inn. It was perhaps, not so fashionable as it had been in the previous century, when Charles I had lost £1,000 in one match to a Turkey merchant at Barking; but it was still much played, and for very high stakes.

The sports of the lower orders of the people, to use an eighteenth-century expression, were often very coarse and cruel. The bear and bull baitings, the throwing at cocks on Shrove Tuesday—a different amusement altogether from cock-fighting—might be shunned by the gentry; but the common people still loved them. It was not until the following century that with many remonstrances against interfering with the sports of the people, bills were finally passed to prohibit them.

There had always been wrestling in many parts of

England; Cumberland and Cornwall were famous for it.

In 1723 the King, having had a ring marked out in Hyde Park for boxing, this sport came into being. It was not, however, until the end of the century, that fashion and wealth were associated with the prize ring. In the early days, it only attracted the mob. Many and curious were the pugilistic advertisements in the papers. William Willis, known by the incongruous title of the "fighting Quaker," announced that he had

fought Mr. Smallwood about twelve months since, and held him the tightest to it, and bruised and battered more than anyone he ever encountered; though I had the misfortune to be beat by an accidental fall; the said Smallwood flushed with the success blind Fortune then gave him, and the weak attempts of a few vain Irishmen and boys, that have of late fought him for a minute or two, make him think himself unconquerable. To convince him of the falsity of which, I invite him to fight me for a hundred pounds, at the time and place above mentioned, when I doubt not I shall prove the truth of what I have asserted, by pegs, darts, hard blows, falls and cross buttocks.

This champion required the bait of £100 before he would go into the ring; but in 1768 two women, one of them known as "bruising Peg," fought for a new chemise. Fighting and boxing among women was not uncommon, and it is curious, as one of the contrasts of the eighteenth century, to notice, that while the women in the upper classes cultivated an extreme and scrupulous delicacy of manner and behaviour, the women of the lower orders often indulged in brutality and indecency, which would not now be tolerated among the most degraded.

Backswording or singlestick was a most popular sport in England. The weapon was a stick or cudgel with a basket hilt, and the aim was to strike the opponent on the head so as to draw blood.

As the century advanced, and the countryman became a day labourer instead of a peasant proprietor, the old English games and sports tended to diminish. The squire still hunted and fished and rode to hounds, the farmer followed in his steps, as far as his income and the law allowed him; but the poor man now slaved from dawn to dusk for a master, instead of working at his own will upon his plot of land. He had no time or energy for sports when the day was done. There were no longer bouts of wrestling and singlestick upon the village green. The infrequent cricket match was supported by men of substance, the bowling green was played upon by the village tradesmen. The labourer " homewards plods his weary way " or turns into an ale-house for some relief from the monotony of life.

The industrial revolution spread its tentacles over the country-side, and, among the other amenities, which it squeezed out of existence, were many of the old English sports and pastimes.

# CHAPTER XIV

## FOLK-LORE

FOLK-LORE and traditions were such integral parts of rural life in the eighteenth century, that no book, which professes to touch it, can neglect the subject. Explorers and students of primitive civilizations paint a dark picture of the life of simple people under the spell of witches and wizards, the terror of medicine men, and the dread of natural phenomena. From such superstitions we flatter ourselves we have entirely escaped. If we have done so—and it may be doubted—the eighteenth century certainly had not. The crusade against witchcraft, which characterized the end of the seventeenth century, was dying down. In 1736 witchcraft ceased to be a capital offence, and Lord Mansfield dismissed a case which was brought before him with the remark that, though the accused might have walked upon her head, as the prosecution declared, he had yet to find among the laws of England one which forbade such a practice.[1] Judges might refuse to convict, and the educated might laugh ; but to the countryman witchcraft was a very real and menacing thing. Witches were not an invention of the seventeenth century, though a wave of witch-finding, and witch-burning seems to have swept the country after the

[1] The remark has also been attributed to Sir John Powell.

Restoration. It has indeed been estimated that 30,000 people were executed in England for witchcraft. There can be no authority for such a statement, and this number in a small population seems incredibly high; but there is no doubt that a great many lives were sacrificed.

Authorities say that witchcraft was the survival of an ancient primitive religion, some old fertility cult which, driven underground by the advance of Christianity, became incredibly debased and horrible. Be this as it may, it is certainly very ancient in its origins. The author of the book of Samuel knew all about witches and their practices. At Benwell in Northumberland, a Roman altar was found dedicated to three witches; and all through the Middle Ages the Church fought against witchcraft, which she declared to be Devil worship. The usual practice of witches and wizards seems to have been to form themselves into groups or covens. There were twelve members in these covens, and a leader. This leader sometimes wore black leather garments, with a black mask over his face, or he would be disguised as an animal with skin and horns. This latter practice may account for the prevailing belief that witches could change themselves into animals at will, and that the Devil, clad in black and sometimes with horns and hoofs as well, appeared at their meetings. These Witches' Sabbaths, as they were called, were held four times a year, on February 2, Candlemas, May Eve, Roodmas, August 1, Lammas, and November 1, All-Hallows. To these meetings many worshippers came from far and near, and the service lasted all night. It consisted of dancing, singing and feasting; and in some cases there is a suggestion of human sacrifice. In the eyes of simple country people the witch was all-powerful. She could overlook their children, their cattle or their crops, and they would dwindle and die. She could foretell the future by consultation with her dog or cat or other familiar. She could destroy her own or other people's enemies by making wax images of them, which she slowly melted over the fire, or into which she stuck pins.

The laws against witches were repealed; but all down the century, and well into the next, are records of attacks upon unfortunate old women who were said to have overlooked someone; who were, perhaps, old and poor and spiteful, and had so gained the ill will of their neighbours. In 1751 Thomas Colley, William Humbles, and Charles Young, otherwise Lee, were tried at Hertford for the murder of an unfortunate woman, whom they had ducked as a witch. This woman and her husband produced pins out of their mouths, overlooked cattle so that they died, and were guilty generally of reprehensible and witch-like conduct. The men pushed the poor woman under the water of a shallow pond and drowned her. The husband managed to escape with his life. He was held to be a wizard and his wife was certainly a witch, as she was drowned in two and a half feet of water. The ringleader was hanged in chains at Gubblecut Cross.

"Many thousands stood at a distance to see him die, muttering that it was a hard case to hang a man for destroying an old wicked woman that had done so much mischief by her witchcraft."

In 1759 according to the *Annual Register*,

one Susannah Hanoels of Wyngrove, near Aylesbury, was accused by her neighbour of bewitching her spinning wheel, so that she

could not make it go round, and offered to make an oath of it
before a magistrate, on which the husband, to justify the wife,
insisted upon her being tried by the Church Bible, and that the
accuser should be present. Accordingly she was conducted to
the parish church, where she was stripped of all her clothes to
a shift and an overcoat, and weighed against the Bible, when to
the no small mortification of the accuser she outweighed it and
was honourably acquitted of the charge.

The power of the witch was almost unlimited.
She could overlook any person or thing, and so cause
their death; she could foretell the future; call up
spirits, if not from the vasty deep, from cauldrons
and chafing dishes; stick pins into the wax images of
enemies, or melt them slowly by the fire, so that they
were taken with pains and incontinently died. She
could cure sickness and heal broken limbs, make up
potions and love philtres, and fly with amazing
celerity from place to place. She could even so
arrange matters, that cows should be found of a
morning milked and standing upon their heads. It
is astonishing that anyone should have set up as a
witch, and so incurred the hatred of her neighbours,
and in earlier times the extreme rigour of the law. In
many cases she made no claims herself to any occult
powers, and was the victim of untoward circumstances,
and the malice and suspicion of her neighbours.
There were, however, men and women who traded
as witches and warlocks, and made quite a good
thing by it. They satisfied two of the baser passions
of mankind, the love of power, and the love of money.
If they could persuade their neighbours that they
were really white witches, and only used their power
for the good of the community, all might be well.
They could sell love potions, salves and herb medicines, which would not do any more harm than those

prescribed by medical men, and in some cases had great curative properties. They could deal discreetly in the future, prophesying smooth things, and taking care to be properly bland and vague ; they could endeavour to remove the spells of other witches. If they conducted themselves in this way, they might escape harm. They never attained to the position of medicine men in savage tribes ; but they were regarded with a mixture of fear and favour by the country people. Men and women went to them stealthily for charms and potions, for ointments and medicines. The danger was that, ignorantly or maliciously, they might be accused of overlooking someone ; of bewitching the cows, in order that they should not give milk, of interfering with the churns so that the butter would not come. If this happened, their fate might be most horrible. Besides conscious impostors, there were some men and women who possessed those occult powers of which we know so little. There were, doubtless, many more who had persuaded themselves, or were persuaded by their neighbours, that they were sold to the Devil, men and women who joined in the curious primitive rites which we have mentioned. The fear and horror of some of these poor creatures who found themselves in the power of Evil, as they believed, must have been very terrible. Horrible too was the position of a harmless villager, who saw his wife and babe pining away under the spell of witch or wizard. There was no doctor at hand to talk of consumption or marasmus. The poor man could only believe, as his neighbours did, that Mother Such-a-one had overlooked his wife and child. It is not surprising that he was filled with a blind insane fury, and that he called the village together, and ducked the wretched witch in the pond until she was drowned. After this, he thought, the spell would be lifted, and those whom he loved would recover. Very often, such is the force of suggestion, this was the actual result. There were of course various means of placating a witch, and charms which could be used against her. If she came to the dairy door when the farmer's wife was churning, and was given a small piece of butter, the churning would be successful. If she was treated in a niggardly spirit and refused this little boon, the butter would not come, unless, of course, the churn should have been made of ash. No witch would go near an ash tree or ash wood, nor did she like horse-shoes. In the north of England the rowan or mountain ash was so used.

" If your whip stick's made of rowan you may ride your nag through any town," was an old York-shire saying. Horseshoes are still considered lucky. No witch would enter a house upon which one was nailed, and it is said the superstition dates from the time of St. Dunstan. That worthy, who seemed to spend his time in worsting an extremely unintelligent Devil, succeeded one day in shoeing him with red-hot horseshoes, and this being still an unpleasant memory, caused him and his satellites to dislike the sight of them. The sacred character of the ash may have been a remnant of the old tree worship exempli-fied in the Yggdrasill of Scandinavian mythology though it has been given another and a Christian origin. It was said that Our Lord as a baby was washed for the first time before a fire of ash wood, and for that reason the tree was held sacred. Country people considered it unlucky to cut down an ash, or an oak tree, which bore mistletoe. A ruptured child, if drawn through the cleft trunk of an ash or a hazel tree would recover. These trees were very carefully preserved, as the patient was not supposed to live longer than the tree. Gilbert White speaks of

a row of pollard ashes, which by the seams and long cicatrices down their sides, manifestly show that in former times they have been cleft asunder. These trees, when young and flexible, were severed and held open by wedges, while ruptured children, stripped naked, were pushed through the apertures under a persuasion that by such a process the poor babes would be cured of their infirmity. As soon as the operation was over, the tree in the suffering part was plastered with loam, and carefully swathed up. If the parts coalesced and soldered together, as usually fell out, where the feat was performed with any adroitness at all, the party was cured ; but where the cleft continued to gape, the operation, it was supposed, would prove ineffectual.

Twigs or branches of the ash tree were also a specific against the ravages of shrew mice. These dangerous creatures, it was said, would creep surreptitiously over the hind-quarters of a browsing sheep, and so baneful was their influence that the animal became instantly paralysed. The cure for this was to take some twigs of a shrew ash, and pass them over the afflicted parts, when the animal would quickly recover. A shrew ash had had a hole made in its trunk by an auger, and in this hole an unfortunate shrew had been imprisoned. In Cornwall and also in Northumberland if disease overtook a flock or herd an animal was offered up as a burnt sacrifice, the farmer quoting Scripture to justify this curiously pagan practice. The old sun worship was responsible for many pagan practices. Baring-Gould tells us of a vandalistic parson who had an old churchyard cross destroyed, because his parishioners would carry

the coffins round it the way of the sun.   At Brilley,
in Hertfordshire, they were carried in the same manner
round a " funeral stone " in the churchyard and it
was said that this prevented the Devil from seizing
upon the soul of the deceased.   The idea that the
left is dangerous may have originated because it is
easier to stab a man upon one's left than upon the
right.   For the same reason, a man always gave a
woman his left arm so that the right would be free
to defend her.

The elaborate celebrations of May Day were probably survivals of the old sun worship.   They took
the place of the Celtic feast of Beltain, for the Church,
finding it impossible to abolish these old festivals,
did her best to substitute Christian feasts, or at least
to make the celebrations decent and harmless.

In another chapter mention has been made of the
maypole, which was set up on the village green, and
round which young men and maidens danced to the
music of a pipe.

At dawn the young people went out into the fields
and gathered branches and flowers for garlands.   In
some villages they went round to all the houses
carrying garlands and a doll wreathed in flowers.
This doll has been thought by some to represent the
Virgin Mary ; but the custom probably came down
from pagan times, as these old customs nearly always
did.   The song that the mayers sang might be
Christianised as the following has been.

> Remember us poor mayers all,
> And thus we do begin
> To lead our lives in righteousness,
> Or else we die in sin.
> We have been rambling all this night

And almost all this day.
And now returnéd back again,
Have brought you a branch of May.
A branch of May we have brought you
And at your door it stands,
It is but a sprout, but it budded out,
By the work of our Lord's hands.
The hedges and trees they are so green
As green as any leek
Our Heavenly Father watereth them
With Heavenly dew so sweet.
The heavenly gates are open wide,
Our paths are beaten plain,
And if a man be not too far gone,
He may return again.
The life of Man is but a grass,
It flourishes like a flower,
We are here to-day and gone to-morrow,
And we are dead in one hour.
The moon shines bright and the stars give light
A little before 'tis day.
So God bless you all both great and small
And send you a joyful May.

Something of the old moon worship still lingered
in the country, though it was not so universal as the
worship of the sun, and its influence was often feared.
Pigs had to be killed when the moon was waxing,
or the bacon would shrink in the pot and melt away
to nothing. "Sow beans when the moon is round,
they'll pod down to the ground," says an old adage,
and several moon superstitions are current even in
our own day. It was not so very long ago that the
girls in a Berkshire village went out into the fields
and sang to the new moon.

New moon, new moon, I hail thee,
By all the virtue of thy body.
Grant this night that I may see
Him who my true love is to be.

In another chapter we have given some account of the beating of the bounds, which usually took place at Rogation- or Ascension-tide. Miss Hull suggests that this may be a relic of the Terminalia, the feast of the god Terminus, the guardian of fields and landmarks. At Warkworth in Northumberland there was a procession on the first of May for the admission of freeholders. Candidates were taken to the confines of a parish, seized by their legs and arms and then dashed against the boundary stones. It seems strange that anyone in that parish should ever have wished to be a freeholder.

The fear of the water or of water spirits was natural at a time when storm and tempest wrought almost uncontrolled havoc. The sailor was often exposed to all the fury of the winds and waters in a little cockleshell of a boat that we should consider unsafe outside a harbour. The country was often flooded, bridges were broken, and rivers in spate carried away the farmers' crops or stock. The sea was regarded with horror. Robinson Crusoe's decent family was filled with scandalized amazement when he expressed his intention of going to sea, and even rivers were considered very dangerous. " The Dart " we are told, " claims a heart." " Bloodthirsty Dee each year claims three, but bonny Don she needs one." The water spirits claimed their victim and it was most dangerous to interfere with them. Anyone who rescued a man from drowning would drown within the year, the spirits would see to it that he did not escape. In Cornwall or North Devon, a hundred years ago, the people would not rescue shipwrecked sailors, or show any hospitality if the wrecked man managed to reach the shore. At Tissington the ceremony of the dressing of the wells is still observed on Ascension Day. In the eighteenth century it was common in many parts of the country and is probably a survival of the worship of the water spirits. The wells were covered with flowers and garlands, or in some cases, as at Tissington, a sort of flower mosaic was made, the petals of flowers being placed upon wet clay so as to form a picture. A service was sometimes held and the well was blessed by the clergy of the parish. Springs and wells of medicinal waters exist in England still, but they are nothing compared to the number of spas and wells which flourished in the eighteenth century. Many of these had medicinal qualities ; but others were nothing more than wells and springs of pure water, the belief that they could heal having come down from very ancient days. Remains of the old stone worship still lingered. At Holme in Devonshire, there is a granite menhir 6 or 7 feet in height ; there on May Day the youths of the parish used to assemble before sunrise with a ram lamb which they had taken from the flock. They would fasten it to a pillar, cut its throat, and then roast it whole. At midday, when the carcase had been thoroughly roasted, a crowd of villagers struggled for pieces of the meat, as the eating of it was said to confer good luck throughout the year. Games then began, which with dancing, singing and drinking continued till midnight.

Like the hollow tree, the hollow stone was believed to effect a cure for rickets, and other diseases of child-hood. In the parish of Madron in Cornwall there is a triangle of three stones, with a hole in the middle, through which a human being could squeeze. It is known as the Men-an-tol or Holed Stone and mothers used to pass their sick children through it, and many cures no doubt resulted. In the same parish is the Crick Stone, or creeping stone. This had to be crawled through on all fours nine times with the back turned to the sun.

Superstitions in connection with birth, marriage and death were innumerable, and varied in different parts of the country. It was lucky for a baby to be born on a Sunday or in the month of July, and very unlucky for it to be born on a Friday, or on the stroke of noon. In the latter case it would certainly grow up to be an idiot. A cat must never be allowed near an infant as it would lie upon it and suck away its breath. The cat, we may remember, was the witches' familiar, and so regarded with some disfavour.

No mother or infant must venture out of the house until the woman went to be churched and the baby to be christened. Until these ceremonies were over both mother and child were open to the influences of bad fairies and ill luck. The right hand of an infant must be left unwashed, so that it might acquire riches throughout its life. The nails must not be cut for a year, but be bitten off lest the child should grow up light-fingered. If an infant were taken into a strange house, its mouth must be filled with salt and then no harm could happen to it. Had it eaten of its host's salt and so was considered to be safe? The awful doctrine, originated by some of the early Fathers, that the souls of unbaptized children cannot be admitted into Heaven was prevalent in country districts. In Yorkshire it was thought that the poor infants were changed into hounds. They were called Gabble Hounds, or Gabriel's Hounds, and they hunted the Devil, whose fault it was that they had not been baptized. In Devon they were known as Yeth or Heath Hounds.

Superstitions connected with marriage, courtship and the choosing of sweethearts are innumerable. On the 14th of February, it is said, the birds choose their mates, and young men and women choose their sweethearts. If the matter did not go as far as that, the young man was at least expected to send his Valentine a present. The festival originated in Roman times when on February the 14th the young man would draw the names of girls in honour of their goddess Februta Juno. The custom lingered like many another pagan rite, and young men drew the names of various girls in the village or neighbourhood, and then each sent his Valentine a present. Sometimes it might be a bunch of ribbons or a gingerbread, but as the century advanced, the Valentine, like a glorified Christmas card, was sold in all the shops, bearing, perhaps, the address, " To my own sweet Valentine," with two hearts entwined, and something in the shape of a dove or a cupid brooding over them. In London the twopenny postmen staggered under a load of two hundred thousand of these Valentines, and it is only within the last forty years that the Valentine has entirely disappeared. There were no twopenny postmen in the country, and the young man, finding the door of his Valentine's house conveniently ajar, would throw in his offering, attached, perhaps, to an apple or an orange. Some village wags chalked on the doorsteps on Valentine's Eve the shape of a letter or packet, and then retired to watch groping fingers trying to pick up the supposed missive. In Devonshire and other parts of the west country, a man's Valentine was the first lass whom he met, on Valentine's Day, who was not a member of his own household.

In Hertfordshire, we are told by a writer in Hone's *Year Book*,

it is customary for the poor and middling classes of children to assemble together in some part of the town or village where they live, whence they proceed in a body to the house of the chief personage of the place who throws them wreaths and true lovers' knots with which they entirely adorn themselves. Two or three of the girls then select one of the youngest among them (generally a boy) whom they deck out more gaily than the rest, and placing him at their head march forward in the greatest state imaginable, at the same time playfully singing :

> Good morrow to you, Valentine
> Curl your locks as I do mine
> Two before and three behind
> Good morrow to you, Valentine.

This they repeat under the windows of all the houses they pass, and the inhabitant is seldom known to refuse a mite toward the merry soliciting of these juvenile serenaders.

In many villages the girls would flock to the nearest wishing-well to wish that the Valentine of the day might be the husband of the future ; at the ruined abbey of Cerne Abbas in Dorsetshire, which tradition says was founded by Augustine, there is a wishing-well. To obtain your heart's desire, if you visit this well, you must pick a laurel leaf from a bush near by, and, making a cup of it, dip it into the well, then turning and facing the church, you wish, but the desire must be kept secret, or the wish will not come true. This was not necessarily a celebration for Valentine's Day.

Wishing-wells were attended at all seasons of the year, by girls who wanted husbands, by wives who wished theirs in the churchyard, by men who longed for fortunes or good harvests or luck through the months to come.

On May Day Eve, and on St. John's Eve, the girls of the village would seek for their coming fortune in husbands. In Somersetshire a lass would put a snail on a pewter plate, and it would mark as it crawled the initials of her future husband.

I hope [said Defoe with his usual unction], that the next twenty-ninth of June, which is S. John the Baptist's Day, I shall not see the pastures adjacent to the metropolis thronged as they were the last year with well-dressed young ladies crawling up and down upon their knees as if they were a parcel of weeders, when all the business is to hunt superstitiously after a coal under the root of a plantain to put under their heads that night that they may dream who should be their husbands.

It is not to be supposed that the young ladies heeded his admonition. They still went out and searched for plantain roots and put snails on pewter plates, and threw apple-peel over their left shoulder in the expectation that it would fall into the shape of their future husband's initial.

On St. Simon and St. Jude's Day they recited as they threw the apple paring the following rhyme :

> St. Simon and St. Jude, on you I intrude,
> By this paring I hold to discover
> Without any delay, please tell me this day
> The first letter of him, my true lover.

On St. John's Eve, his flower, the St. John's wort, would be hung over doors and windows to keep off evil spirits, and girls, if they were not searching in the fields for plantain roots, might be making the dumb cake. Two girls made the cake, two baked it, and two broke it. A third person then put it under the pillow of the other six. The whole performance must be conducted in dead silence—if a word were spoken the thing would end in failure. The girls, having kept silence, went to bed and fell asleep to dream of future husbands. Something of the same sort was occasionally done on St. Faith's Day, October 6. A cake of flour, water, salt and sugar was made by three girls in the way we have described, but each of the girls subdivided her part into three, put the portions through a wedding-ring and then as she ate it recited the following rhyme :

> Oh good St. Faith, be kind to-night
> And bring to me my heart's delight
> Let me my future husband view
> And be my visions chaste and true.

On the Eve of St. Mary Magdalene's Day a sprig of rosemary might be dipped into a mixture of wine, rum, gin, vinegar and water. The girls, who must be under twenty-one, were to fasten sprigs of rosemary in their dresses, drink three sips of the concoction and then go to sleep in silence and dream of their future husbands. It was well that the drink was confined to three sips or the dreams might have been very strange indeed.

According to another superstition if a girl ate an apple alone looking into a mirror by candlelight, her future husband might be seen in the glass, peering over her shoulder.

On Hallow-e'en a girl going out alone might meet her true lover, a very natural occurrence, one would suppose, and in no way connected with magic. There was a story, however, of a young servant-maid at a farm, who, going out for this purpose, encountered her master coming home from market rather later than usual. The girl rushed in and told her mistress,

who, being in a low state of health, took to her bed
and very shortly died. On her death-bed she implored
the maid to be kind to her children. "For you,"
she said, "will be mistress here when I am gone."
It was said the farmer married the girl very shortly
after his wife's decease. . . .

Sowing hempseed at midnight was another custom
of St. John's Eve. It must be done at midnight and
the maid must recite the following :

> Hempseed I sow, hempseed I hoe,
> And he that is my true love come after me and mow.

Her future husband would then appear.

In Dorsetshire the girls would go out and pick ash
leaves. Putting one into the left hand they would
say :

> The even ash leaf in hand,
> The first I meet shall be my man.

Then, shifting the ash leaf under their glove, they
would continue :

> The even ash leaf in my glove,
> The first I meet shall be my love.

Then, thrusting the leaf into her bosom, the girl would
end the incantation by the following rhyme :

> Hoping this night my true love to see,
> I shall place my shoes in the shape of a T.

The future husband would then appear in a dream.

Incantations were always in some verse or rude
rhyme which reminds us that an incantation was a
thing that was sung.

A bride was often carried into church or across the
doorway of her husband's house. Great danger from

witches or evil spirits lurked upon the threshold, and horseshoes, ash twigs and St. John's wort were hung up over the lintel to scare away the powers of Hell. The horseshoe must always be one that had been picked up, and not made for the purpose. If it were cast from the near hind leg of a grey mare it would be the more efficacious. Grey horses were always lucky and were used to draw the bridal carriage at a wedding.

How far such superstitions were generally believed, it is difficult to say. Fielding declares that they were confined to the uneducated, but in Jane Austen's *Mansfield Park*, a novel written in 1814, we find the rector's widow believing in the efficacy of charms. Perhaps Fielding would not have called Mrs. Norris an educated woman, and there was at the close of the century a large body of men who were frankly sceptical.

Dr. Johnson's attitude to apparitions was that of a modern member of the Society for Psychical Research, and he, in company with others, investigated the matter of the Cock Lane ghost. It was the story of a poltergeist, which has a curiously modern and familiar ring. Johnson and his friends exposed the whole thing as a most palpable fraud, but his friends were highly intelligent men, who scorned all tales of the supernatural. We can hardly think that in the country there were many men who did not believe or half believe in ghosts and charms and omens, even if they had discarded old superstitions about wishing-wells, and snails on pewter plates, witches and black cats. There were haunted houses in which no one would live, glens and footpaths, where no one would walk at dusk, rivers which even the salmon poacher would not fish. No doubt there was far less credulity than in the previous century. The works of Thomas Paine were sold on barrows in the market-place. Astrology, which had been a science in the seventeenth century, was beginning to lose ground in the eighteenth. Swift ridiculed it in his predictions for the year 1708 by Isaac Bickerstaff Esq., other writers imitated him and by the nineteenth century it had almost disappeared. In the early days of the eighteenth century there were still a good many professors of the pseudo science. In 1728 a list of books on astrology included quite a dozen, and as late as 1774 weekly prophecies of political events were inserted in the London *Evening Post*. Nowadays we still have our "Old Moore," and a hundred superstitions, and relics of black magic remind us that we are not so very far from the eighteenth century with its belief in witchcraft and charms and incantations.

# CHAPTER XV

## TRAVEL

TRAVEL increased enormously during the eighteenth century. In the early years, only the very wealthy made a practice of travelling. The poor could not do so without a permit from the authorities, and it was even discouraged in the well-to-do. In the seventeenth century a Sussex squire was fined £1,000 for residing in London rather than at his country house, and many proclamations were issued enjoining country gentlemen to live at home and " to perform the duties of their several charges . . . to be a comfort to their neighbours . . . to renew and revive hospitality in their respective counties."

The habit of staying at home lingered long after proclamation and fines were things of the past. If the country gentlepeople journeyed at all, it was to the nearest county town, where they had a house for the winter. There was thought to be something giddy and dissipated, something almost morally wrong, in travelling about the country. That it was always most uncomfortable, and often dangerous, no one could deny.

What advantage [says a writer in the early days of travel] can it be to a man's health to be called out of bed into these coaches an hour or two before day in the morning;

to be hurried in them from place to place till one or two hours within night, insomuch that, after sitting all day in the summer time stifling with heat or choked with dust, or in winter time starving or freezing with the cold, or choking with filthy fogs, they are often brought into inns by torchlight, when it is too late to sit up and get a supper, and next morning they are forced into the coach so early that they cannot get breakfast. What addition is it to a man's health to be laid first in foul ways, and forced to wade up to the knees in mire, afterwards sitting in the cold till teams of horses can be sent to pull the coach out ? Is it for their health to travel in rotten coaches, and to have their tackle or perch or axle tree broken, and then to wait three or four hours (sometimes half a day) and afterwards travel all night to make up the stage ?

The country gentleman who posted in his own carriage, and the rider on horseback had not to put up with the humours of fellow-passengers or the rottenness of decaying stage coaches, but for all travellers the roads were equally bad.

The Spanish prince, who paid a visit to the Duke of Somerset in 1703, took fourteen hours to journey from Portsmouth to Petworth in Sussex.

We set out [says one of his attendants], at six o'clock in the morning, to go to Petworth, and did not get out of the coaches, save only when we were over turned, or stuck fast in the mire.

'Twas hard service for the Prince to sit fourteen hours in the coach that day, without eating anything, and passing through the worst ways I ever saw in my life . . . the last nine miles of the way took six hours to conquer.

The Duke of Somerset, himself, had a house at Guildford, where he or his family broke the journey when any of them were travelling to London, a distance of fifty miles. This was on the main roads ; the smaller roads and lanes were sloughs of despond.

An Essex apothecary, being so unwise as to ride along a by-road, found himself sinking into a bog. He called to a boy in an adjacent field, and asked if there was a good bottom. The boy assured him that there was; but as he progressed he found himself sinking deeper and deeper into the slough.

"I thought," said the indignant doctor, as he struggled on, "that you said there was a good bottom to this road."

"So there is," the lad answered, "but you have not come to it yet."

People of rank always had four horses to their carriage, and these horses were not the light, elegant creatures which drew the broughams and victorias of the nineteenth century; but strong, heavy animals of the cart-horse type, known as Flanders mares. Defoe tells us of a lady near Lewes, who was drawn to church in her coach with four oxen. These Sussex roads were unusually bad, so bad indeed that the judges at the spring assize only ventured as far as Horsham or East Grinstead, the jurymen, prisoners and others being left to plough through the mud as best they might.

The roads of Sussex were indeed surpassed by those of Devonshire, which could not be used by wheeled traffic at all, goods being carried by pack horses, or dragged on a kind of sledge.

"This infernal highway," says Arthur Young, of the road between Preston and Wigan, which he had just traversed. "Let me seriously caution all travellers to avoid it as they would the devil."

"My dear sir," he exclaims on another occasion, "what am I to say to the roads in this country—

the turnpikes, as they have the assurance to call them, and the hardness of heart to make one pay for."

I had a very bad journey into Bucks [we read in the Verney letters], and like to have been overturned twenty times. The passengers alighted several times, up to the mid legs in dirt, and walked for miles in dirty splashy ways ; but I ran all risks in the coach, being unable to walk. At length I returned to London about 9 at night. At Clayden the family were frightened, and rang the dinner bell and shot a gun.

In the spring of 1706 the following advertisement was proudly exhibited in the bar of the Black Swan of York.

Your four day coach begins on Friday, 12th of April, 1706. All that are desirous to pass from London to York, or to any other place on that road, in this expeditious manner, let them repair to the Black Swan in Coney Street, York. At both places they may be received in a stage coach every Monday, Wednesday and Friday, which actually performs the whole journey in the short space of four days (if God permit). The coach sets out at five in the morning.

This would no doubt have been termed a flying coach, and these were reckoned to do as much, sometimes, as four miles in the hour, in the summer, and upon good roads. Later in the century there was a marvel called the Rumsey Machine, hung on steel springs, " which begins flying on the 3rd April (1774) from London to Poole in one day."

By this date, main roads in the south of England had begun to improve, though the coach from Edinburgh to London in 1760 still took sixteen days to do the journey. The old custom of making up the highways by statute labour had fallen into abeyance. Everybody was liable for the upkeep of the roads.

The squire and the farmer sent horses and carts, poorer men gave their labour. The waywarden saw, or was supposed to see, that each man did his share ; but his supervision was not very strict. The men loafed and gossiped, dawdled and sang, and at the end of the days of statute labour, the road was often very little the better for it. In some parishes a money contribution was accepted instead of service. A man owning a waggon, with four horses, lent it to the parish for four days, or paid a sum of £1 10s. Gradually it became the accepted thing, that a rental of £50 was equivalent to a waggon and four horses, and the owner of the property was charged accordingly. The roads, however, were still bad, and the authorities conceived the brilliant idea of farming out the main roads, just as they farmed the workhouses, the postal services and the gaols, and as in France, the taxes were farmed.

Turnpike trusts were set up all over the kingdom. There were the high, white turnpike gates at every five miles or so of the road, with little, queer-shaped houses for the turnpike man, who ran out when the rattle of wheels, or the sound of horses' hoofs were heard, and did not open the gates till the toll had been paid. These men were generally very unpopular. No one had ever paid such tolls before, and to stop every few miles on a journey, and pay out good money was extremely irksome. In 1728 it was necessary to pass an act imposing severe penalties on " ill designing and disorderly persons," who had " cut down, pulled down, burnt and otherwise destroyed several turnpike gates and houses." There were riots in many parts of the country, and in Yorkshire a serious rising of the country people, against the obnoxious turnpikes, had to be quelled by the military. The life of the pikeman was not an easy or a pleasant one.

In the dead waste and middle of the night [says a contemporary writer], when sleep steals over him wearily, how many calls of the coachman, the chaise driver, the stanhope gentleman, the important bagman, and the drover, is he obliged to obey. The imperative " Pike—Gate—Hullo ! " are like so many knells rung in his ear. . . .
Who that has looked upon the pikeman's contracted span . . . his little white painted hut, like a showman's figured canvas, but shrewdly guesses that the best portion of his sunside of comfort are on the outside ? What a Jack in the Box ! He seems in his room like a singing bird in a cage. His cat and dog are his companions, save when the newsman, postman, or in short, any man arrives.

Tolls varied ; though they were supposed to be uniform ; but in cases where the turnpikes were farmed they were often very high. When coaching was at its height 20,000 pikemen were employed in collecting tolls at 7,800 gates. This was in the early nineteenth century, when the exertions of Telford and Macadam had made the English roads the best in the world.

Miss Hutton, noting the improvement, says a statue ought to be erected to Macadam, and adds that " the man who mends roads confers a greater bene-fit on mankind than the general who slaughters thousands."

No one dreamed of travelling in winter who could possibly avoid doing so. Spring was the season when, as Chaucer says : " longen folk to gon on pilgrimages."

In the spring, the road ploughs went out, dragged by a team of horses, to scrape the highway free of mud and stones, and the accumulated obstructions of the winter. The Swiss pastor, Moritz, who gave us his interesting account of travels in England in the eighteenth century, speaks of the goodness of the roads ; but that was near the metropolis. The roads in the north and west, according to travellers, remained as bad as ever. The unfortunate pastor met with much rudeness at the hands of innkeepers, because he chose to go on foot ; and that this attitude was not the result of his being a foreigner is shown by Richard Warner, a clergyman, who went for several walking tours at the end of the eighteenth century. He complains of meeting with the same rudeness from innkeepers and street urchins.

Pedestrians, according to Boniface, were either cut-throats or else they were impecunious. In both cases they might go to ale-houses, which were places of entertainment for the poorer classes. In England, if a man did not ride, he travelled in his own carriage drawn by his own horses ; or if he were going a long distance, by post-horses ; or he went in the stage coach, or the waggon if he could not afford the coach.

Pennant, travelling from Chester to London in 1739, the first day with much labour got from Chester to Whitchurch, twenty miles, the second day to the Welsh Harp, the third to Coventry, the fourth to Northampton, the fifth to Dunstable, and as a wond-rous effort, on the last to London, before the commencement of night.

The strain and labour of six good horses, sometimes eight, drew us through the sloughs of Mireden, and many other places. We were constantly out two hours before day, and as late at night ; and in the depths of winter proportionately later.

The London Royal Mail

Families, who travelled in their own carriages, contracted with Benson and Co., and were dragged up in the same number of days, by three sets of able horses.

The single gentlemen, then a hardy race, equipped in jack-boots and trousers, up to their middle, rode post through thick and thin, and, guarded against the mire, defied the frequent stumble and fall ; arose and pursued their journey with alacrity : while in these days their enervated posterity sleep away their rapid journeys in easy chaises, fitted for the conveyance of the soft inhabitants of Sybaris.

The road was often so narrow that a stage coach took up the whole of it ; other vehicles were forced to back, or, in unenclosed country, driven into the fields. Pedestrians often walked in the fields when the roads were impassable. Farmers grumbled at destruction of crops ; but the custom of the day upheld the walker.

The stage coach was a great lumbering vehicle, covered with black leather. It had four windows, a boot for luggage, and a basket behind. The inside passengers, of whom there could be six, paid the highest fares. The outsides paid much less, for it was a difficult job to climb up to the roof and still more difficult to cling on. There were no seats on top, except one beside the coachman, which was much coveted, and for which the driver accepted a handsome gratuity. The other " outsides " sat on the shiny sloping roof and clung on by straps or handles at the corners as best they might. According to law, not more than six passengers might be accommodated on the top of a coach ; but nearly twice that number was sometimes taken. Poor Pastor Moritz, finding his quarters so insecure, slipped into the basket at the back. This was very well as long as they were going uphill, and the pastor was nearly asleep among the trunks and packages, when the coach began to descend. The luggage now fell upon him, and he was so bruised and shaken that he was glad to climb back to his insecure place upon the roof.

The difficulties of travelling are well set forth in this letter of John Byrom's, written in 1725.

This day, about twelve o'clock, I set out for London (from Manchester). We went to Holmes Chapel, and came there before five o'clock. Mr. Stopford and his brother came to us about seven. Tuesday. Rose at five. We had a pint of wine mulled, reckoning 5/10, horses 17d. a piece. My mare had a peck and three quarters of oats every day. We set out as soon as it was light. They called at Talk o' the Hill and drank a tankard of ale, but I could drink none ; thence to Stone where we dined ; I was much tired and lay down in a couch chair ; they had a boiled fowl, I some broth, and was much refreshed. Tuesday night we came to Lichfield to the King's Head, a very good house, had many good things to supper, but I could scarce eat. We baited to-day at Ouseley Bridge a quarter of an hour.

Wed. Feb. 3rd rose at five. Mulled wine to breakfast, reckoning about eight or nine shillings. Went as soon as light to Coventry to the White Horse. I was tired, but not quite so much as I used on former journeys. Dinner leg of mutton, the family dinner ; two officers dined with us. I ate a little, not much. The landlord a comical fellow. Thence, about two o'clock, set out for Daventry, baited this morning a little, but at Coleshill met Mr. Bullock.

Dunchurch lanes very dirty or else all the way was very good. I could not well follow Mr. Marriott and theirs through the field way ; I came not into Daventry with them, but about half an hour after ; the older Stopford stayed to bring me up but missed his way.

Henry Clark and I followed a pack horse. To-night, at Daventry, I began to have a good appetite, and ate heartily.

Thursday we did not set out till near seven, being a large company, for the house was very full. Our reckoning very reasonable. Paid 2/3 for my share in the house. The road but bad ; they all took the field way for the most part to

Towcester, and rode so hard that I could not keep pace with them.

At Towcester, Mr. Marriott and Stopford stayed for me; but just at the town's end, I would go by myself if they rode so hard, so we all light and drank a glass of wine and ate some bread and cheese, and then went on to Stony Stratford, where we dined at the Swan. Thence we rode to Dunstable, and lay at the Windmill. . . . It was the worse house we had met with and the dearest.

Friday set out about seven to St. Albans; we baited and stayed two hours, had bread and cheese and cold pork, thence to Barnet at the Green Man, thence to Highgate, a mile short of which I met Fidler and Mr. Wright. I swopt horses with him, for he had a horse that proved to be lame, and was going to Manchester. . . . I rode after them to Highgate, where Parker, who came along with us from Dunstable, was "sworn," [1] but before I came so I saw not the ceremony.

It is satisfactory to note that next day Byrom had "three poached egges for breakfast," instead of the somewhat heady and unsatisfactory mulled wine.

Persons of rank and position drove in their own carriages, or, later in the century, in post-chaises, changing horses at each stage. The post-"boy," who was often a man who had been at his job for years, sat upon one of the horses. The post-boy, Humphry Clinker, when the squire's generosity enabled him to get his clothes out of pawn, appeared in "a narrow brimmed hat, with gold cording, a

---

[1] The "swearing in" on the horns at the inn at Highgate was a farcical affair, a "popular amusement and private annoyance" much practised in the eighteenth century.

"It's a custom at Highgate that all who go through must be sworn on the horns, sir, and so, sir, must you. Bring the horns. Shut the door. Now, sir, take off your hat. When you come here again don't forget to mind that."

cut bob, a decent blue jacket, leather breeches and a clean linen shirt puffed above the waist line."

He was a workhouse lad; "but could read and write, and do the business of the stable indifferently well." He could also "make hog's pudding and bob nails, mend kettles and tin sauce pans." He knew

something of single stick and psalmody, could play upon the Jews harp, sing "Black eyed Susan" "Arthur o' Bradley" and divers other songs. He could dance a Welsh jig and "Nancy Dawson," wrestle and fall with any lad of his inches, and could find a hare when his honour wanted a bit of game.

He had, in short, a fine and varied education. He did not know Greek like the coachman on the Tonbridge road who spent Sunday studying the Greek testament and who translated οὐαὶ ὑμῖν ὁδηγοὶ τυφλοί [1] as "Whoa, whoa, ye blind leaders."

Coachmen were fine people, in their many-caped coats, buttoned to the chin. The best of them were fine drivers, with a good knowledge of horses, and of the world of coaching England, and a useful gift of repartee. No wonder the young bloods, the Corinthians of a later date, got themselves up to resemble coachmen. It was, however, a hard life. Some coachmen who drove good cattle, on a popular route, made as much as £400 a year; others were lucky if they got 12s. a week. Should a man be put to drive a night coach, he might find himself with a mouldering vehicle, rotten harness and poor horses. Anything did for the night coaches. Few people travelled by them. Anyone who could afford the money or the time stopped at an inn for the night.

[1] Woe unto you, ye blind leaders.

Drink and bad company ruined many a good driver. At every inn, where the coach stopped, there was a mug of ale, or a glass of hot gin and water for the coachman.

"Timothy! What! You on the box!" said a gentleman to a driver who had been his servant. "What's become of old Tom?"

"Why, Tom, your honour, hath lifted his whip so often to his head, 'tis almost over with him."

"And Frank?"

"Didn't your honour hear? Why, Frank drove for speed against another coach for a crown's worth of punch. Both were upset. Frank had his collar bone and an arm broken ; but that's a trifle compared with what befel some of the passengers."

"And Jack? What's become of Jack?"

"Jack's in limbo about this 'ere parcel, what dropped out of our coach."

"And Dick?"

"Why, some pheasants were found yesterday in Dick's care. The squire made a terrible pother about it, and I'm hanged if Dick ain't gone this very morning to list for a soldier. Before he set off though, he went to Master, and told him he knew as I could drive, and so here I be, come to his place."

Mr. Palmer, the M.P. for Bath, had, according to de Quincey, " accomplished two things, very hard to do in our little planet. He had invented mail coaches, and he had married the daughter of a duke." By the first exploit he certainly benefited the travelling public, and his own family, for mail coaches, which were started in 1784, and belonged for many years to the Palmers, brought in altogether the sum of £100,000. Before this time, letters were conveyed

by post-boys, upon horseback. On lonely country
roads they could be, and often were, attacked and
robbed. Possibly the number of letters was not
very great, for on one occasion the post-boy set out
from London to Scotland with only one letter in
his bag.

Highway robbery has always existed in some form
or other ; but in the eighteenth century it reached
its zenith. If roads were improved for coaches, they
were also improved for highwaymen. Crimes of
violence increased.

" Thieves and robbers," says Smollett, " are now
become more desperate and savage than they have
ever appeared since mankind was civilized."

To carry a purse full of bad money, to give to highwaymen, was a common practice, and boots were
made, with cavities in the heel, in which valuables
might be put. The laws became more stringent, and
rewards of £40 each were offered for the apprehension
of highwaymen.

The turnpike men, in the little toll-houses, were
even given speaking trumpets, that they might send
warning of the approach of robbers ; but these precautions were of little avail. Bow Street runners
from London, or some of the larger towns, might
occasionally penetrate into the country to arrest a
notorious criminal; but the police were, otherwise,
utterly ineffectual.

Highwaymen terrorized the countryside, but if
opposed with resolution would sometimes beat a very
hasty retreat. In 1752 the Devizes chaise was stopped
near the half-way house between Knightsbridge and
Kensington. William Norton had been asked to
go in the vehicle and if possible arrest the high-

wayman, who had attacked several coaches at that spot.

As we came near the house [he says], the prisoner came to us on foot, and said " Driver, stop." He held a pistol tinder box to the chaise, and said, " Your money directly. You must not stay. This minute your money."

I said, " Don't frighten us ; I have but a trifle, you shall have it." Then I said to the gentlemen (there were three in the chaise) " Give your money." I took a pistol from my coat pocket, and from my breeches pocket a five shilling piece and a dollar. I held the pistol concealed in one hand, and the money in the other. I held the money pretty hard. He said " Put it in my hat." I let him take the five shilling piece out of my hand, and as soon as he had taken it, I snapped my pistol at him. It did not go off. He staggered back and held up his hands and said, " Oh Lord, oh Lord." I jumped out of the chaise, he ran away and I after him, about six or seven hundred yards, and then took him.

If there was seldom honour among thieves there was apparently a very high political feeling. At the time of the famous Middlesex election, a certain Captain Stapleton was stopped by highwaymen at Gunnersbury Lane when he was returning to London from Richmond. As they demanded his money, he called out " Wilkes and Glynn for ever," whereupon they told him to drive on, assuring him that they would never rob a friend of liberty.

The reward of £40, offered for the apprehension of highwaymen, often led to an increase of crime. Jonathan Wild was not the only man who made his fortune out of criminals.

In 1768 five men induced some poor wretches to commit highway robberies, and divided among themselves £960, which they collected as informers. Many more highway robbers must have died in their beds, or perhaps in brawls, than ever came to the gibbet; though these dotted the country-side.

" Thank God," said a traveller, returning from barbarous lands, and espying one of these erections, " I must now be come to a civilized country."

Disbanded soldiers, spoiled by the wars for every other profession, turned highwaymen; sometimes a tradesman, in desperate need of money, went out on to the country turnpike, and cut a purse. The only way to avoid these knights of the road was to travel on a Sunday. Sunday travelling was forbidden by law; but it was sometimes possible by paying double to secure a horse or a chaise.

In 1772 a French traveller, Grosley, paid a guinea to go from Dover to London in a " flying machine " on a Sunday. The road was one of which Arthur Young, writing about the same date, declared that " it would be a prostitution of language " to call it a turnpike; but the Frenchman and five companions arrived safely in London.

Poor people, if they travelled at all, walked, or journeyed in the waggon. This vehicle took passengers and luggage, and was covered with a large hood. It was in fact the carrier's cart of a later date. The driver walked at the head of his eight horses, which never went at more than a foot's pace.

When Roderick Random, after various adventures on foot, resolves to take the waggon to London, he is told that " the waggon from Newcastle to London had halted here two nights ago, and that it would be an easy matter to overtake it." Random and his companion, Strap, accordingly pursue the vehicle on foot, and overtake it next day. Random bargains

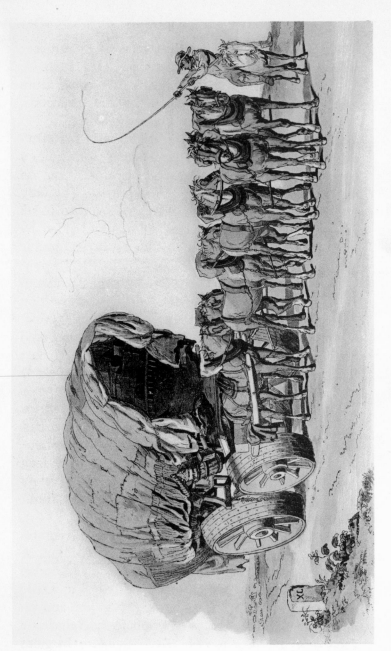

A Waggoner and his Team

with the driver for one place in the waggon, which he and Strap occupy alternately, and for this he pays 10*s.* Considering the value of money in those days, the fare seems very high.

When the roads were so bad and so dangerous, and vehicles very expensive, it is not surprising that other methods of travel were popular. Heavy goods were always, if it were possible, sent by sea or river, and later in the century by canal. Coal came to London by sea, and to the country villages by river or canal. The cost of carriage seems to have been enormous. Coal which cost 5*s.* the chaldron (about a quarter of a ton) at the pit's mouth, cost 20*s.* or 30*s.* in country towns and villages. It cost 12*s.* a ton to send goods from Manchester to Liverpool by water; but 40*s.* a ton would have been charged had they gone by land. In 1656 Francis Matthew had proposed making a canal between the Isis and the Avon, but the times were not propitious, and it was only in 1760 that the first canal in England was begun. This was constructed by James Brindley, to carry coals to Manchester, from the Duke of Bridgewater's pits at Worsley. Before he died, in 1772, Brindley had planned 365 miles of canals, and others were following in his footsteps. By the end of the century England was covered with waterways, and a great internal transport was being done.

> How oft doth man by care oppressed,
> Find in an inn a place of rest.

After long, tiring, tedious journeys, in hard weather, over bad roads, no wonder the weary traveller welcomed the glow and light and warmth, which streamed out of the inn window. How he would stamp his numbed feet, and hold out chilly hands to the blaze, call for a quart of mulled ale, and ask what was for supper.

That is a pleasant inn, on the great north road which Smollett describes in *Sir Launcelot Greaves*:

> The kitchen in which they were assembled, was the only room for entertainment in the house, paved with red bricks, remarkably clean, furnished with three or four Windsor chairs, adorned with shining plates of pewter and copper saucepans, nicely scoured, that ever dazzled the eyes of the beholders ; while a cheerful fire of sea coal blazed in the chimney.

Until the end of the century, the kitchen was often the only common sitting-room in an inn. The quality, who came in their own chaises, the inside passengers in the coach, the gentlemen who rode attended by servants, were shown into private sitting-rooms. Foot passengers, if they were received at all, were entertained in the kitchen, and there, too, might be found the outside travellers on the coach, passengers from the waggon, the bagman and the soldier.

De Quincey gives an amusing account of how three outsides " made a vain attempt to sit down at the same breakfast table, or dinner table with the consecrated four. The waiter, being equal to the occasion, sang out, ' this way, my good men,' and enticed those good men to the kitchen."

Very many of the old inns are still with us. Some have been improved out of all their ancient delights, and given lounges and cocktail bars, and other horrors ; but there are some like the " George " at Huntingdon, or the New Inn at Gloucester, with old courtyards and galleries, which are much as they were, when fine gentlemen in curricles, and bagmen on horseback clattered in and out.

Moritz mentions inn signs which stretched across the street. The wrought-iron work of these was very beautiful. The signs themselves were often extremely ancient. The oldest of all, the ivy bush, which denoted that wine was sold, dated from pagan times and the worship of Bacchus. The Chequers was an inn sign in the streets of Pompeii, though some have thought it really derives from the arms of the Earls of Warwick, who at one time granted licences to sell beer. The hosts of dragons, bulls, bears, swans and lions red and green, black and blue, still emblazon the country-side.

The King's Head is still sometimes that of George III. Queen Anne's portrait hangs outside an inn at Pinner. The " Ship and Shovel " has nothing to do with a spade. It commemorates Sir Cloudesley Shovel, the idol of his sailors. The Duke of York was popular with the soldiers. He might not be a great commander ; but he looked after the commissariat, and his head is on many an inn sign.

Arthur Young, who travelled all over England, must have had a wide acquaintance with inns. At the end of a volume he gives a list of hostelries, good and bad.

Dunstable. Bull, very good ; mutton steaks 1/– ; ducks, 2/– ; bread 2d. a head.

Swan at Newport Pagnell middling.

Kimbolton White Lion shabby.

Grantham George. Very good, uncommonly civil, very reasonable.

Newark. Saracen's Head. Disagreeable and dear.

Rotherham. The Crown. Very disagreeable and dirty; but
very cheap hashed venison, potted macarel, cold ham, tarts
and cheese and a mellon at 1/– a head.

Leeds. Old King's Arms. Dirty and disagreeable. Veal cutlets, tarts and cheese for supper at 8*d.* a head without malt
liquor being charged.

Driffield. Nag's Head. Very civil and cheap. Mutton steaks,
ducks, tarts and cheese. Mushrooms, capers, walnuts and
gherkins and other pickles, 2/–.

Richmond (Yorks). "King's Head." Good. Brace of partridges, leash of trout and cheese 1/– a head.

Newcastle. Civil, but extravagantly dear. A boiled fowl,
oysters and one woodcock 2/6 a head. Also a roast fowl
and very small haddock and ten smelts 2/6 a head.

Cambridge. "White Hart" where you will find a haughty
landlady, who lays it down as a maxim of conduct, never to
come, send as often as you please.

Penrith. "New George." Exceeding good, reasonable and v.
civil. The dinner was roast beef, apple pudding, potatoes,
celery, potted trout and sturgeon 1/– a head.

In *Roderick Random*, the hero, and his satellite Strap,
are shocked and amazed at the rapacity of a landlord
who charged them 8/7 for a night's lodging, bread,
beer, fowl and sausages, four bottles of liquor, fire
and tobacco, and a breakfast of hasty pudding and
ale. The man quoted Horace too, which made it all
the more unbearable. How welcome such a bill
would be to the modern traveller!

Catherine Hutton describes how she and Mrs.
Andrée (the widow of Major Andrée) travelled alone
together, and of their adventure in an inn.

The house was full, and we were stowed in a miserable room
with two beds, and without either lock or bolt to the door.
Mrs. Andrée had the precaution to place chairs against the door,
but about midnight they yielded to the efforts of two post boys,
whom, by the light of the rushlight, we saw staggering into the
room, in a state of complete intoxication. I sunk away under

the bed clothes, and left the management of them to Mrs. Andrée, who demanded, in a tone of authority, what they wanted. They replied, that they wanted to come to bed. And, drunk as they were, they wanted no more than their own, for the beds were certainly theirs. After some loud remonstrances and threats, on the part of Mrs. Andrée, and some hearty curses on their own, they left us in full possession of their dormitory, and our guardian chairs were replaced.

This was at the end of the century, when the roads and the inns were safer. In early days, few women travelled without a male escort, and ladies never went in a stage coach, or entered the public rooms of an inn. A hundred years before Miss Hutton and Mrs. Andrée travelled together, an intrepid woman, the Rosita Forbes of her day, journeyed through the length and breadth of England alone on horseback. This lady was Celia Fiennes; but such women were very rare.

Much merchandise came to London, and to other large towns by canal, river and sea; but there would be seen on all the roads leading to the metropolis, flocks and herds of creatures driven in to be slaughtered. There would be strings of sheep and cattle and pigs going to Smithfield.

At Christmas-time quantities of turkeys, geese and poultry were driven up to the London markets. Their feet would be tarred to preserve them from the roads, and at night they were turned into stubble fields, where for some months after harvest, a living was to be picked up. Turkeys were sent, in this way, from Norfolk right up to London, taking weeks on the way.

The main road near any large town presented a lively appearance. Men built houses overlooking the turnpikes, that they might see the coaches going by. They put up little wooden summer houses in their gardens.

Moreover [said Mrs. Jennings, in one of her raptures concerning Delaford], it is close to the church, and only a quarter of a mile from the turnpike road, so 'tis never dull, for if you only go and sit up in the old yew arbour, behind the house, you may see all the carriages that pass along.   Oh, 'tis a nice place !

# CHAPTER XVI

## GARDENS—NATURE

THE English have loved gardens from mediaeval times. As early as the twelfth century, Neckham, the Abbot of Cirencester, wrote a book, *De Naturis Rerum*, in which he set down what should be grown in a " noble garden." In the seventeenth century, however, there was a great advance in garden knowledge. Evelyn and Parkinson wrote their celebrated treatises, and Charles II, if he brought nothing else good out of France, carried away an admiration for the French gardens and the genius of Le Notre.

By the eighteenth century, the French models were not so much copied. Dutch William and his English wife had brought in the fashion for the formal gardens of Holland. In such a picture as Grinner's " Spring " in the Antwerp Museum, in the sunk garden at Kensington, we may see such pleasant alleys, beds of flowers, canals of water, statues, and leaden cisterns, clairvoyées, or ornamental grilles. The trees were trained into formal shapes, the lower branches being cut off, and the whole looked like the conventional trees of a Noah's Ark. Topiary work, which has had a revival in late years, was a great feature in many Dutch gardens ; in others were statues and tall hedges of yew or box.

Pope very justly protested against the excessive artificiality of many gardens, and quotes the catalogue of topiary work sent out by " an eminent town gardener." This included " Adam and Eve in yew. Adam, a little shattered by the tree of knowledge in a great storm. Eve and the serpent very flourishing." Used reasonably, however, and in its proper proportion, topiary work could be very interesting and beautiful.

" To make one in love with yew hedges, you need only take a walk either in Paradise or the Physic gardens of Oxford," says John Lawrence in the *Gentleman's Recreation*.

When Pope writes to Lord Bathurst in 1732 he describes the garden enthusiasm which then prevailed, how some wanted art, and others Nature ; how one " advised peremtorily there should not be one lyme tree in the whole plantation," while another described horse-chestnut trees as : " not to be trees but weeds."

There were some [Pope continues], who could not bear evergreens, and called them nevergreens ; some who were angry when they were cut into shapes, and gave the modern gardeners the name of evergreen tailors ; some who had no dislike to cones and cubes, but would have them cut in forest trees ; and some who were in a passion against anything in shape which they called green walls.

A great stimulus was given to horticulture by Linnæus's book on the sex of plants in 1735. As communication with foreign lands became less difficult, it was possible to bring home exotic trees and shrubs. It is interesting to read of the treatment accorded to some so called tender plants. The larch, for instance, which was " nursed up as a rare exotick," languished in spite of all the care expended upon it. The exasperated owner threw it out upon a rubbish heap, where it promptly took root, and became the ancestor of all the larch plantations in Britain. The forests of England supplied the needs of the navy. In the New Forest, Mr. Lascelles tells us, there are oaks which were planted to supply the ships of eighteenth-century England. " Pits or beds," he says, " of three spits of ground each were dug a yard apart, and three acorns planted triangularly in each bed." To each planter of these acorns was given half a bushel to plant in one day, and the result has been the wooden walls of Rodney and Nelson, and the glorious ancient oaks which still survive in the New Forest.

In 1750 Dr. Richard Pocock describes in his diary the garden of Sir John Colliton at Exmouth. This gentleman had a magnolia, a tulip tree, the sword blade aloe, and such curious specimens as the kidney bean tree, and the artichoke or orange myrtle. He had a son living in America, who sent him the seeds of rare trees and shrubs, so that his garden was scarcely typical.

Henry Compton, who was, perhaps, a keener horticulturist than he was bishop, made a beautiful garden at Fulham Palace, and in a catalogue of the trees to be found there in 1750, is the " black Virginian walnut tree, the honey locust, the pseudo-acacia, the Virginian flowering maple, the red horse chestnut, the cotton tree and the evergreen oak. The number of trees and shrubs that was known in England in the eighteenth century was remarkable. Of flowers there was also a great wealth ; but they had not attained to the size and vivid colour of modern garden

flowers, and many which are now common had not
been discovered.    The dahlia and the chrysanthemum,
the delphinium and the aster were unknown, and so
were many other flowers which grow in our con-
servatories, or adorn herbaceous borders.

The azalea, though it was introduced into England
as early as 1734 by Peter Collinson, who imported
many American shrubs, continued to be a rarity, and
was sold for as much as £20 a specimen in 1784.
Such common shrubs as the spiræa, the escallonia,
the weigelia, and the cotoneaster were unknown;
but the rhododendron and the buddleias were grown
in many gardens, and the kalmia, whose pearl-like
flowers make it appear rare and exotic, was grown
in England by Peter Collinson in 1734, and was called
at first the mountain laurel. Linnæus, when he
named and classified American plants, called it the
kalmia after the Swedish botanist Peter Kalm who
discovered it in 1748. The fuchsia, though it was
called after Leonhard Fuchs, a German herbalist,
who was born in 1501, was first grown at Kew in
1788. A Captain Frith had found it in Chile. About
the same time a nurseryman of Hammersmith, James
Lee, saw, in a cottage window, in that village, a
beautiful plant, which was quite unknown to him.
He was told that it had been brought home by a
sailor from South America, and he accordingly bought
it, took it to his nursery, nurtured it with care, and
sold cuttings of it at high prices. The fuchsia was,
however, considered by him, and by the gardeners
at Kew, to be a greenhouse plant. The immense
bushes, which now grow in Devon and Cornwall,
and the west of Ireland, were later productions.

Samuel Gilbert, a great authority on gardens,

writes of snowdrops, anemones, daphne-mezereum, candytuft, meadow saffron, crown imperials, columbines, cowslips, crocuses, violets, daffodils, wallflowers, hyacinths, double daisies, fritilleries, guelder roses, flower de luce, asphodels, sweet williams, gilliflowers, dittany, sweet johns, ladies' slipper, peonies, poppies, larkspurs, nasturtiums, marvel of Peru, Princes' feathers, and African marigolds, lilies and roses. He also mentions tulips and auriculas, on which flowers he was an enthusiast, and he tells us that people would give as much as £20 for an auricula root.

At the beginning of the century, it is said, about one thousand different kinds of exotic plants were known. By 1800, the number had increased to 4,000. In Miller's Dictionary of Gardening, in 1724, only twelve species of evergreens are mentioned, and by the year 1768 the number had rather more than doubled. Men were willing to journey to the ends of the earth in order to find rare plants. In 1787 Archibald Menzies, of the Royal Navy, saw the flowering currant growing upon the shores of North-West America, and a year or two later, he joined in Vancouver's expedition, with the express purpose of finding it, and other rare plants, and bringing them home. Sir Joseph Banks fitted out a ship and went at his own expense to such far distant lands as Labrador, Vancouver, the Pacific Islands and Australia. Botany Bay, the fame of which as a convict settlement was to be so notorious and terrible, was named by Banks after his own pleasant hobby.

The poet Gray asserted that: " Our skill in gardening and laying out of grounds is the only taste we can call our own and the only proof of original

talent in matters of pleasure." Gray should have
known something of the gardens of Italy, even if he
had not seen those of Holland ; but undoubtedly a
great advance was made in what we now call garden
architecture. The man who built the Horse Guards
and Devonshire House did not think such designs
beneath him, and laid out the gardens of Kensington
Palace, and those of many another great house.

By this time, there was a reaction against the formal
Dutch or French gardens. Bridgman, the superintendent of the royal domains, conceived the idea of
throwing down the enclosing walls or hedges, and
opening out a view of the surrounding country. His
invention of the ha'ha was so called, says Walpole,
because country people uttered, or were supposed to
utter, this ejaculation in their surprise at finding
themselves suddenly upon the confines of the garden.
Bridgman's successor, Kent, went further in his
attempted conformity to nature.

"Nature," he asserted, "abhors a straight line,"
and so he abolished the long walks between yew
hedges, the rectangular pools and beds. Adam and
Eve and the Serpent were swept away, together with
the leaden statues, the clairvoyées, the pleached
alleys. In their place, Kent and his followers, who
went to greater length than their master, made winding
paths and meandering streams which wandered nowhere in particular. They planted dead trees to give
a natural appearance to the landscape, and, as in
Hyde Park, joined two ponds to make a " real lake."
" Capability Brown " was so called, because he
always declared that a garden had capabilities. He
might have said capabilities of destruction. It is
grievous to all garden lovers to think of the beautiful

avenues, the ancient yews, and flower beds, that were
sacrificed to this new mania for landscape scenery.
Every garden owner did not succumb to these new
fashions.   De la Rochefoucauld describes a charming
garden at Mistley, near Colchester.   There he found

groups of rare trees, carefully tended and tastefully disposed
on a carpet of turf which is mown every week, and is admirably
fine and smooth.   The drive is a gravel path, which runs in a
graceful curve round all parts of the garden, and is designed
to pass at the foot of all the fine trees.   Amongst the rarest of
these trees I observed two tulip trees, which must have been
from sixty to eighty feet high. . . .   The hot houses are very
large and well exposed to the sun.   One of them is a double
one, and is so arranged, that with very little stretch of imagination, you might think as you stand beneath a bower of ripe
grapes, that you were in the month of July.   The dwarf cherry
trees which adorn this hot house were all red when I saw them,
and produced a charming effect ; there were plenty of peaches
and pine apples large enough to make one's mouth water.

Lawns, in all periods of English gardening, have
held an important place.   They were usually sown
with grass, sometimes with trefoil, and in some old-
fashioned places, with camomile.   Good grass seed
was, as we have said, in the chapter on agriculture,
very difficult to obtain.   If turves could not be
secured, it was better to sow with trefoil or camomile
than to sprinkle dandelions and docks all over the
grass plot.   Lawns were, of course, mown with the
scythe, and much care and skill would have been
necessary to keep the surface of the English bowling
green smooth and short.   The work in a garden
must have been laborious, but labour was cheap, and
far more men were employed than is the case in these
depleted years.   In the Verney letters there is a
description of the inroads made by birds, which
were far more numerous then than now.

I have pretty well beat off the jays and crows and magpies,
from the gardens [says the writer], but there is a great many
blackbirds and threshes that come to the cherries and other
fruites, of which I have killed a great many, and still they
increase. I am forced to follow them close or they will destroy
all the fruite.

Boys were often employed to scare birds in the
garden, or scarecrows were used, called in some
counties mommets, a relic of crusading days, when
Mahommet took the place of Guy Fawkes. The
growing of vegetables increased during the century.
Potatoes, which were at one time a delicacy for the
wealthy, became, by the end of the century, the food
of the poor. Skirrets, which Evelyn described as
being " exceedingly nourishing, wholesome and delicate, and so delicious that the emperor Tiberius
accepted them as tribute," have entirely vanished
from our gardens. Scorzonera is rarely seen, and a
kind of spinach called Good King Henry has almost
disappeared. Rampion and alisander, which were
used in salads, have gone ; but numbers of other
vegetables took their place. During the eighteenth
century the consumption of vegetables greatly increased.

Greenstalls in cities [says Gilbert White], now support multi-
tudes in a comfortable state, while gardeners get fortunes.
Every decent labourer has his garden which is half his support
as well as his delight, and common farmers provide plenty of
peas, beans and greens for their hinds to eat with their bacon.

Mustard did not form part of the many sallets which
were then served, but was grown for its seeds, and
for medicinal purposes. The yellow crocus produced a cordial, and also a hair dye. An ounce of
saffron was distilled from four thousand flowers. No

wonder there was an old saying, " as dear as saffron." A great number of other medicinal herbs were grown, to be distilled in the still-room, under the superintendence of the mistress of the house.

Frames and greenhouses were the invention of the seventeenth century. For a long time greenhouses were roofed with tiles and slates, like the Orangery at Kensington. The growing of oranges was much the fashion, and at a time when foreign fruit seldom penetrated into the country, it was much appreciated.

Cuthbert Clark, whom we have mentioned as the inventor of a threshing machine, conducted an experiment on plants with electricity, which, we should have supposed, was only thought of a century and a half later.

He planted two turnips in two boxes, each containing twenty-four lbs. of earth. He kept them in the same exposure and all circumstances the same to each, save that one was electrified twice a day for two months, at the end of which time it was in full growth, the skin bursting, and weighed nine lbs. The other at the end of four months, did not quite reach that weight.

It has often been said that the people of the eighteenth century had no eye for natural beauty, and took no interest in the things of the country. That the centre of enlightenment was the town, cannot be denied, but there were certainly men, living in the country, who noticed its beauties with delight, and who even sang its praises and painted its loveliness.

Gray and Collins, Shenstone, Akenside and a host of other poets wrote verses in praise of rural scenes. Some of their poetry seems to us stilted and artificial ; but every age has its own form in poetry, except indeed those periods when there seems to be no form in it at all. Gainsborough and Wilson and Morland have painted the beauties of rural England. Gilbert White has given us the most minute and interesting of nature notes. White was one of the few men of his time who sought out animals without any desire to kill them.

He remarked the migrations of the birds, but he did not shoot them. He planted acorns, where he thought oaks were needed, and the row of beeches which is still in existence, was grown from the beech mast which he scattered.

He tells us of the birds and beasts which are now, alas, extinct, or dwindling. He saw grouse in Woolmer forest, near Selborne, and the fine red deer, which Queen Anne regarded with such pleasure when she took the Portsmouth road.

This fine herd of five hundred or so gradually dwindled in numbers until the Duke of Cumberland "sent down an huntsman and six yeoman prickers in scarlet jackets laced with gold, attended by the stag-hounds, to convey the deer in carts to Windsor."

Gilbert White also writes of the hoopoe and the goatsucker, the red-backed butcher bird, the little auk and an osprey which was shot upon Frensham pond about six miles from Selborne. In the woods he finds the sundew, the daphne mezereum, the autumnal gentian, the wild lathryrus and the green hellebore, and many another flower.

The daphne mezereon

> Though leafless, well attired and thick beset
> With blushing wreaths investing every spray.

was so named, it is said, on account of its poisonous qualities. The name mezereon comes from a Persian word Madzaraon, meaning "destroyer of life," and

A Typical Country Market Place, Morpeth

its berries are most deadly. In spite of this, it was used as the principal ingredient of the Lisbon diet drink, much recommended by the faculty, and dried pieces of its root were used as a cure for toothache.

The beauty of England has been terribly destroyed in our own day. Those of us, who are middle aged, can remember a far more lovely countryside. In the eighteenth century there was a feast of natural beauty, unspoiled by railways and factory chimneys. Quiet narrow roads wandered through woods and over commons. Forests, though they might have dwindled here and there owing to the demands of the iron smelters, often covered hundreds of acres. There were rolling downs, with clumps of broom and gorse, purple commons that stretched for many miles, lovely sea beaches, where the trees and flowers crept down to the sands, quiet and beautiful places, untouched by man and his hideous civilization. Large cities were rare, and the little country town, with its quiet old streets, had a charm almost as great as that of the country-side. These towns were not as they are now, the enemies of natural beauty, eating up the land round them, and spreading their crops of hideous bungalows over wood and field. They were the centre of rural life, and they were built on the prosperity of rural England. The country may have been difficult of access, and sometimes even impenetrable ; it was often unhealthy from damp, and ague-bearing fens ; but that it was very beautiful no one can deny.

How grievous it is that the loveliness and charm of England has been, and is, being destoyed before our eyes. Fielding, alarmed by the very moderate increase of London, prophesied, that in a hundred years, the whole county of Middlesex would be covered with brick.   It has taken nearly two hundred years for his prophesy to be realized ; but Middlesex is not the only county to be defaced, and it may be that at the end of another century, the beauty of England will be like the Dodo, a thing to read about, and to see in museums and in picture galleries.

# ACKNOWLEDGMENTS

I WISH to acknowledge my debt to the novelists and essayists and other writers of the eighteenth century. I am much indebted to the Rt. Hon. Henry Holland, the editor of a *West Country Physician*, for permission to quote from his book, and also to the Oxford University Press for leave to make use of *The Diary of a Country Parson*, by Mr. J. Beresford. Mr. George Binns had kindly allowed me to publish an extract from his grandfather's diary, and I must also acknowledge my indebtedness to the following books.

| | |
|---|---|
| *English Farming* . . . . . | LORD ERNLE. |
| *The English Labourer* . . . . | J. and B. HAMMOND. |
| *English Folklore*. . . . . . | E. HULL. |
| *History of the Eighteenth Century* . . . | LECKY. |
| *English Diaries* . . . . . | LORD PONSONBY. |
| *More English Diaries* . . . . | LORD PONSONBY. |
| *Coke of Holkham and his Friends*. . . | MRS. STIRLING. |
| *English Local Government* . | LORD and LADY PASSFIELD. |
| *Charles James Fox*. . . . . | J. DRINKWATER. |
| *Memorials of the Thackeray Family* | J. PRYME and A. BAYNE. |
| *Ancient Streets and Homesteads of England* | |
| | A. RIMMER and J. HOWSON. |
| *The English Village* . . . . . | SEEBOHM. |
| *Sussex Archæological Societies' Collections* | |
| *The Essex Village* . . . | ELIZABETH VAUGHAN. |
| *Memoirs of a Royal Chaplain* . . | A. HARTSHORN. |
| *Doctor Darwin* . . . . . | H. PEARSON. |
| *The English Parish Church* . . . | A. R. POWIS. |

*Society in the Eighteenth Century* . . . L. STEPHEN.
*The Diary of William Jones* . . ED. O. F. CHRISTIE.
*Social England* . . . . . H. D. TRAILL.
*England in the Age of Anne* . . . TREVELYAN.
*The Ladies of Llangollen* . . . . BELL TRAVERS.
*The English Peasant* . . . RICHARD HEATH.
*Morwenstowe since Stewart Times* . . . F. C. HAMLYN.
*The Industrial Revolution in the Eighteenth Century* . MANTOUX.
*John Wesley* . . . . . . C. E. VULLIAMY.
*Verney Letters 1717–1799* . . ED. F. and M. VERNEY.
*Nottinghamshire in the Eighteenth Century* . J. D. CHAMBERS.
*Popular Novel in England* . . . HARVEY DARTON.
*Childrens' Books in England.* . . HARVEY DARTON.
*The Eighteenth Century* . . . . . ANDREWS.
*This was England* . . . . . H. A. VACHELL.
*Health, Wealth and Population 1760–1815* . . . BUER.
*The English Church in the Eighteenth Century.* C. J. ABBEY.
*The Autobiography of George Pryme* . . ED. A. BAYNE.
*Henry Crabbe Robinson's Diary* . . . . SADLER.

# INDEX

Acland, Rev. John, 216
*Agricultural Magazine*, the, 188
Agricultural wages, 10, 141, 204, 215, 207–10; rents, 68, 71, 142
Andrews, —, author of *The Eighteenth Century*, 314
Anne, Queen, her reign, 1, 8, 11, 34, 37, 42; her income, 55; religious revival, 75, 82; the Bounty instituted, 76; trade unions, 221; the press gang, 227–9; her racing stud, 254
*Annual Register*, the, 13

Bakewell, Robert, cattle breeder, 11, 69, 71, 151–2; his system, 154–7; his death, 159
Bangor, Bishop of, 83
Bayne, A., 313
Bayne, Ed. A., 314
Beltain, feast of, 268
Beresford, J., 313–14
Binns, George, 313
Binns, Jonathan, visit to Holkham, 72
Blackstone, Sir William, 223
Bowls, game of, 258
Boxing, 259
Bray, Dr., founder of the S.P.C.K., 189

Brooks, Henry, author of *The Fool of Quality*, 195
Buer, —, author, 314
Burney, Fanny, 52, 109
Burrell, Timothy, 58, 253; dinner menu, 56
Butler, Lady Eleanor, 113, 161
Byrom, John, 39, 46, 54–5, 161; letter to his son, 186–7, 231; journey to London, 288–9
Byron, Lady, 215

Carrington, Lord, 161
Cave, Sir Thomas, 248
Chamberlain, Rt. Hon. Joseph, 3
Chambers, J. D., 314
Church fabrics, 87; furniture, 88–9; music, 90; "ales," 242
Churchwardens, elections of, 23, 27; duties of, 28–9, 62
Clark, Cuthbert, 309; invented a threshing machine, 145
Clerks v. Parish
Coaching, 280, 293
Cockfighting, 247
Coke of Holkham, Thomas, 11, 16, 61, 139, 143, 151, 158, 182, 255; his Norfolk farms, 68–74

Made and Printed in Great Britain by Butler & Tanner Ltd., Frome and London

# OUR FOREFATHERS' WAY OF LIFE

## GAINS AND LOSSES IN 200 YEARS

*English Country Life in the Eighteenth
Century.* By Rosamund Bayne-Powell.
(Murray. 10s. 6d.)

### Reviewed by ARTHUR MACHEN

" The beauty of England," says the
author, in her last chapter, " has been
terribly destroyed in our own day." Indeed, it has come to this, that, even now,
measures are under official consideration to
restrain the wholesale horrors by which the
loveliness of the country is being laid waste,
even as we look at it. It is something, no
doubt, that the Hard Fact fellows have
been brought at last to acknowledge what
will turn out to be the hardest fact of all:
that the amenities and beauties must be
brought into the great debit and credit
account of life. But what intolerable out-
rages upon these amenities have been perpetrated, before the smoke of the iniquity
has got into the nostrils of the occupants
of the Front Bench.

### Countryside Pleasures

Once, as Miss Bayne-Powell remarks, the
English countryside was a very different
matter.

In the eighteenth century there was a
feast of natural beauty, unspoiled by railways and factory chimneys. Quiet, narrow
roads wandered through woods
and over commons. Forests,
though they might have
dwindled here and there owing
to the demands of the iron
smelters, often covered hundreds of acres. There were rolling downs, with clumps of
broom and gorse, purple commons that stretched for many
miles, lovely sea beaches, where
the trees and flowers crept
down to the sands, quiet and
beautiful places, untouched by
man and his hideous civilisa-
tion. Large cities were rare,
and the little county town,
with its quiet old streets, had
a charm almost as great as that
of the countryside.

With the author's leave, she
may almost leave the railways
out of the account of destruction and desolation. The ugly
zone of the railway was, after
all, strictly limited. It brought
into being, doubtless, nasty
suburbs, large and small, about
the towns where it touched.
Dickens and the Victorians are
eloquent on the horrors of the
railway hotels, all raw plaster,
draughts, and discomfort. A
row of little villas would
sometimes spring up by lonely
stations in quiet country places.
But put a mile or so between
yourself and the line, and you
were safe. Twenty years ago,
the lad who drove me in his
trap on an errand from such a
lonely station in Suffolk knew
that the plural of " pea " was " peasen."
Now he would call them " pai-ees "—
though there are no known characters which
can fitly render the curst compounded
vowels of our Cockney speech.

### The Ubiquitous Car

It is not the railway that has done the
mischief; it is the motor-car. The locomo-
tive has to stick to the permanent way.
The car goes everywhere. It turns the
beautiful winding lanes into hideous " cuttings." It lops down the hedges so that
the driver can see where he is going. It
blasts the fourteenth century bridge so
that something may be built that will bear
the motor-lorry's weight. It knocks down
the fifteenth century houses that the cars
may save one minute in getting through
the town. And it makes every green hill
and every lovely valley accessible; places
where people may swarm; plots ripe for de-
velopment and the floriferation of Builders'
Bungalow Bacillus.

And then comes the question: how
should we like it if we were to find ourselves suddenly transported into English
country life in the eighteenth century?
Perhaps one man in 10,000 would think
that he had strayed into Heaven; the rest
of us would be acutely wretched. As I
write, I strike a match wherewith to re-
kindle my pipe—and think of the process
that would have been necessary in 1750;
of the flint and steel and tinderbox, of the
clumsy rappings with untaught, unaccus-
tomed fingers, of the bruised knuckles, of
the groping with the sulphur match in the
feeble, wandering fires of the smouldering
tinder. We should have to learn the craft
of living all over again, before the life of
those days could become tolerable to us.
If we could manage it, I think we should
find it worth while.

# A FARM FOR TWO POUNDS
## By HAROLD BALDWIN

An enthralling volume of reminiscences. An emigré's life in Canada before the war was not an enviable one, but, to a man to whom creature comforts meant nothing as compared with the thrills and dangers of winning a livelihood under conditions of the utmost hardship, it meant all the things which we are apt to narrow down and limit by the phrase 'self-expression.'
With Frontispiece. 7s. 6d. net.

# MODERN MYSTICS
## By SIR FRANCIS YOUNGHUSBAND, K.C.S.I., K.C.I.E.

Sir Francis gives a general explanation of what the Mystic is. Then he illustrates his theme from the lives of modern mystics of such apparently different nature as a High-caste Hindu, a French nun, a devout Mahomedan, an English Society lady and a Welsh miner.
10s. 6d. net.

# ENGLISH COUNTRY LIFE IN THE 18TH CENTURY
## By ROSAMOND BAYNE-POWELL

The object of this book is to show in a simple, clear and attractive way, without the frills of artificial romance or the dullness of official statistics, how the village lived.
With Illustrations. 10s. 6d. net.

# BEYOND THE SUNSET
## By CHARLES DOUIE
### Author of *The Weary Road*

This story opens on the battlefield on the morning of Armistice Day and continues the adventures of the subaltern of *The Weary Road* in many lands and in many callings, soldier, scholar, civil servant, teacher, journalist, traveller, mountaineer.
7s. 6d. net.

# HARK BACK!
## By COL. WILFRID JELF, C.M.G., D.S.O.

A brilliant series of episodes of the South African and European Wars, with tributes to the author by Field-Marshal Lord Milne, Mr. Charles Tennyson and Brig.-General C. C. Lucas.
5s. net.

## BOOKS BY WALTER STARKIE
## SPANISH RAGGLE-TAGGLE
### ADVENTURES WITH A FIDDLE IN NORTH SPAIN

' Last year Dr. Starkie gave us his fascinating " Raggle-Taggle." Now he brings us an even better book.'—*The Sunday Times*.

' This delightful book is as readable as it is vivid.'—*The Observer*.

' His fiddle has opened for him the hearts of an underworld unknown even to George Borrow. As a vivid picture of the essential Spain it is unsurpassed.'—*Morning Post*.

Second Impression.
Frontispiece by ARTHUR RACKHAM. 10*s*. 6*d*. net.

## RAGGLE-TAGGLE
### ADVENTURES WITH A FIDDLE AMONG THE GYPSIES OF HUNGARY AND ROUMANIA

' One of the immortal travel-books.'—E. B. OSBORN in the *Morning Post*.

' An entrancing book. I guarantee continuous entertainment.'—COMPTON MACKENZIE in the *Daily Mail*.

' A remarkable book. His thousand-and-one adventures make extraordinarily interesting reading.'—*Country Life*.

' Fascinating and disturbing. Far away from ordinary comparisons.'—*The Listener*.

Fifth Impression.
Frontispiece by ARTHUR RACKHAM. 10*s*. 6*d*. net.

## THE VALLEYS OF THE ASSASSINS
### By FREYA STARK

' Belongs to something bigger than geography. This adventure that she has so magnificently recounted may be read with joy. A rare and delightful book.'—HOWARD SPRING in the *Evening Standard*.

' This truly enthralling record ought to take its place among the classics of travel.'—Miss V. SACKVILLE WEST in the *Observer*.

Third Impression.
With 6 Maps and 34 Illustrations. 12*s*. 6*d*. net.

"English Country Life in the Eighteenth Century." By Rosamond Bayne-Powell. (John Murray. 10s. 6d.)

## (BY ARTHUR BRYANT.)

The theme of this book is England as she once was—a little England of six million souls, mostly country dwellers, of market town, village street and open field, of lonely woodlands and great heaths where only the ale-house and the gibbet stood, of solitudes where the church bells rang after sundown to guide the hapless traveller to his bed. It was an England poor in many things by modern standards, but, like Chaucer's parson, passing rich in others: there was a cow, it was reckoned, for every man, woman, and child, there was rough freedom, there was local self-government—a homely democracy in the little things of life that matter, more real than all our vaunted countings of heads, and which, more even than the unbroken beauty of its landscape, was the crowning glory of the England of the eighteenth century. Of all these things, and of many others, the author writes with knowledge, understanding, and love. "Teach us," wrote Goldsmith,

that states of native strength possest
Though very poor, may still be very blest.

*∗*

Out of this rich country England came the true-hearted, rough men who manned Nelson's ships, who dared to mutiny when all Europe was banded against them and yet forgot their grievances to man the guns the moment an enemy sail appeared, whose semblances still look out from Morland's and Rowlandson's pictures to remind a more anaemic age of how heartening a thing free, coarse, full-blooded humanity can be. Miss Bayne-Powell is never shocked by them, but accepts them joyfully with all their rude, rustic implications. What could be more rich, or, to the true lover of rough life, more moving, than the description on page 21, taken so skilfully and appropriately from Hones Year Book, of the perambulation of the parish boundaries:—

if the boundary be a stream, one of the boys is tossed into it; if a broad ditch, the boys are offered money to jump over it, in which they of course fail, and pitch into the mud, where they stick as firmly as if they had been rooted there for the season; if a hedge, a sapling is cut out of it, and used in afflicting that part of their bodies upon which they rest in the posture between standing and lying; if a wall, they are to have a race on the top of it, when in trying to pass each other they fall over on each side—descending, perhaps, into the still, Stygian waters of a ditch, and others thrusting "the human face divine" into a bed of nettles; if the boundary be a sunny bank, they sit down upon it and get a treat of beer and bread and cheese, and perhaps a glass of spirits. When these boys grow up to be men, if it happens that one of them should be asked if a particular stream were the boundary of the manor he had perambulated, he would be sure to say, in the manner of Sancho Panza, "Ees, that 'tis, I'm sure o't by the same token that I was tossed into 't and paddled about there like a water rat till I wore half dead."

If he should be asked if the aforesaid bank were a boundary, "oh it be," he would say, "that where we squat down and tucked in a skinful of vittles and drink."

*∗*

Miss Bayne-Powell knows a lot. She even knows her Commination Service and explains the mysterious passage in it about removing one's neighbour's landmark. She introduces us to characters like Thomas Turner, the mercer and general dealer of East Hoathley, and Walter Gale, the boozy schoolmaster of Mayfield, whom I fancy she first met, as I did, in Lord Ponsonby's treasured pages. Yet she gives us no references and hardly any footnotes, and her bibliography is curiously artless with its citation of a popular modern biography like Mr. Drinkwater's "Charles James Fox," and its complete omission of the Historical Manuscript Commission's Appendices—those great repositories of English social life which the muniment rooms of our country houses have given to modern historians. But, for all this, and though she does not perhaps sufficiently distinguish between the value of contemporary literature (which nearly always tends to distort life by magnification or by caricature) and such direct evidence of daily life as is provided by diaries and letters, the author has balance and judgment and intuitive feeling for the living past that takes her nearer the truth than ten times her technical equipment carries many a learned pedant. And her book throughout is enriched by a lovely rhythmic style and a hatred of the unseeing enemy that slays beauty, which endears it to the discerning reader from the first to the last page.